BILL BENNETT

BILL

BENNETT

A MANDARIN'S VIEW

BOB PLECAS

DOUGLAS & MCINTYRE
VANCOUVER/TORONTO

To my wife, Pauline Rafferty, the person in my life who makes everything—even writing a book—possible.

06 07 08 09 10 5 4 3 2 1

Douglas & McIntyre Ltd.
2323 Quebec Street, Suite 201
Vancouver, British Columbia
Canada V5T 4S7
www.douglas-mcintyre.com

Library and Archives Canada Cataloguing in Publication
Plecas, Bob, 1944–
Bill Bennett : a mandarin's view / Bob Plecas.
Includes bibliographical references and index.
ISBN-13: 978-1-55365-228-1 (bound) · ISBN-10: 1-55365-228-2 (bound)
ISBN-13: 978-1-55365-177-2 (pbk.) · ISBN-10: 1-55365-177-4 (pbk.)

1. Bennett, W. R. (William Richards), 1932–. 2. British Columbia—Politics and government—1975–1991. 3. Prime ministers—British Columbia—Biography. I. Title.
FC3828.2.P54 2006 971.1'04 C2005-907898-7

Editing by John Eerkes-Medrano
Jacket and text design by Ingrid Paulson
Jacket photograph by Nigel Dickson
Printed and bound in Canada by Friesens
Printed on acid-free paper that is forest friendly (100% post-consumer recycled paper) and has been processed chlorine free.

We gratefully acknowledge the financial support of the Canada Council for the Arts, the British Columbia Arts Council, and the Government of Canada through the Book Publishing Industry Development Program (BPIDP) for our publishing activities.

CONTENTS

Introduction 1

1 A WISE FATHER DOES NOT SEE EVERYTHING 7

2 A GOOD TIME OR A LONG TIME 23

3 BORN AGAIN 39

4 THOSE GUYS ARE TOAST 52

5 STEERING, NOT ROWING 71

6 WORK TO LEARN 87

7 FACEOFF '79 103

8 THE BEST-LAID PLANS 118

9 BRINGING IT HOME 139

10 TOUGH GUY? 170

11 RESTRAINT 201

12 IT ENDS WITH EXPO 237

A FINAL WORD 269

Acknowledgements 283

Sources 285

Bibliography 290

Index 294

INTRODUCTION

"Mandarin n. 1. A high public official in the Chinese Empire. 2. A high government official or bureaucrat."

ITP NELSON CANADIAN DICTIONARY

BILL BENNETT was premier of British Columbia from 1975 to 1986. For much of that time, I was a senior official or deputy minister in the B.C. government. A couple of years ago a few of my colleagues and I, "the old-timers," decided it was important to provide a public record of Bennett's accomplishments during his years in office. I drew the short straw.

To carry out my task properly, I knew I would need Bennett's co-operation. While he agreed to co-operate, one of the first things he told me was: "This will be your book. It is not *my* book, it is not *our* book, it is *your* book." He repeated some variation of this each time I interviewed him—seven times in all.

The second thing he said—and he said this only once—was: "Others have approached me, but I didn't think the timing was right, or I was concerned they might write a puff piece. Tell the story as you see it, and let the people judge." Perhaps he thought that a retired deputy, with an inside view of government, would be fair.

I have tried to be objective. If I have failed, it is because I admire Bill Bennett. He was the best premier I worked for—and I have worked for six premiers, from both the centre-right Social Credit Party and the centre-left New Democratic Party, serving in ten ministries under twenty-five ministers.

I also recognized—in fact, I knew before I started—that I am not a historian, not a political scientist. But I love hearing and telling stories, especially political anecdotes. To be a good deputy minister you have to live and breathe politics. The business your boss is in is politics, and the first rule of work is to understand your boss. Deputy ministers are not partisan; they can't be, if they are to be effective. As one of my federal colleagues observed, deputies are the permanent custodians of the permanent problems.

My interviewing the ministers and the other people who played significant roles in the Bennett government was one of the most enjoyable parts of this exercise. All the people I interviewed for this book have one trait: being away from the cut and thrust of politics, they have mellowed. Most of them are now getting on in years, and the sharp edges they once had have rounded off.

I did not, however, interview every minister and every key player. Some of Bennett's ministers will be disappointed because this book does not include the admittedly important things they accomplished. If these people don't like my interpretation or feel I have left out something important, they can do as I did: write a book!

This book is not a biography of Bill Bennett. It focuses on the period of roughly 1973 to 1986, beginning when he entered provincial politics. It includes a chapter on his background and upbringing and another on Dave Barrett, and ends when Bennett left the political stage at the Socred leadership convention in Whistler that chose Bill Vander Zalm as his successor. After that time I remained a deputy minister and lost track of what Bennett was doing.

It is a sad but true commentary on politics that once you are gone, you are forgotten. Many British Columbians have forgotten Bill Bennett and do not appreciate his contributions. That is a shame. The events described in this book have had a permanent influence on the government of British Columbia, and I hope this book helps Bill Bennet's contributions to be remembered.

This book is not, however, a comprehensive overview of the Bill Bennett years; neither is it an academic account. I wanted to write about leadership and about how public events play out behind the scenes as well as in front of the cameras. This book is about honest men and women making tough decisions to the best of their ability. The story is often told in their own words; I hope this approach makes the wonderful world of B.C. politics come alive for the reader. And I hope it will provide academics with primary data so that they can write a more scholarly analysis than the one I provide here.

I remain surprised at how Bennett analyzed issues and disseminated his ideas. What amazes me is the one message he never tried to communicate: who he was. Here's a guy with a high school education, who in the beginning spoke in public in a wooden, inflexible, stiff, incoherent way but went on to lead the province for eleven years, winning three elections with a very high percentage of the popular vote. The media painted him as a tough guy—uncaring, callous, bottom-line driven, stiff, inflexible. He let that happen; it didn't bother him.

Those who know Bill Bennett and who have worked with him know the public image isn't true. He is funny, witty and warm. Tough, yes. A loner, yes. But great fun to be around. In office, Bennett was a contradiction, a public–private split personality, and I try to explore that in this book.

Bennett ran against Dave Barrett three times, and won each time. Barrett accomplished a lot in his three years in office, much of it good: the Insurance Corporation of British Columbia (ICBC) and the Agricultural Land Reserve (ALR), for example. However, only a few of Barrett's accomplishments survive today. The two men never got along, but Barrett was a foil, revealing both Bennett's strengths and weaknesses.

Bennett's legacy is much broader than Barrett's. This is to be expected, since he was in office almost four times as long. And many of the things he accomplished still have an immense impact on present-day B.C. Those accomplishments are described in this book. Some other things he did were undone by his successors, such as achieving the financial discipline of living within one's means. Within a few years of Bennett's retirement, unsustainable expenditures were rolling out of government. They began with the Socred administration of his successor, flowed through the NDP years and ended with B.C. becoming a "have-not" province. This is disgraceful mismanagement, which I believe he never anticipated, especially from his own party.

Some people who heard I was writing this book asked me about an incident in which Bennett was involved in the late 1980s. I give it no attention here because it falls outside the time he was premier. William Rayner, referring to the issue in his book *British Columbia's Premiers in Profile,* put it this way:

> On May 12, 1989, [Bill Bennett], brother Russell and lumber baron Herb Doman . . . were cleared of insider trading charges by a Vancouver court. The three had been charged after the Bennetts sold Doman company shares in November 1988 for $2.1 million shortly before trading in the shares was suspended. However, the B.C. Securities Commission later found the trio guilty of substantially the same charges and imposed penalties of its own in October 1999, after a lengthy legal battle.
>
> For William Richards Bennett, the case was an annoying distraction. Now a respected senior citizen, he divides his time between Kelowna, where he still has business interests, and his retirement home in Palm Springs.

I leave it to others who have studied the issue to comment further.

Bennett's party, Social Credit, has ceased to exist in any meaningful way. That need not have happened, and it bothers him. But not as much as seeing mistakes being made that damage his beloved British Columbia. I say this because I discovered, in my two years of researching and writing this book, Bill Bennett's incredible sense of public service. He felt—he feels—an obligation to give back to British Columbia, a place that was good to him and his family. Public service is what he expected of himself and of others. He did his best, and when his time was over he disappeared from the stage.

Two final comments.

The first honours the age-old tradition of B.C. political administration concerning the relationship of premiers/ministers and deputy ministers. If in this book you find observations that you agree with or think are particularly astute, remember that they came from my interviews with and the direction I received from the premier, Bill Bennett, or one of his ministers. On the other hand, if you find something you disagree with or think is particularly stupid, blame the deputy minister, in this case the author. This was the way of my world.

Second, a comment that will probably annoy Bill Bennett. One of the things I enjoyed was discovering a little—all that he would reveal—about his obvious love for his wife and family. Though it was always kept private and separate from his public life, this strong tie sustained him through some tough years. It was demonstrated during weekends at home in Kelowna, with his family and perhaps a few friends, as well as those times when Audrey came down to visit Bill in Victoria—often when no one else knew she was there. It is a lifelong devotion that we might all strive to emulate, irrespective of political stripe.

1

A WISE FATHER DOES NOT SEE EVERYTHING

"That was always Dad's attitude: he wasn't out to make the most money... His first love was family, his second was politics."

BILL BENNETT

THE AIR CANADA flight from Kelowna to Vancouver left on time for a change. In aisle seat 7B, the newly elected member of the legislative assembly for the province of British Columbia quietly flirted with the stewardess. It was a harmless flirtation, and it came so naturally to him that he did not even realize he was flirting.

Bill Bennett, age forty-two, was heading to the provincial capital, Victoria, and tomorrow, September 19, 1973, he would be sworn in as the new MLA, taking the seat his father had held for thirty-two years. His "new" briefcase was not really new; he had lucked into a used one at a neighbour's garage sale for two dollars last month, and the patina provided a more seasoned image for its owner.

The stewardess returned more often than was required, as she found the young, fit passenger in 7B very attractive and witty. And while the name on her call sheet was familiar, she was certain this easy-going guy couldn't be one of the famous Bennetts of Kelowna. She did not feel comfortable asking him personal questions because, while friendly, he seemed somehow guarded.

The seat next to him was empty, and he had time to think about next steps. Although not given to introspection, he was naturally inclined to planning and thinking through the way ahead.

He knew one thing above all else: he could not make a mistake. He would be cautious, he would learn. The pressure would be on, especially from his own caucus. He would have to prove himself to all his colleagues, and to some he would be a threat to their own leadership ambitions.

The NDP government members were going to have a field day with the rookie. "Daddy's boy" was going to be given a lesson. He was more than just a new member of the legislature, he was the former premier's son, a pretender to the throne, and there was a lot of getting even to get done.

The media would watch the blood sport called politics in British Columbia with great interest and report with glee if he stumbled and fell. Any mistake, and he was in danger of looking incompetent. He must not let that happen. He might be described as wooden, or nervous, but no one would question his competence. Bennett remembers these days well:

> I was nervous because I did not want to make a mistake. That was in the early days. You don't want to trip early, because you can never recover.
>
> There was no pressure on the other guys because they're not out there. Half my colleagues in my caucus in the first year were waiting to see me fall. They weren't cheerleaders. I had to get out and prove it, and the only way I could do that was to learn to do it! If you're brought up the way I was, I didn't really understand how you could be so phony in the legislature, with a lot of speeches that are made in there and the outrageous things that people get away with and that aren't correct. I couldn't do that.
>
> Still couldn't, but you find a way to speak to it without putting on a show. They were used to W.A.C., who had for years put on a show; Barrett put on a show, Bob Strachan put on a show, that's the way they did it. But it's my nature to be perfect, to do it right. I was fidgeting because I wanted it to be right.

Most MLAs, as well as the general public, were sure Bill Bennett would quickly prove he was much less a politician than his father was. How could he not be?

But he would not give them a reason. He would be completely under control, would give short answers to questions and would not say anything that would give his opponents any ammunition. He did not need to immediately light the world on fire with new ideas—that would come.

He kept returning to the thought: one mistake would be deadly, two would be the end of his dreams to follow his father and be premier. He would be careful, and most of all he would control his mouth, the wisecracks, the witty one-liners that some people in this new environment would jump on. He would have both a public persona and a private one.

A reporter he knew in Kelowna had prompted a one-liner when he asked Bennett what subjects he had studied in school. Bennett had replied: "I did take all the courses, Latin and French. But I don't know why I took Latin. Obviously the Roman Empire was not coming back." Had he uttered this line in the legislature, he would have had the Teachers' Federation all over him, demanding an apology.

He knew he had a long way to go, and this was a different journey from the one his father took:

> I always had an interest in politics, as did the whole family. I would never have had a chance if my dad hadn't been defeated.
>
> When I went into politics, that meant striking a difference. You undertook the job a different way. B.C. had lots of colourful politicians—Phil Gaglardi, my dad, Dave Barrett. I knew what I didn't want to be like.
>
> People saw my father as very outgoing, but they saw him after he was fifty years old. When he was young he was very shy, very quiet. He didn't have a great sense of humour when we were growing up. These things he developed over the years, after getting into politics.
>
> He became very demonstrative because that was the way he saw things had to be sold. That was the age of stump speakers. I came in in the age of television. That was the medium my father had difficulty dealing with.

The last few weeks had been stressful, and as the wheels lifted off the tarmac Bill Bennett settled into the happy state of planning his future. As the plane banked over the lake he relaxed and looked down at the train tracks running along the shore. He found himself doing what he very rarely did: thinking back on how this new phase in his life had begun.

TWO TRAIN JOURNEYS had had powerful impacts on his life. The first occurred when he was just six years old.

He had been a sickly child, born just five pounds, with jaundice and bad allergies. To avoid the allergies, one spring his mother convinced his father to take him along on the train across Canada to the national Conservative convention in Ottawa. Each day his father gathered in the club car and talked politics with his cronies, whose ranks grew with each train stop.

Just out of Regina, young "Billy" Bennett was tossing a quarter into the air from the dollar he had saved from his ten-cents-a-week allowance. The quarter fell out of his hands and landed in a spittoon, which he had witnessed steadily filling with tobacco spit. The quarter was in there, gone, and he burst into tears.

One of his father's fellow travellers had watched the disaster unfold. He soothed the boy by reaching into the spittoon, withdrawing the quarter, cleaning it on his hanky and returning it to Billy. And, magic upon magic, giving him a second shiny new quarter.

For the rest of the trip Billy would try to catch that quarter somewhere near the top of the spittoon and drop it, hoping for a repeat.

It never happened. The quarter never fell back into the spittoon, never earned him another quarter. But today some of his friends would, while laughing, tell you that he could still show you the first one he earned.

Bennett's second train trip was with his brother R.J. when he was twenty. They were headed to Windsor, Ontario, on a furniture-buying trip. A couple of friends from Kelowna on a jewellery-buying trip were on board, and they and twenty other middle-aged male passengers took over the club car the first night out. The booze flowed, and the next night it flowed again, and again. Every night smashed, every day hung over. On the way back, Bennett remembers learning a lesson: "I talked to my brother, and we agreed that we had a lot to do when we got back, a lot of responsibilities, and we wanted to make things happen. So we wouldn't take a drink during the formative years of our business, and we didn't. I didn't take a drink, a social drink, until I was over thirty."

Stubbornness runs in the Bennett family. His mother's father stayed with the family for long periods of time. They called him Bumpy, and he and Bill Bennett did not get along. Bumpy was an old soccer player, and his idea of discipline was to give you a good kick in the backside. He was prejudiced and outspoken about other races and religions, and young Bill Bennett delighted in asking his father's view of Bumpy's comments when they were together at dinner. The next time they were alone, Bumpy would chase him to kick his ass. Bill Bennett became quite a fine runner. But his family says his stubbornness comes from Bumpy.

He chuckled to himself as he remembered what a holy terror he had been as a child. As a toddler he refused to wear clothes in the summer, and it took his mother, Aunt Winnie and sister Anita to keep him in bathing suits while at the same time keeping him from drowning in irrigation ditches. Anita resorted to tying him to the cherry tree in the yard. Small for his age, he charmed his way through grade school as a good-looking, quick-witted kid.

His mother, the former May Richards, was a tall, imposing woman. She ran the home, while W.A.C. ran his business until he had earned enough money to enter politics. Their home had strict moral standards, and adherence to duty and the work ethic were the order of the day. That day was structured around a list of tasks posted in the kitchen, and only after they were completed and the school work done was it time for play. Bennett remembers those days:

> I think I had a typical upbringing, being shown what was right and what was wrong, all the old-fashioned virtues that were stressed in the country.
>
> That is my family. From the time I can remember in the house, every kid had to make his or her own bed. You were given jobs, which were rotated between the kids—dust the stairs, take out the ashes for the furnace and so on.

> They rotated, so nobody got a special deal even when it came to doing dishes, washing and drying. These were the things you did because it was expected of you. Then there were the things you did to earn some money, like ten cents to go to the show. We used to burn wood and store it in the wood room, so we had to bring it in, and got maybe ten cents.

But money as a goal was not the driving force. Rather, it was how you could use it:

> Being able to spend what you earn was important, and if you didn't have money you were limited in what you could do, so it wasn't money for the sake of money but what it could do for the things that you wanted to do. That was always Dad's attitude: he wasn't out to make the most money. If you gave him a safe place to build up his business, then he would have enough money to do the things he wanted. His first love was family, his second was politics.

His sister Anita, ahead of him in school and a voracious reader, took Bill in the same direction. No one realized that the smart-aleck kid who got along well in school with little effort had read all of Dickens before he finished elementary school. No book was off limits; reading was considered good preparation for living and the next-best thing to getting out and doing things. Anita read the encyclopedia from cover to cover, and young Bill did the same. Every weekend she brought home armloads of books that she and Bill read and discussed:

> Not just the library books people talk about, which my sister sort of lent me. But later, I think we had just about every magazine that ever came, except one: what I wanted was *Fortune* magazine, so eventually when I got a paper route and a job in the store I bought my own subscription to *Fortune*. I used to read it diligently. Now that was business, and it was interesting because it helped show the way you come to make decisions by seeing what companies do and what drives people.

He started to work in his father's store when he was thirteen.

The family also encouraged musical training, and young Bill Bennett not only sang in the school musical HMS *Pinafore* but also played the trumpet for five years. He was good enough to be asked to join the Kitsilano Boys' Band, but that would have meant too many trips to Vancouver:

> I played the trumpet because I started out in piano, and the lady who gave me the piano lessons after about four or five lessons said to my mother, "You know, he may look like an angel, but he is no angel." She suggested that I move elsewhere, so I took up the trumpet.
>
> They had a boys' band, and every Christmas the band would go out in the back of a truck in the cold and play carols. That went on for some time. Once I hit junior high I played the French horn for just one season, and then I really got more interested in sports.

As well as his mother and sister, there was the irreplaceable Winnie Earle. Winnie had joined the family in 1932 to help out for six months, and never left. Her special charge—not by design, just by love—was Billy. Simmering not far below the surface of this charming, quick-witted youngster was a raging temper. He was stubborn, small and fiercely competitive, and when he lost he became angry. The family called him "Pepper Pot." Sometimes Aunt Winnie would lecture him, and sometimes she would just break out laughing. And she gently taught him, by example, how to bring his temper under control.

His father was an important man, a successful businessman in a small town, the local MLA and then premier. He worked long hours and was away from home for long periods of time. His brother R.J. was away at a boarding school in Vernon for a few years, and Bill was raised by three women.

His father had a firm hand, and on half a dozen occasions he used it on Billy's bottom. But, by and large, even though he lived in the biggest house and had a famous father, his upbringing was normal for a kid in a small town. In elementary school, Bill's allowance was determined by his mother phoning Barrie Clark's mom and asking her what Barrie received weekly. Barrie's family had little money, so the allowance was only twenty-five cents per week, and that is what Bill got. Out of that he was expected to save, and he did.

Everyone in Kelowna knew the Bennetts were richer than most and lived in the big house on Ethel Street that his father had bought for $5,500. The house sat on 7.65 acres and had been built in 1912 by former Kelowna mayor Frank DeHart. Under the entry hall carpet the tiles were arranged to show a large "D" framed inside a heart. The property when first purchased included an old blacksmith shop, a lofted barn and a silo. Bennett remembers, "Nobody had money. I can remember the phone number was 676—that tells you how many phones there were in Kelowna at the time. In my dad's hardware store, the phone number was 1."

Before becoming premier in 1952, his father caught the train to Vancouver and ferried over to Victoria every January, returning in late May or early June every year. One year when he was at home, a visitor had measles and the house was quarantined for six weeks. W.A.C. moved out prior to the doctor's arrival and stayed at a local hotel. He was a highly motivated man with a passion to succeed not just for himself but for the province he had adopted. He believed in his vision of what was right and was convinced that the majority of people in B.C. agreed with him. Having won six elections as premier, he seems to have been proved right.

Yet W.A.C. never proselytized to the family. He never criticized his children for their teenage Friday and Saturday night parties. Although he was a teetotaller, he did not push his views onto Bill or his friends. W.A.C. did bet Bill's best friend, Tony Toser, that he could not quit smoking until he was twenty-one. The bet was a hundred dollars. Tony lost, and paid.

It was at the dinner table that the family came together. And it was here where the sparks flew as they were encouraged to argue and think for themselves. Bill was the most rebellious and strong-willed one in the family. His mother was the peacemaker. About his father he remembers: "When I was growing up we were encouraged to speak at the dining room table. There would be lots of arguments and a lot of politics, amongst other things. My father was very patient with smart-ass kids who were expressing things before they knew better." Once he asked his father how he put up with him, and W.A.C. replied: "A wise father does not see everything." He recognized that he would have driven his son away if he had told him what to do or how to do it.

High school was good for Bill. It provided an outlet for his fierce competitiveness in playing basketball. He made the team despite his small size and lack of natural ability. The team had its own social sphere. One stop was Don Terry's ice cream parlour, but it was expensive. Bill figured out that rather than all of them paying thirty cents each for a float, if instead they bought a brick of ice cream and ordered just soft drinks they could save five cents each.

There was always the hardware store, where Bill and R.J. worked every day after school and all day Saturday. Bill could play basketball because they practised at night, after working in the store. He could skim along in school without doing much homework. On weekends, they chopped wood using an old tractor they had converted.

As the hardware store branched out into furniture and appliances, the brothers became the delivery men. Moving furniture and refrigerators made strong backs for playful minds. They branched out into the propane business and were able to give up woodcutting. They sold the converted tractor for a profit and replaced it with a propane truck that they loaded after work. Then they would make the rounds to customers.

W.A.C. BENNETT served as premier of B.C. for over twenty years. He was elected six times. He represented the Social Credit Party, but not the Social Credit dogma.

Social Credit was an economic doctrine whose principles were developed by Major C.H. Douglas, an English engineer. He argued that the wages paid to people, which he called "A," would always be less than the cost of production, which he called "B." Without social credit, there would be insufficient money to purchase all the goods produced. More simply put, people were poor because they didn't have enough money, so give them some.

This wacky idea had little traction anywhere in the world, but in Alberta during the Great Depression a radio evangelist named William "Bible Bill" Aberhart became convinced that it was a way to drag Alberta out of the depression. Desperate times produced desperate results, and he was elected premier in 1935 with 54 percent of the popular vote. In 1936 he issued "Prosperity Certificates" to the people of Alberta. However, the legislation underpinning the social credit scrip was struck down. The Social Credit Party morphed into a fundamentalist conservative government that judiciously spent Alberta's burgeoning oil revenues. Aberhart and his successor, Ernest Manning, won nine elections.

Meanwhile, over in British Columbia in 1941, W.A.C. Bennett was elected Conservative MLA to represent the Okanagan and first sat as a backbencher in the coalition government. He served in B.C.'s Post-War Rehabilitation Council but found the coalition of Liberals and Conservatives to be unworkable. He left the coalition and crossed the floor to sit as an independent.

In 1952 an election was called and W.A.C. was looking for a party. A ragtag group of disparate people had rallied around the Social Credit banner and were running candidates across the province. He joined, immediately adding credibility to the party. The election used a system that allowed voters to rank-order their chosen candidates, and if a candidate did not receive a majority, second- and then third-ranked votes were counted. The Liberal and Conservative Coalition had dreamt up this scheme believing that their voters would cast their second-choice votes for each other, never for the social democratic Co-operative Commonwealth Federation (CCF), and that the CCF voters would never vote for the two free-enterprise choices.

The great minds had not considered that disgruntled Liberals, Conservatives or CCFers might vote for this new party, Social Credit, as their second choice. But they did, in sufficient numbers to elect them to a minority government.

As the most experienced Social Credit MLA, W.A.C. Bennett became premier. A year later he engineered an election, threw out the goofy electoral system and went on this time to win a majority.

He presided over the opening up of the province, riding a wave of economic prosperity. He deservedly took credit for the construction of highways, the extension of the Pacific Great Eastern Railway and the major hydroelectric projects on the Peace and Columbia Rivers. He acted as his own finance minister and ran a tight, fiscally conservative ship that was able to proclaim the province debt free in 1958.

Although he was a free enterpriser, W.A.C. knew when to exercise government power for the public good and nationalized the province's hydroelectric service to form B.C. Hydro and the Lower Mainland–Vancouver Island ferry service to create B.C. Ferries. He fought with the trade unions, limited social welfare spending and kept the public service small, but he expanded public and post-secondary education.

He was a populist, and was never home in Kelowna; he purchased an apartment in the capital. He was fifty-two when elected premier, and in his seventies when he lost power in 1972. His son felt that W.A.C. had stayed too long—a mistake he intended not to make.

BILL BENNETT was two years out of high school when his father became premier. Two days after that election, W.A.C. turned the business over to his sons and told them to not come to him for any advice but to get on and make it successful. He also told them that the existing store was not their inheritance—it was going to the grandkids, but they could have what they built. They were put on salary plus. It was all they needed.

They became builders and developers. They put together Kelowna's Orchard Park shopping centre. They bought the old Eldorado Ranch and logged it, paying for the purchase price with log sales. They opened more hardware stores and now called them "Bennett Stores." Bill, who looked after the marketing, loved the psychology of selling and the promotional end of the business. He would have an idea or see an opportunity. He would do his homework, carrying out exhaustive due diligence on any deal. He could read a balance sheet better than his brother or father and loved the creative use of real estate. For example, the Bennetts didn't buy the Ashdown's hardware chain; they bought their real estate and leased it back to them. They bought the Marshall Wells firm, amalgamated it with the Bennett Stores and leased out the real estate. Bill's competitors said that he knew instinctively what would be a good business deal and what would not.

One morning the two brothers went skiing. They took the furniture van up the hill and bought half-day passes. One brother fell on the first run and broke his leg. The other brother helped him into the back of the truck and made him lie down and be as comfortable as possible. He then went back to the lift sales office to get his money back. The office refused, so he returned to the truck to tell his sibling that he would be back at noon to take him to the hospital, once he had used up his pass. After all, you might give up one pass but not two, and it was only a broken leg.

In the middle of all this hard work and hard play, at the ripe age of twenty-two, the unexpected happened. On a blind double date, Bill met Audrey Lyne James.

A week later he asked Audrey out. Well, not exactly. He was out of town and the call would have been long distance, so he had R.J. phone Audrey and pretend he was Bill. He told her two weeks later. She was mad, but she already knew this was the one. Two months later they were engaged.

Audrey was a medical receptionist who was a couple of years younger than Bill. She knew he was the right guy for her, but it was intimidating to meet his parents: "When I first met Mr. and Mrs. Bennett I was overwhelmed, especially with him. I was in awe of him. She was a sweet, sweet lady. I was a little terrified, but then as I got to know them, especially him, he was kind of a pussycat."

Audrey wanted to get married right away. Bill said he would not marry until he turned twenty-three, and two days after his twenty-third birthday they married. He built a house for them, but then a business deal came up where they could buy a motel. They sold the house, moved into one of the units of the motel and stayed there for three years, until the third of their four sons was born. She cleaned the rooms, booked in the guests, dealt with the complaints and raised the kids.

Eventually they built their dream house and had a fourth boy. About a week after W.A.C. lost the 1972 election, Bill and Audrey had a long talk. His father was certain to resign, and Bill was thinking of going into politics.

They talked about the pros and cons. The boys were young, and Audrey knew that Bill would throw himself into the new job. He would be away much of the time. Audrey knew he was not running merely to be an MLA; her husband would want to be premier. She had her doubts:

> He has always needed a challenge. I think this is why he went into politics. He was getting bored with what he was doing. It didn't matter what I

> said to discourage him. Our youngest was ten, and Brad the oldest was fifteen. I used to think, What is going to happen?—especially in the teenage years. It wasn't easy. But he had made up his mind. It was a family thing, a sense of public service.

His winning argument was the one that pointed out what they both felt: that many of their acquaintances in their age group had made their money and were now playing, and playing around, with lots of money and parties and trouble. Neither Audrey nor Bill wanted that.

Over the past few years, with his financial future secure, Bill had begun to turn towards public life. He joined Toastmasters to overcome a natural shyness and stiffness when speaking before even small numbers of people. He joined the Chamber of Commerce, and when Kelowna was identified as a special high-unemployment zone by the federal government, and therefore eligible for federal grants, he organized the area's response.

Robert Stanfield, the leader of the opposition in Ottawa, had phoned him in 1972 asking him to be a candidate. Bennett turned him down. He could not imagine going to Ottawa, and in any event he felt Stanfield would lose. He had thought his father would step down in 1969 or in 1972, creating a vacancy, and he would have run. There was no vacancy then, but now there might be.

He decided to test to see if it was possible. He understood there was no sense in talking to his brother or to his friends—they would support him whatever he did. He phoned Grace McCarthy, a defeated Social Credit MLA and former cabinet minister now working for the Socred caucus, to determine if she knew anyone in the Kelowna area who might have a dispassionate view. Grace told him that a first-rate young woman who had worked on her campaign had just moved with her husband to Kelowna. Their names were Meldy and Hugh Harris. Meldy puts it this way:

> Hugh got a call from Bill Bennett saying that he would like to talk to him. Grace had mentioned that Bill should call Meldy and Hugh and talk to them if he wanted some perspective on organization or on some of the things he might have to do to win the election.

> Hugh and Bill talked, and there was a great fit. I think they probably put their heads together at that point and said, "What do we have to do?"

After they had spoken for an hour or so, Hugh remembers saying: "Bill, Meldy and I will help you. I can figure out how to do this with Meldy's help. But we are not interested in helping you be an MLA. The commitment we need from you is that you will also seek the leadership of the Social Credit Party, and indeed be the next premier."

That had been Bill's plan anyway, but to hear someone else say it seemed to prove to him that it could be done. He agreed. But it must be kept secret. He went home and told Audrey what Hugh had said. Before he could finish his story, she jumped in and said, "I certainly hope you told him you would do it."

On June 5, 1973, W.A.C. Bennett resigned his seat after representing Kelowna for thirty-two years. He indicated that he would stay as leader of the Social Credit Party until November 24, when the party would hold a leadership convention. In his press release he mentioned that he believed Les Pedersen, who had been his attorney general, should be the new leader.

The leader of the Progressive Conservative Party had failed to win a seat in the 1972 general election. After W.A.C.'s announcement, Derril Warren went straight to Kelowna to discuss with the local Tories the possibility of running and winning the seat. He decided the following Tuesday, June 11, 1973, to run in Kelowna.

Bennett was ready and waiting for Warren's announcement. He needed Warren to run in Kelowna, so he kept a very low profile, not commenting one way or the other as to his intentions. He had two reasons. First, if Warren ran and beat him, then his electoral career would be over and he would go on and do something else. Second, when he beat the leader of the Conservatives he could make the first move towards destroying the other free-enterprise parties that had previously split the vote and allowed the NDP to win.

On June 12, he told Audrey, "I announce tomorrow."

She replied, "There is someone you have talked to, but not told any details. I think you should, tonight."

"Who?"

"Your father."

THE PILOT announced their arrival in Vancouver. The passenger smiled warmly at the stewardess as he left the plane and walked quickly to the connector for the short flight to Victoria.

Once airborne, he went over his immediate plans. How to get from the airport to town? He was sure that if he took a taxi into town he could get the government to reimburse him as a legitimate expense, but that would be more expensive than riding the shuttle bus. He would take the shuttle and find somewhere to stay that was not expensive.

He was looking forward to one aspect of going into the legislature, even with the rough ride he knew was coming. For the first time since February 1971, when now NDP cabinet minister Bob Williams had accused him and R.J. in the legislature of insider land deals with B.C. Hydro, he could fight back. He had sued and won; the charges were untrue. But his blood was up, and he still carried a grudge. He wouldn't get mad, he would get even. Those who knew him and his competitive drive knew this battle had only just begun. Pat Annesley, in the April 1984 *Equity* magazine, described Bill Bennett's approach:

> If you play games at all, sooner or later you run across the type. He can be a good player or a so-so player. It doesn't matter. Sometimes he's a beginner. That's when he really shines. He's barely heard of gin rummy, you understand. Or chess or golf or whatever it is. But well, what the hell, he'll give it a try. So you teach him the rudiments of the game. And very shortly thereafter, he beats the pants off you. Luck, naturally. So you play him again. And again. And after a while you realize that luck has very little to with what's going on here. He plays with a fierce single-minded concentration. Presses every advantage. Wills the breaks to come his way. It's fun, and all that. The usual banter goes on, with maybe a little more of the parry-and-thrust flavour to it. Just a game, right? Then why does it feel like you're in a hand-to-hand fighting match on the front lines of a world war? And will the bastard ever lose?

If he ever does lose, god forbid, you're in trouble. A kind of manic, steely determination sets in. And you'd better hope the gods are going to smile on him early on. Otherwise you'll be there for hours. Days. If the demands of life and work are such that a re-match isn't possible until next Christmas, rest assured that he will regard the intervening months as a mere interruption. He'll have the board out, or court set up before you're through the front door. Playing with him is exhausting. Draining. Bruising. Never dull, mind you. But the psychological pitch is too much for ordinary folk like you and me. And let's hope you never got so foolish as to play for money. Such men are rare, for which we can all be thankful.

Bill Bennett is one of them.

Deplaning into sunshine, he walked quickly to the terminal. He was focused. On a mission. He didn't realize it, but he had put on his game face. Unlike the friendly, witty, wisecracking, charming young businessman completely at home in Kelowna, he was now guarded, tightly wound, walking stiffly. It was as though the plane trip had changed his personality. This would continue for several years, well into the time that it took for the media to define him. He had a private face, only to be shown to family, friends and colleagues in small groups, and a public one, mistake-free, intense and wooden.

Then he was surprised, and had to laugh. Standing there, with his hand out, was the MLA for South Peace, Don Phillips, who in his booming voice that had heads turning said, "Welcome Bill! Come on, let's get your bags. We've got work to do."

Driving into town, Don told Bennett who in caucus was friendly, who would not be, where he was staying (with Don), where his office was and how Don was going to work for him: "We'll just put our nose to the wheel and shoulder to the ground and get you elected leader and then get these godless socialists the hell out of here."

2

A GOOD TIME OR A LONG TIME

"I didn't get elected to come in here cap in hand and have you tell me what I can and can't do. I am bringing this up in cabinet, and you had better figure out how to pay for it."

BILL KING

DAVE BARRETT possesses an intuitive way of capturing the media's attention. He appeared in the public view for the first time in July 1959, when he was fired. The *Vancouver Sun*'s front-page story read:

> The provincial government has fired an employee from his $510-a-month job for working actively with the CCF party. He is David Barrett, 29, staff training officer for the Haney Correctional Institute.
>
> Barrett has been in the government service for six years and is seeking the CCF nomination to run against Labour Minister Lyle Wicks in Dewdney constituency in the next provincial election.

Attorney General Robert Bonner confirmed the move:

> This man, unfortunately, made a series of platform appearances for a political party. This is not in keeping with employment in the government service. One of the achievements of modern government is a politically independent civil service.

Dave Barrett was born on October 2, 1930, the youngest of three children. He grew up in the east end of Vancouver in a working-class neighbourhood. His father, a Fabian socialist, made his living selling vegetables and fruits from the back of a half-ton. His mother was a communist who voted CCF and spent her free time fundraising for causes like Dr. Norman Bethune's missions in China and Spain.

Their marriage was arranged and a failure. Both sides were very bright, very stubborn, and both refused to compromise. They separated when Dave was twenty. The home was not very religious: the family was Jewish but observed Jewish cultural traditions by exception rather than rule.

They were poor, and lived in a rough part of the city where everyone was poor. Dave sold newspapers, he shook hides at a packing house, and every Saturday he peddled fruit and vegetables from the back of his dad's truck. They worked on margin, sold large volumes, generously handed out free bananas and watermelon slices. Advertising was by word of mouth. Eventually his dad bought an old store on Powell Street, and through hard work and low margins became successful. However, successful did not mean rich. Sam Barrett, the outgoing owner, was easy-going with money: people got credit without giving their names, they got bags of fruit for whatever they had in their pockets, not the selling price. The store would simply give away the produce when Sam thought they had made enough money for one day.

Education was important to both parents. Dave followed his brother to Britannia High School. He was extremely bright, but by grade eight he was having too much fun to worry about marks. He joined the army cadets. He hated the discipline. He joined the rugby team. He loved it but was not good enough to play first string on the first team and was kicked off, even while riding the pines, for discipline reasons. Then he played second team, and played well, because on the intermediate team there was no discipline.

One September Dave was given a year's detention, to be served after school. The drama club was having problems getting enough boys to stage an operetta, and the teacher traded the year's detention for participation in the operetta. A whole new world opened up for Dave; he found he loved the stage and the drama.

The east end of Vancouver was an ideal place for a young guy who loved to fool around. This part of the big city had it all—drug users, bars, fights, bootleggers, prostitution and petty thieves. It was a rough place, where while shooting pool you could watch people shoot up. This was the real, big-city world, and if you wanted to play you became street smart. Dave was street smart.

He was also expected to go to university, and he attended Seattle University in 1948. His classmates were returning service men and women who had no time for the old university social rules and norms. They had fought for freedom and would not be shackled by outdated traditions. Dave loved this atmosphere. He remained on academic probation most of the time and took six months longer than normal to graduate.

He graduated in 1953, and that summer he met Shirley Hackman, his wife-to-be. They were soon married. They were young, broke, their families did not approve; they did it anyway. Even when it meant eating nothing but Savoy cabbage, they would always overcome.

He was a case worker at the Children's Aid Society when they married. He borrowed two dollars from his wife to buy a tie. He quickly turned against the social-work establishment and began to fight it. It was too rigid, uncaring, bureaucratic. Kids were falling through the cracks. Dave left.

He went to work at Oakalla Jail. He worked with young offenders. Once again he immediately found himself at odds with management. Far too rigid. Far too structured.

Dave found himself realizing that to beat the system he needed more credentials because his ideas were being ignored. He applied to the University of British Columbia to do graduate work. He was turned down.

An old professor at Seattle University intervened, and through the old-boys' network Dave was accepted at St. Louis University. The Jesuits saw something in this passionate, fun-loving, caring young man that Canadian institutions had missed. He excelled and received his master's degree. He was offered a job in the Haney Correctional Institute and accepted it. He was back in B.C. for good.

His work at the new $5 million institute soon sent him searching for ways to change the system. Politics came naturally to him, and the best way for him to support the reform of the system was to join the CCF. That led Dave to seek the nomination in Dewdney to run against the Socred minister of labour, Lyle Wicks, in the 1960 provincial election. He had lost his job but won his constituency. Socreds, however, were in power again.

Dave had never seen the legislature. He had no idea how government worked. He was nervous.

Two weeks after listening to the first throne speech he had ever heard, he rose to respond. In 1960, MLAs were not permitted to have any notes or speech prompts. He was allowed a glass of water to quench a parched throat. He started, he stumbled, he paused. Reached for the glass of water. Hands shaking so badly he spilt the glass. (To this day, he never pauses in a speech to take a drink of water.) But he survived, and slowly learned the art of House politics.

On a trip to Saskatchewan, he heard one of Canada's finest orators, federal NDP leader T.C. Douglas, speak. He was spellbound. Tommy Douglas could lecture, tell jokes, make you laugh, make you cry and, most importantly, deliver the message. Dave loved the approach and made it his.

His first two terms were fairly lacklustre, but after the 1966 provincial election he was coming into his own and becoming a recognized party leader. This election also brought in new NDP members Tom Berger and Bob Williams. Berger began to agitate to get rid of long-time leader Bob Strachan and was finally successful. In 1968, Strachan announced he was stepping down and a leadership race was on.

Berger beat Barrett by thirty-six votes, and Williams ran third. They did not have to wait long for an election call. W.A.C. Bennett regularly called elections every three years, and true to form the provincial election was called for August 31, 1969.

Dr. Pat McGeer had been elected leader of the B.C. Liberal Party in 1968 and sat with four colleagues in opposition. They felt sure it was their turn to govern.

W.A.C. Bennett toured the province in the summer of 1969 showing a government-produced film about how great B.C. was, entitled *The Good Life*. A favourite trick was to hold dinners to which the town elite would be invited. A happy hour kicked off the evening, and of course the premier, being a teetotaller, did not attend. Guests were asked to be seated. The piano struck up the first few bars of "God Save the Queen." The audience rose to their feet. The piano stopped. W.A.C. walked in. The next day the newspapers screamed: "W.A.C. Gets Standing Ovation."

W.A.C. ran against the big-city lawyer Berger and the academic brain researcher McGeer. The socialist on one side, the egghead on the other. Both from Vancouver.

Berger ran on the slogan "Ready to Govern." The public did not agree. W.A.C. had for twenty years hammered the "godless socialists" drum. The NDP was okay in opposition but not as a government.

The media were captured by W.A.C. He was the B.C. success story. In Nanaimo, the young Liberal candidate was told by the newspaper that no matter what he did, including standing on his head to give answers at all-candidates' meetings, he would get no coverage. The newspaper was supporting W.A.C. and local candidate Frank Ney. Not surprisingly, W.A.C. won and Berger lost his seat. Barrett became the NDP's interim House leader.

Dave would have one major obstacle to overcome in moving from "interim" to permanent leader: the B.C. Federation of Labour, whose leadership opposed him. They tried to undermine him at every turn because they did not see him as a "labour guy," and he wanted to put some distance between the party he led and the labour movement. He made this clear in a report in the *Victoria Times* on May 31, 1970:

> *Interviewer Street:* "To be blunt, you are saying you don't want the party identified with labour leaders as distinct from men or women who may belong to labour unions?"

Barrett: "To be blunter, we are not a labour party. And I think that should be clearly understood. That's my position."

He worked hard, travelling to many constituencies, and when the convention rolled around the following year Barrett had built up sufficient support to be elected leader.

Dave approached opposition differently than his predecessors had. Prior to his leadership the caucus always approached issues with a serious-minded, morally superior attitude. W.A.C. would bait them by calling them godless socialists. And, every time, they rose to the bait with haughty moral superiority. But Dave refused the bait and defused its effectiveness. W.A.C. called him a Marxist. Dave replied, "Which one: Groucho, Harpo or Chico?" When W.A.C. called him a waffle, referring to the left wing of the NDP, Dave called W.A.C. a pancake. It was childlike, but it made Dave appear funny and non-threatening. He would not make the mistake Berger had made, of appearing to think he could replace Bennett as premier; he would just be Dave.

True to form, W.A.C. was touring the province before calling an election in 1972. At the Royal Hotel in New Westminster, while his cabinet was heading to UBC for a tour, a protesting construction worker lowered a two-by-four onto Cyril Shelford's shoulder and broke it. W.A.C. blamed the incident on organized labour and Dave Barrett. Following another B.C. political tradition, Barrett sued Bennett. This effectively removed the issue from the election because it was before the courts. (The suit was, of course, dropped shortly after election day.)

W.A.C. called the election for August 30, 1972. The political landscape had changed since 1969; the NDP ran on a platform of "Enough Is Enough." Dave headed upcountry, working the crowds, never mentioning forming the government. Just friendly, slightly overweight Dave. Non-threatening. Easy-going and funny. You could trust him to stick up for the little guy.

The Liberal leader, Pat McGeer, stepped down and was replaced by Mr. "Full of Himself" David Anderson. Arrogant, a foreign-service officer, silver-medal-winning Olympian, environmentalist, political amateur and one-term federal MP who had never given a formal speech to Parliament. He had made his name by mastering the thirty-second voice clip for radio as he warned of the dire environmental consequences of an oil tanker from Alaska crashing on the shores of Vancouver Island.

The Conservatives had a new and energetic leader in Derril Warren, who had been elected in 1971. In the Vancouver business community he was the young W.A.C. replacement.

In fact, the two new leaders of the Liberals and Conservatives foretold the breakup of the centre-right coalition of people who had elected Social Credit for over twenty years. They also visually reflected the reverse image of an old, tired government in power.

Television was becoming the medium for all communications. W.A.C. had a mind that raced ahead of his mouth, often leaving out chunks of sentences, but he knew what hot buttons to push and how to get a crowd going. Television was not kind to this old-style politician. The contrast with his three young opponents was too great. Twenty years in power was too much. His ideas were old, his rhetoric was old-fashioned and his party was splitting up.

The NDP won with thirty-eight seats. Socreds, ten. Liberals, five. The most remarkable era in B.C. political history was over.

DAVE BARRETT, his wife Shirley and their three kids drove off the ferry and stopped in Sidney at a pay phone to call Government House for instructions. He had been called earlier in the morning by Deputy Provincial Secretary Lawrie Wallace to come over to Victoria because Premier Bennett was stepping down that afternoon. He was told to come straight up, so he did, and accompanied by his family, a secretary and a staff person he was sworn in. He did not realize that he could have arranged anything he wanted. He just did not know how this worked.

A week later, his cabinet was sworn in. Again, a quick ceremony. The criterion for cabinet membership was simple: if you had been a former caucus member you were in, if not you were out. None of the new blood made it to the front bench, irrespective of ability, intelligence or geography.

Barrett's first cabinet meeting dealt with two issues. The first was in the form of a question Barrett asked: Were they there for a good time or a long time?

The cabinet agreed: fundamental change, quick. If they had only one term, so be it, but they should use it to get things done.

The second issue saw the premier describe his, and therefore cabinet's, operating style and their relationship with the bureaucracy:

> I insisted on a hands-on cabinet. There would be no delegating of political decisions to the bureaucracy. The bureaucracy was there to serve the political masters, not the other way around.
>
> There were open and frank exchanges that led to sharp disagreements in cabinet, and that was important, but I deliberately kept a tight rein on meetings. We kept with one simple agenda model all the way through government. I refused to have any report given to me that was over one page long, and I refused to have any memos discussing political matters even written. We did not permit bureaucrats at cabinet meetings. Occasionally a deputy minister would be invited to give a rundown on technical problems or some other aspect of what we were discussing, and then politely asked to leave.

Dave Barrett inherited a horse-and-buggy government largely run by one man, W.A.C. Bennett. With his deputy minister of finance, Gerry Bryson, carefully controlling spending (Bryson was referred to as Little Treasury Board, W.A.C. as Big Treasury Board) and the deputy provincial secretary, Lawrie Wallace, running grand events, W.A.C.'s government sailed along for twenty years. It was not until 1970 that the province's total budget reached $1 billion.

Civil servants could not phone out of province without a deputy minister's prior approval. Staff could not travel without the comptroller's prior approval. Senior staff were not allowed to attend any out-of-province events without the premier's approval. The premier was the paternal figure who set the pay, the tone and the style.

Minister of Labour Jim Chabot told a graduate student writing about the Mediation Commission Act in 1971, just before the provincial election, that "I would like to change the law and have some ideas on how to make it more workable, but the old man told me to keep my ideas to myself... He would tell me what to change and when."

Dave Barrett set out to change this climate with a vengeance. To start, civil servants were given bargaining rights.

Norm Richards, the president of the B.C. Government Employees' Union, and staff person John Fryer presented a package of demands to the chair of the Public Service Commission, Art Richardson, and Commissioner Meryl Campbell, the employer representatives in the first round of negotiations. The commissioners had never bargained and had no experience acting for the employer in collective bargaining. Thus they did not know how to proceed and presented no ideas or demands. They accepted all the union's proposals and contract language, with two exceptions, which they indicated they must take back to their minister, Ernie Hall.

On presenting them to Hall, they were told that of course they were accepted. Hall then went through the proposed contract and found what he, not the union, thought was missing and added several more benefits for the workers. He decided, for example, that lifetime job security would be granted to employees who had worked for the government for two years. It was a hell of a way to teach public servants how to vote.

People began to be hired at an ever-increasing rate. The bureaucracy grew from about 31,000 to 39,000 in three years: 8,000 new permanent positions. The Ministry of Labour grew from just over 100 employees to more than 700 in three years.

The NDP and its predecessor the CCF had been waiting for decades to form the provincial government. Every policy under the sun had been debated, and now was the time to get the program underway. The first session of the legislature opened in October 1972. The minimum wage was raised to the highest in Canada (at $2.50), a $200 Mincome was established for all old-age pensioners, the Mediation Commission was struck down, the cap on teachers' salaries of 6.5 percent per annum was repealed and a ban on liquor and tobacco advertising was thrown out.

The spring session brought in the Agricultural Land Commission Act, the Labour Code, the Insurance Corporation of B.C. Act, the B.C. Petroleum Corporation Act and the Mining Royalty Act, all major pieces of legislation and all very controversial. Many other bills were driven through, covering every aspect of life.

The government bought the pulp mill at Ocean Falls. It bought Columbia Cellulose. It entered a joint venture with Brascan to develop a coal field. At the end of Barrett's first year in power he was at the top of his game, and no one in the disorganized opposition could lay a glove on him. He went to New York and Europe on trade and investment missions.

Then Barrett made his first political mistake. W.A.C. Bennett resigned on June 5, 1973. A week later, on June 13, W.A.C.'s son Bill announced he would run to fill the vacancy. Barrett could have waited up to six months to call the by-election; this would have allowed the Social Credit leadership convention to be held before the by-election date, making it much harder for the young Bennett to win. He did not care. He had slain the master, the father, and he would make mincemeat of the son.

The government expanded its legislative agenda. It expanded the bureaucracy. In power only 1,200 days, it passed 367 pieces of legislation—more than double the number passed in the previous three years. It was a dizzying array: a human rights code, pharmacare, legal aid services, housing and consumer affairs ministries, a rentalsman and rent controls, aid for post-secondary students, reformed welfare schemes that increased rates and expanded categories eligible for claim, community resource boards, increased urban bus service and a doubling of the park base in the province. To run all the programs, new staff, new offices.

Strong ministers drove their agenda and the weaker ones stumbled along behind. Bill King, the minister of labour, told Gerry Bryson, still acting as Little Treasury Board, five minutes into their first meeting on the way out the door, "I didn't get elected to come in here cap in hand and have you tell me what I can and can't do. I am bringing this up in cabinet, and you had better figure out how to pay for it." And Bryson did. Actually, both of them did.

The great irony here is that the social democrats, a party of social planners and academics, had no plan. As NDP staff person Wally Ross said:

> With the exception of just a couple of ministers, they never had any more control than a guy caught in an avalanche. Nobody ever sat down and said what our priorities were and what's going to be done this year. Beyond welfare, which consistently received strong emphasis, no priorities were ever evident, with health, housing and other areas being but holding operations. It was like a house of casual pleasure run by the girls.

Human Resources Minister Norm Levi put it this way:

> The government never had a blueprint for office. It lacked one when it took office and failed to develop one subsequently. Our basic interest and ideas were right, but the needed refinement of them never occurred. Effective management was lacking. Anyway, you can't advance on the broad number of fronts we did and maintain a blueprint.

But one minister had a blueprint, if only in his head. Bob Williams, the "resource minister," was viewed by many as the real power in the government. No one disputed his brilliance, his competence, his desire to do right by the downtrodden. Just as no one disputed his acid tongue, his disdain for those he perceived to be of lesser intelligence (that is, most people) or his willingness to step into the gutter.

Williams waded into areas whenever he wanted, staying away only from tough ministers like Bill King. He dominated in cabinet, pushed the agenda where he wanted and was ruthless with those who opposed him. But he could neither control nor direct the tidal wave of activity that rolled ahead of the government's ability to manage it.

PAUL TENNANT, in his article "The NDP Government of B.C.: Unaided Politicians in an Unaided Cabinet," spelled out a view, supported by interviews, personal observation and other studies, that the fundamental structure of cabinet government in B.C. had not changed much from the time when B.C. entered Confederation. British Columbia's government was organized around common program theme areas, such as health, finance, education, transportation, labour. Success was often measured by balanced budgets. Governmental goals related to economic development. Economic policy was segmented into forests, mines and highways, with little need for interdepartmental coordination. This was held together by a strong authoritarian leader; in B.C. it was W.A.C. Bennett.

The NDP left the cabinet structure the way it had found it. However, it changed the policy agenda. Social policy, not economic policy, became the driving force. And social policy requires coordination. Leaving in place the old-time cabinet structure might still have been successful, but the problem was exacerbated because Barrett did not act as an authoritarian leader. The cabinet became a debating society.

Policy was driven by strong ministers who got their way through force of personality. There was no consistent source of information, no consistent financial oversight and monitoring, no reference, other than in vague ways, to party policy. Legislation went forward poorly drafted, with little or no consultation with affected groups. It was often withdrawn, rewritten and re-introduced. This approach left the impression that the government was bungling and out of control. And it angered the public.

Proposals at cabinet were often adopted with no fiscal impact planning. Minister King introduced to cabinet in January 1974 a $20 million plan to hire summer students, starting May 1. It was accepted. The ministry had no staff available to run the program, no offices, no plan. No one in cabinet asked how it could be done; they just assumed it would be done. A week later, King phoned his deputy and said that someone had said what a good idea the summer student employment plan was and cabinet agreed to put in $5 million more. Two weeks later, the minister phoned his deputy after cabinet and said that Bob Williams had not been in cabinet the day the program had gone through and had just heard of the plan. Therefore $5 million more was being allocated to be directed specifically at forest-related projects.

With a program design and a one-page summary to go to cabinet, a $20 million program was passed with no thought given to the delivery infrastructure. This was increased by $5 million for the simple reason that one cabinet minister thought it a good idea. And it was raised by $5 million more when another cabinet minister agreed two weeks later. The program was delivered on time and on budget, but with this kind of planning it is little wonder that the bell finally tolled for fiscal mismanagement.

The reasons for this situation are not complex. First, the premier chose his cabinet from the eleven old hands, not from the twenty-six newly elected members. They had sat in opposition together and had dealt with a traditional and successful government—a model they understood and admired. They saw no need to change.

Their approach to policy making was based on a combination of trust in their own knowledge of what must be done and mistrust of the bureaucracy to help them. They believed that the critical thing was to have the right minister in the right job making the right decisions, with no thought about how that actually translated into structures and delivery systems.

The economy helped. Rolling along as it had for most of the past twenty years, it continued to generate revenues that allowed for undisciplined spending. Education spending increased 13 percent in the first year and then 23 percent in each of the next two years. As long as revenues kept ahead, this did not matter. The financial management system of W.A.C. was likely the crudest in all provincial governments, largely carried in the heads of W.A.C. and a few senior finance officials, and it remained unchanged under Barrett. They just did not think they needed to pay more attention. In the words of one senior finance official: "Stop and go. Revenues in, then revenues out. No financial planning. No financial forecasting. No priorities established. They frowned on economists and would wait until the revenue numbers and expenditure numbers came in and then would draw up their budgets."

The macho nature of cabinet aided this deception: they just did not think budget planning was necessary. Their reasoning was: W.A.C. did it, and we are better than him! Some even argued that they were on a mission; central control and planning would slow the process down, there was too much to get done, and therefore those who suggested planning and controls were suspect. Paul Tennant quotes one minister: "'We simply didn't have the time to develop complex organization around the cabinet. We had so much to do we thought it better to put general things aside until later.' The statement is antithetical to any conscious attention to overall planning and is at the same time supportive of the unaided politician in the unaided cabinet."

Barrett, the social democrat in a hurry, with a huge caring heart for society's downtrodden, had an answer for all of life's woes. He would fix everything with taxpayers' money, irrespective of cost. He had an inherent inability to organize a structured solution. His cabinet followed him.

DAVE BARRETT faced the fall of 1975 with trepidation. He was fearful that the decades-old symbol, a balanced budget, was not within his grasp. If he waited to call an election, he would prove that the NDP were not good managers. On the other hand, as he travelled around the province on his annual fall tour he found great grassroots support. He thought that perhaps all he had to do was demonstrate strong leadership and ride the issues hard. Once he got onto a platform with Bennett Junior, he would win.

Barrett's first opportunity to set the stage for a possible election was presented by an old foe, organized labour. In the summer of 1973, B.C. Ferries workers went on strike. The government caved in order to get them back to work. Bob Strachan, the minister of transport, said he gave in because "it was like having a gun to my head."

After that, Bill King stepped in firmly to control the labour agenda. Organized labour discovered that "their" government would act responsibly to serve the public interest. But the battle was on.

The next year, firefighters went out on a bitter strike, followed by ICBC workers. In the summer of 1975, the IWA went on strike. A bitter inter-union squabble broke out between them and the Canadian Paperworkers Union. Then the Teamsters who delivered propane gas around the province struck. They were followed by food industry workers, retail employees and railway workers. By early fall, nearly sixty thousand workers were on strike.

The government acted on October 7, 1975, introducing the Collective Bargaining Continuation Act. All disputes, public and private sector, were covered. The strikes were to end in forty-eight hours, and a ninety-day cooling-off period was enforced. The bill passed quickly, with only three NDP members voting against it.

Organized labour was furious. The business community was dumbfounded. The public was very pleased. Beating up organized labour had always been good politics in B.C., and would continue to be, but this time the "heavy" was the labour unions' best friend, their own political party, the NDP. And for the first time ever, back-to-work legislation was to be applied to private-sector unions. To the public it appeared that the government had acted in the public interest.

The second opportunity was presented by the federal government. Over the Thanksgiving weekend in October 1975, Prime Minister Pierre Elliott Trudeau called a First Ministers Conference in Ottawa to unveil his anti-inflation plan. Inflation in Canada was running in double digits, and strong action was required.

Trudeau proposed wage and price controls. There was heated debate. The Canadian Labour Congress was opposed. The national NDP was opposed. But all the premiers, including Barrett, signed on. Again Barrett was sideways with organized labour and with the mainstream thinking of the NDP.

To mitigate this mainstream sentiment, the B.C. cabinet introduced by order-in-council a freeze on the prices of food, fuel and essential services. It also raised the minimum wage to $2.75 and Mincome rates. This angered both the large and the small business community.

British Columbia was the only province in Canada to take action on prices. Again, organized labour, the CLC, cried out about the failure of the provinces, particularly NDP provinces, in not standing up to Trudeau.

Barrett called his last caucus meeting in late October. The northern B.C. MLAs were in favour of an election call—they had seen the good crowds on the premier's tour. The urban MLAs were against. They were led by Richmond MLA Harold Steeves, who argued that polling numbers in his riding showed a clear defeat. The party polls, however, were not shared with caucus. They showed trouble.

The cabinet was split. Two ministers, Jack Radford and Ernie Hall, led the anti-election arguments. Hall went around the cabinet table and told each of the ministers what their Achilles heel was and how it would be used against them; Norm Levi's overrun, Bill King's back-to-work legislation, ICBC's deficit.

Barrett was left to think about it. He turned to two people for advice. Bob Williams and his new cabinet secretary, Marc Eliesen, both argued for a quick election. They argued that the NDP might lose some ground, but if it waited it would be worse.

Barrett couldn't decide. Maybe he would win a smaller majority, but he would win. Maybe, if he lost, he wouldn't lose much, and he would make a comeback after the public had had a taste of Bennett Junior.

He rationalized that no B.C. government since the Great Depression, and no CCF or NDP government, had ever failed to win a second term. And in a TV debate he would whip Bill Bennett's ass. But if he lost, would all his reforms be rolled back? Would the last three years be for naught?

Surely the province was not ready for "Daddy's Boy," little Billy. Surely not.

3

BORN AGAIN

> *"I went into the office, in a building that had probably been built in 1917–18, on Broadway. There were two half-time girls there, and they couldn't be paid. They couldn't meet the payroll the week I was elected president."*
>
> GRACE McCARTHY

AFTER THE election loss in 1972 W.A.C. had clung to power for a few weeks, as if reluctant to let it go. Perhaps he thought the nightmare would end and he would awake. But no, it was time to give it up. He called his cabinet together.

The cabinet members were all gathered, except for Ralph Loffmark, who decided that since it was over, it was over, and he would get on with life. W.A.C. went around the room and thanked them all personally. They were good friends saying goodbye, and all of them secretly wished the old man had died in office rather than having faced defeat. They quietly went their own ways, and W.A.C. went to Government House.

Grace McCarthy describes why he lost: "He lost because he was there for such a long time, and the NDP sold the idea that he was getting old, long in the tooth, couldn't handle the present situation, the new economy, *et cetera*. There was no one reason; frankly, it was just that people were tired, he'd been around a long time, the hippie age was with us, people were bare-footed and pony-tailed and flower children, and this guy didn't suit the times."

Bill Bennett sees it this way:

> Social Credit lost the election because they had always ridden on the strength that was unique to W.A.C. to lead the election. Organizationally they had the usual things, the constituency and workers that were supposed to get out the vote, but it wasn't really structured to make sure all the ridings worked. They were not of the modern generation where they really went out and had a structure for campaigning.
>
> The NDP had Yvonne Cocke and her machine, the best organization in the country. They didn't have the best policies, maybe, but they could get the vote and they had the organization to get it out.
>
> And that was lacking—we were in a change generation, with television now a major factor, and it hadn't been in other elections. Combine that with the age of W.A.C., who was turning seventy-two. The reported remarks of Phil Gaglardi that the old man was losing it didn't help. W.A.C. felt that was the killer blow.

Grace McCarthy and Dan Campbell, both defeated, had been asked by W.A.C. to stay on and work in caucus: Campbell as administrative assistant to the leader of the opposition, and Grace McCarthy as caucus research assistant. Their personalities dictated that they had no choice but to put aside the sackcloth and ashes. The Social Credit Party had shrunk to fewer than four thousand members, many of them paper shadows of days past.

W.A.C., Grace and Dan decided to rebuild the party. The place to start was not Victoria, but around the province. The party had no real head office and no money; membership lists were fragmented and often non-existent. The rebuilders knew the secret to success in the next election would be an army of members. First they had to stabilize the existing base and convince the faithful that this was just a setback, not the end of Social Credit. Grace McCarthy remembers:

> The party was in disarray, not because of the defeat, although that added to it, everybody was dispirited. But before we went to the election the machinery had run down, there was no machinery. There was no organized volunteer organization, there was no party organization. There were probably one hundred paid-up members. That was all.
>
> I went into the office, in a building that had probably been built in 1917–18, on Broadway. There were two half-time girls there, and they couldn't be paid. They couldn't meet the payroll the week I was elected president.

The new caucus was left to struggle with being the opposition. Let Barrett have his day in the sun. W.A.C., Dan Campbell and Grace McCarthy hit the road in Bill Dale's Cadillac Coupe de Ville. Week after week, they barnstormed the province. Bill Dale drove and made the hotel arrangements. The other three ran the circus.

Dan and Grace would take turns leading off, shamelessly stealing each other's best lines from the night before. They snuffed lighted candles to show freedom being snuffed out by the socialists. They were given a leg up by the NDP's introduction of a brilliant but poorly drafted bill. Marjorie Nichols, the tough-nosed *Vancouver Sun* press gallery reporter, recalled the legislation in her book *Mark My Words*:

> The Act that set out to put a freeze on agricultural land was the most damaging, the most contentious of all. It started out as something which would have allowed the government of B.C. to designate all land in the province according to various categories. I remember asking Barrett what I thought was an absurd question at the time: "Are you telling me that this bill would give you the power to designate the spot upon which the Hotel Vancouver sits as a cabbage patch?"
>
> Unbelievably, he said, "Yes."

> I recognized this immediately as a pretty stunning document. I ran down to the harbour, chartered an airplane and flew the Act over to Vancouver. They ripped out about four pages of grocery ads and ran the entire Act in the *Vancouver Sun*. Years later, people still had that on their refrigerators.

AFTER THE WARM-UP band, the finale was always W.A.C. A folk legend. He recaptured people's loyalty with good old pump-priming rhetoric about free enterprise versus the socialist hordes at the gates.

They stabilized the party. Stopped the decline. Gave hope. And started to sell memberships. Grace remembers the revival:

> Our first meeting was in Nanaimo. W.A.C. Bennett took the Agricultural Land Act, and he waved it in the air and just gave them the whole load. One fellow, I can see him, he came from the back of the hall, at the end of the speech, and he had his NDP membership—you'd think we staged it, but we couldn't have staged it as well. We had TV cameras and everybody there, and he came from the back, and he's from Europe, and he said, "Mr. Premier, I've been an NDP member for years."
>
> My heart sank and I thought, "Oh, no, this guy's going to deride the Socreds."
>
> But he said, "I'm going to tell you, where I came from," and he named wherever he was from, and he said, "I'm going to tell you, that's exactly how they treated us there, exactly." And he had everybody just transfixed. He had tears in his eyes and he said, "It's how they do it, it's how they do it."
>
> We didn't think we'd go this far, but this guy could go this far. They were all communists as far as he was concerned, and the whole crowd started to surge towards the front stage to sign up memberships. It was like you were giving away ten-dollar bills. But they were pushing five-dollar bills at us.
>
> I couldn't write up the memberships fast enough. Dan and I are sitting there writing, and I'm looking at him saying, "God, this is incredible!" And we went home with all these memberships.

ON JUNE 5, 1973, Hugh Harris knew he was up against it. W.A.C. Bennett had just resigned his seat in the legislature, and his son Bill, Hugh's new friend, fully expected Hugh to put together a winning campaign for him.

When Hugh had told Bill he would support him if he agreed not only to run but to go all the way to the premier's office he had, as always, gotten carried away with his own enthusiasm. He had no idea how to organize a modern election campaign. He had never done it before. But that had not stopped him before.

Hugh had been born in the east end of Vancouver in 1941. Raised in foster homes, he claimed the rough and tumble of growing up turned him into an entrepreneur. He was a hell-raiser as a kid and a tattooed member of the Aces street gang. He had married Meldy and settled down, moving to Kelowna in 1972. He didn't vote in the 1972 election because it was held on a Wednesday, his golf day. The Socred loss infuriated him, and when Bill phoned and asked for help he was ready.

While a confirmed right-wing business guy, Hugh was not your typical white-shoes, white-belt Socred. He was a witty, easy-going, pipe-puffing, jean-wearing rumpled bear of a man. His nose was crooked and slanted, having been broken by Emery Barnes when Hugh tried out for the B.C. Lions. Although a political neophyte, he was also a political junkie.

Hugh figured out how he would learn the tricks of running a campaign. Down to Vancouver he went, and out to NDP headquarters. His enthusiasm was obvious, their politics different, but Hugh walked out with all the non-classified NDP material on how to run campaigns like the NDP did.

He returned to Kelowna and organized an NDP-type campaign in the by-election. First he had to ensure a nomination victory, which turned out to be a one-sided contest between Bennett and constituency president Fred Stevens. Taking no chances, Hugh jammed the hall with Bennett supporters wearing red-white-and-blue boaters displaying the slogan "Build with Bill." Bennett won going away. His father, proud enough to burst, said: "Here tonight we see the rebirth of the Social Credit Party in the province of British Columbia. The rebirth here will increase in momentum throughout the province and the coming by-election. In two or three years from now the NDP will only be a bad dream. Happy days are here again."

Hugh immediately turned his attention to the September 7 by-election. Within days, hundreds of volunteers were door-knocking. Every person's vote preference was noted and written down and recorded at headquarters. Undecided voters were visited twice or even three times. A drive-to-the-polls team was readied for election day to ensure that all the committed voters got to the polls and voted. As Allan Fotheringham noted in the *Vancouver Sun* on September 8, 1973: "The offices of Bennett, most unusual for the Socreds, were filled with meticulous charts on canvassing and poll-by-poll enumeration, the NDP-invented technique copied by other parties that seldom perfect it. The gung-ho younger business types brought in by Bennett, once taught the techniques, revelled in their execution."

This by-election was about more than who would represent the Kelowna constituency. Many members of the Vancouver business establishment had seen the Conservative candidate and leader, Derril Warren, as the heir apparent to W.A.C. Bennett. Just as Peter Lougheed had rallied a dormant Progressive Conservative Party in Alberta to beat Social Credit, Warren was expected to repeat the feat in B.C. If Derril lost, it would be the end of his political career and foreshadow the end of the Conservative Party in B.C. If Bill Bennett won, the Vancouver money and business community would have second thoughts about going Conservative and would, at least, be willing to consider Social Credit as an alternative.

Bennett knew the risk he was taking: "I had to set the trap. First of all I had to wait and wait, making it possible so he could be drawn in... I wanted him, because if he could beat me then it was all over. Warren had said, 'Well, if I don't make it I will stay here and work in Kelowna and set up my office,' which he did. It was the end of his political career."

The Warren camp also made a last-minute tactical error. The Vancouver *Province* editorial page, reflecting the Vancouver business establishment's view, had endorsed Warren as the best pick to take on the Barrett government. Ten thousand tear sheets were distributed across the riding. It reinforced the anti-Vancouver sentiment, the big-city-knows-best feeling, that many Interior residents feel. Suits from Vancouver seldom understand the Interior, and the backlash hurt Warren.

On September 7, 1973, Bill Bennett won with 39 percent of the vote, less than his father attained, but the same as Dave Barrett's provincial total in the 1972 election. The NDP ran second, with 26 percent, and the Conservatives third, with 25 percent. The Liberals came in a distant fourth at 10 percent.

Once the nervous, newly elected MLA had given his victory speech at campaign headquarters, the beginning of the transformation of the party was evident. The crowd was young, affluent, anti-Vancouver, upwardly mobile, hard-working, hard-playing college and business people.

The little old lady in tennis shoes and the elderly man in full Nanaimo (white shoes and belt, polyester shirt and pants) may still have been part of the party W.A.C. had founded, but they were in the minority. And they were in the backrooms, sipping tea. Social Credit had moved to scotch and water and a quick shake your booty on the dance floor. This model was about to be emulated across the province.

The significance of the win lay in the defeat of Derril Warren. The death watch began for the Conservative Party. Warren refused to comment on what his future might be, but Bennett wasted no time in calling the win "a victory for free enterprise, and I appeal to the Conservatives and Liberals to unite behind Social Credit."

Importantly, even the Vancouver papers began to recognize that Social Credit might not be dead. The *Sun* editorial page grudgingly commented the next day:

> With the victory of William Bennett... the Social Credit Party may have begun something of a recovery after its smashing defeat in last year's general election...
>
> However, the election was not a serious defeat for Premier Barrett...
>
> For Derril Warren, the gallant Conservative, it could mean the end of a political career already overshadowed by defeat in the general election. He can no longer lead from outside the legislature... the Conservative Party... obviously must find another leader...
>
> The result for the Liberals is a major disappointment. In truth, it seems to leave Social Credit as the possible alternative to the NDP at the next general election.

DON PHILLIPS hosted a cocktail party in Victoria on September 20, 1973, the night Bill was sworn in as the new MLA for Okanagan. The plan was to meet the caucus and the press gallery, bend a few elbows and get to know the new guy. A penthouse suite in the Harbour Towers was rented.

The only problem was, it was the night of the Bobby Riggs–Billie Jean King tennis match. The only way to watch the spectacle, which included Billie Jean walking in with a pig on a leash (perhaps symbolic of the new age, the young woman beating the pants off the old man), was to turn on the only television set in the place, which was situated in the bedroom.

A dozen or so opposition MLAs and reporters sat on the bed and on the floor or leaned against the walls—shouting, laughing, drinking and eating hors d'oeuvres. Reporters went away shaking their heads. They had just borne witness to a new era. The difference between Bill and W.A.C. for old caucus members and old press gallery hands was immense, almost unbelievable. Perhaps the rumours that he wasn't just "Daddy's Boy" were true. For one thing, he drank Johnny Walker Red. For another, he was funny. Could this be true?

On September 26, Bill Bennett gave his maiden speech in the legislature. It was brief and dealt with constituency issues, calling for the establishment of an Okanagan Basin Authority made up of the three levels of government. For a scant ten minutes he spoke about becoming a constructive opposition critic who would offer positive alternatives to unacceptable government programs. He called for turning Highway 97 into a four-lane freeway. He argued for the immediate removal of the 12 percent federal sales tax and the 5 percent provincial sales tax on building materials used for housing. He said: "The proper role of government is as an arbitrator. No party has exclusive rights on a social conscience, and the philosophical differences among the parties has to do with method rather than ultimate objective."

He was starting to stake out his position as different from others in the caucus. In an interview with Peter McNally in the *Province,* Bennett argued that Social Credit had to move to the centre: "There's not enough people in this province to elect a right-wing government. A responsible alternative to this government must be a centre-of-the-road party."

He also recognized that it takes foot soldiers, not generals, to win elections: "When the troops start to believe that the generals win the war, they leave the work to the generals, and that happened to our party."

The general, his father, had lost the last election. It would not happen to him; Bennett recognized his father's impact. "I take it for a fact that in inheriting his friends, I inherit his enemies."

ON OCTOBER 11, Bennett announced that he was seeking the Social Credit Party leadership. From the Socred caucus, Newell Morrison, Pat Jordan, Frank Richter, Don Phillips and Alex Fraser decided not to run for the leadership. The rest, however, would run: Jim Chabot, Ed Smith, Bob McClelland, Harvey Schroeder. They were joined by Burnaby accountant Jim Mason.

There were no leadership tours and only two debates. Most arm-twisting was done by telephone, on the convention floor and in hotel rooms. Bennett took the convention by storm: "My focus was my team and my group, and of course when we hit the convention I had all these young people coming out, people who had never been to an election. They were nineteen or twenty, and this really socked it to them because the other delegations were all older people. They had never seen anything like this. What I really needed to do was just not misstep..."

Marjorie Nichols handicapped the race in the *Vancouver Sun*, on November 22, 1973:

> As the first of an expected 2,000 convention delegates began arriving today at the Hotel Vancouver for the opening session Bennett appeared to be holding firm on the inside track... The point is that the six contestants for the mantle being handed down after 21 years by W.A.C. Bennett represent a surprisingly broad philosophical spectrum.
>
> The future direction of the party could thus be markedly altered as a consequence of the election of the leader.
>
> Bennett has staked out his position on the left wing, and has made it clear that under his stewardship there would be a conscious swing toward the ground now occupied by the Liberals.

Candidate support was first tested at the convention in the election of a new party president. Grace McCarthy, Bennett's campaign manager, had thrown her hat into the ring hoping for a one-two punch. Trying to decide whether to run was party Vice-President Ken Kiernan, a former cabinet minister and very popular with the old guard membership. When Kiernan decided to run on voting day, it was felt this might signal a movement away from the young Bennett.

Bennett did not particularly care; he had spoken to Kiernan, who had told him he would stay neutral in the leadership race and support him if he won, which he expected. Bennett could see advantages to Kiernan winning: it would mollify the segment of the party that still yearned for the old man and the old ways.

However, this time W.A.C. intervened. He phoned his son and asked that Bill rally his troops behind Grace because she had remained loyal. He wanted this as a favour. Bill agreed. He phoned Hugh Harris and told him he wanted to swing behind Grace. Hugh disagreed. Bill looked at him with a steely-eyed stare that Hugh had never seen before and said: "Just do it." Hugh blinked and said: "OK, you're the boss."

Grace won by twenty votes.

The next day was the leadership vote. Bennett's followers staged a raucous celebration. For three days he had the largest group, and the youngest, noisiest delegates. Pompoms were swung by dancing cheerleaders. There was a brass marching band, hundreds of helium balloons, boys in raccoon coats, a St. Bernard dog, conga lines of middle-aged businessmen and women and students wearing Styrofoam boaters with "Build with Bill" buttons.

Bennett won on the first ballot. He collected 883 votes, more than the rest of the candidates combined. Bob McClelland ran second, with 269 votes; Harvey Schroeder had 204, Jim Chabot 97, Ed Smith 74 and James Mason 10.

After Bennett's acceptance speech his supporters revved up the band, marched around the hall and out onto the streets of Vancouver carrying banners and balloons and giving away Okanagan apples. It was the largest political leadership convention in B.C. history, and the first with all the flash and pomp of an American-style convention. It foreshadowed a new, dynamic television-driven event for parties to elect leaders.

Although issues were not central in picking the new leader, it was clear that an ideological swing, from right to centre-right, had occurred. From one-man leadership to a collegial, all-inclusive style. Bennett remembers:

> I think there was a generational change. It had happened in other provinces, you could see it in the Atlantic provinces; in Alberta, Quebec, Ontario, Manitoba. It was a generational move, and it was not just a change in attitude. Some of the ones running against me were taking very extreme positions. People wanted to have a common sense of direction, not ideologically driven fights: "Where are we going to go, what's going to get us there, what is society going to be like?"

Bennett's acceptance speech had two themes, which were to be repeated over and over again in the weeks and months ahead:

> Let it be clearly understood, by friend and foe alike, that as your new leader I am my own man.

And:

> Now we are a new party, and I am dedicated to making this an open party. We've shown that this party, and only this party, is the free-enterprise party of the future.

BETWEEN THE leadership convention and Christmas, Bennett began the constant travel that was to be his life for the next few years. A few days in Victoria, watching, listening and learning. Occasionally speaking to the media. Rarely speaking in the legislature. However, one incident in the spring session of the legislature served notice that he would not be pushed around. The government was in full voice, taunting the new leader of the opposition. The favourite taunt: Daddy's boy—Did Daddy write that for you? Have you checked with Daddy? Most of it, he took. But finally he had heard enough.

He stopped, looked directly at one of the more vociferous members of the government—one of his oldest adversaries—leaned forward and quietly said: "At least I have a daddy."

The government benches were stunned, and so were his colleagues. No one knew this fact, which obviously hit home. Bennett quietly finished his presentation, nodded to the Speaker and left the floor. The member across from him remained staring down at his desk.

The razzing from this day forward took on a different tone. The comments about his father ended. The kid from Kelowna had served notice.

Most of Bennett's time was spent travelling around the province, speaking to groups of people of various sizes, every day and night. He was tireless. His travelling companions were always either Grace McCarthy or Dan Campbell. Often Dave Brown came along to give media advice. Some days Dave would go jogging with Bill in the morning. Dave was recognizable as the one in the three-piece jogging suit.

The first stop after the leadership convention was Comox. Dan Campbell had been the MLA for many years, until being soundly defeated in the previous election. But he still could fill a hall of people curious to see the young Bennett. Dan describes the event this way:

> In the beginning, Bill's chief handicap was that his public speaking ability would have done credit to a cigar store Indian. On the other hand, in private talks he was outgoing, charming and persuasive.
>
> Bill was not the showman type his father was, but he did not stammer either when he did speak. On a public platform he was a great fidgeter. He kept playing with water glasses. He liked to bring about a maximum of distraction by putting his hands in and out of his pockets. He had a particular fetish for paper napkins and often ripped up enough to look after a fair-sized wedding...
>
> We chose the Comox Legion Hall for his first exposure as premier-to-be. It was to prove a hairy experience. Our plane had weather problems out of Vancouver. We were about two hours late.

I could see the crowd was a little restless. So I got up and immediately introduced Bill as the next premier of B.C. My friends in the audience were too polite to take out their waiting frustration on the new boy. They gave him a rousing welcome.

He quickly blew that by telling the crowd that he was glad to be in Courtenay, which is a no-no in Comox. He followed that by dumping over his water glass on his scribbled notes. During his speech he devastated all the paper napkins within reach at the head table.

Bill at this time was not the world's greatest speechmaker, but he was a good question-and-answer performer. This night the crowd sat on their hands during the speech, but when he got to the audience participation part, things came alive.

After the meeting we both agreed that the audience free-for-all was to be a foremost attraction for all future meetings.

Following this and every other meeting, whoever was travelling with Bennett was encouraged to critique the performance. He was always his own harshest critic, but he combined his self-flagellation with outside peer criticism that enabled him slowly to improve his speech performance. He would never lose the public and media's perception of stiffness, of being a wooden public performer, but he learnt how to get his message across. But once the media had branded him as a lacklustre speaker, they never gave up. Even after Bennett became an accomplished public speaker, the media never acknowledged it.

And, every weekend, he would go home to Audrey and the kids. There he would be revived and refreshed.

4

THOSE GUYS ARE TOAST

"I intend to get up, have a good stiff drink of gin, go to the polls, vote Social Credit, come home, spend two hours washing my hands, and then finish off the bottle!"

ANONYMOUS LIBERAL, AS QUOTED BY ALLAN FOTHERINGHAM

IT WAS THE WEEK between Christmas and New Year's, 1973. Bill Bennett was home with his wife and family in Kelowna. He had been home for the past six days and was scheduled to stay until January 3, when he would head out on the road again. Audrey could see the strain and pressure slip off him as he slowly returned to his normal wise-cracking self.

But Audrey knew something was stuck in his craw. And until Bill had thought it through and got it out in the open, it would make him behave like a bear with a thorn in its paw. She had seen this before, when he had gone into a new business, especially in the earlier years. She knew he was wrestling with all the information he had absorbed in the past six months. The transition from successful businessman to leader of the opposition to premier-in-waiting had its stresses. He would keep them bottled up, and

Audrey knew to wait: "At those times when Bill is forced to bring his work home, he is encapsulated in his own world, totally alienated from his family. We just sit and watch; there's not much you can do about it."

She also knew he was close to figuring out a general strategy of how to go forward. During the last few days of skiing he had thrown himself at the mountain, a sure symptom that her overly competitive husband was driving himself against the different hill that needed climbing.

In his mind the plan for the next three years was taking shape. He had gone to—more accurately, been taken to—school in the past few months. Quietly assessing colleagues in caucus. Listening to their ideas. Reading everything he could get his hands on. Talking with Dan Campbell on how to strengthen the caucus. Working with Grace McCarthy and hearing about the strengths and weaknesses of the party.

Although the government members had heckled him the few times he spoke in the House, it did not bother him. He knew what he was going to say and kept it short. He was able to watch them in action during the scant time he spent in the House and to assess their strengths and weaknesses.

His few meetings with the Vancouver business community had been less than satisfactory. He clearly was not their first choice. Not their choice at all, in fact. Although the young businessman Jimmy Pattison had stood up for him, other more senior members of the business establishment, like Forrest Rogers, had been outspoken critics. In the larger scheme of things they were not important. Grace McCarthy describes one of these meetings in Vancouver:

> Bill was trying very hard. One day—he was now leader—we were called to the Bayshore Inn to a meeting of either the Majority Movement [a right-wing coalition group] or just a group of business-people, and Mike Burns of IBM. It was one of the worst meetings I had ever attended.
>
> It was in a small room in the Bayshore. Bill and I were sitting there, at a long boardroom table, everyone kind of squeezed around the table, and there were maybe eleven people. And this group of people, I remember them being so critical. It was like they weren't accepting Bill, and

they were very angry at Bill's dad. Their businesses were threatened, these socialists were coming in, they were overtaxing us already, their attitude about business was terrible, this is all your fault, your dad should never have stayed as long as he did.

When they came out with that really rough stuff, the son was sitting there taking this. I was absolutely livid. I didn't know what I'd do, I was so angry.

And Bill just very nicely said: "This is our plan, we're sticking with the program and this is what we're going to do, and we'd like you to come along," as if to say, "If you don't want to come along it's up to you, it's in your hands."

We walked out of the Bayshore, and I said I could kill them, I'd never been so angry in my life. And he put his hand on my shoulder and said, "Grace, don't worry. We'll have the last laugh, be patient."

THE CAMPAIGN SIGNS from the 1972 general election had not all been taken down when the province began to buzz about forming an anti-NDP party. Or anti-socialist party, as it was simplistically called. By January 1973 there were hundreds of groups forming across the province. The logic was simple.

In the 1972 general election, the wheels fell off the Socred wagon. Social Credit's popular vote fell to 31.6 percent from 46.8 percent in 1969. It won ten legislative seats. The Liberals' popular vote fell slightly, to 16.4 percent and five seats. Unfortunately for them, all these seats were in Vancouver and as a result they were perceived as a big-city party. The Conservatives received 12.67 percent of the vote after having run only one candidate in 1969. They won two seats in Victoria, but their leader, Derril Warren, failed to win his seat. The NDP moved up in the popular vote from 33.9 percent in 1969 to 39.59 percent in 1972 and won a solid majority with thirty-seven seats.

The reasons for the turnaround were put aside. People jumped on the simple arithmetic: 60 percent non-socialist, 40 percent socialist. The naïve argued that all you had to do was get all the non-socialist vote together and happy days would be here forever.

At the beginning of 1973 a small group met at Jarl Whist's home in Kamloops. It included Rafe Mair and several other lawyers and businesspeople. Whist, a wealthy immigrant from Norway, despised socialism and led the way in becoming the leader of S.O.S., Stamp Out Socialism. This group took out newspaper ads which argued that they were about to restore free enterprise in B.C. and would unify the three parties of the right or, "failing that, the free enterprise vote."

This led them naturally to join up with Vancouver groups interested in the same sort of movement, and a final name change. Under the joint leadership of Whist and Burnaby lawyer Arnold Hean, the Majority Movement was born in April 1973.

Then, as often happens to well-intentioned one-issue groups, summer arrived and support disappeared. The anti-socialist warriors were off on the golf courses and sipping martinis on their yachts. Except for a few public outpourings when they came back from the nineteenth hole, they had missed the important Kelowna by-election.

DECEMBER 28, 1973, was a cold day on Big White, and Bennett attacked the mountain relentlessly. Big White could be challenging, and he was not the greatest skier in the world, but he attacked, attacked, attacked. Finally he was satisfied and exhausted. Three clear themes had formed in his mind.

He was determined to build an open party that attracted a wide spectrum of people, including younger professionals and businesspeople who were already making a real difference in their communities. With encouragement, they would join and make a greater contribution. He applied the marketing skills he had learnt and fine-tuned in business. He knew he had a branding problem. There were two sides to the coin in attracting new Socreds.

On one side, he needed to remake Social Credit into a large, busy, middle-of-the-road-to-right party that looked a lot like, well, his friends in Kelowna. He had to replicate the group of people who had rallied around his campaign. Young and not-so-young businesspeople, professionals, the upwardly mobile, who would eventually be called yuppies. He had to go into every community and convince these people that it was good and necessary to join Social Credit and make a difference. It would be a reverse takeover: a certain segment of the public would take over a political party. Bennett recalls his strategy:

> Most governments, whether Liberal, Conservative or NDP, like to keep control. They don't want a lot of new people coming in, because they're troublemakers, they're going to ask questions and have their own ideas. But that's what I wanted and exactly the tack I did take. We did two things.
>
> We got the party which had a new president, Grace McCarthy. I used to go to head office and see the volunteers she had and they're all doing it by hand, no computers. They were doing these small mailouts. Later on it got more sophisticated, but you know, it was all people doing the work, getting memberships...
>
> Over the next two years I tried to contact everybody who'd run as a candidate against Social Credit in the last election, whether Liberal or Conservative. I asked them what it was they wanted when they ran and said we were an open party and we would love to have them join us, bring their ideas. I'd talk to them and then I'd make announcements. These people might be very obscure—for example, a third vice-president from the Esquimalt Conservatives—but it was important to make an announcement every day, or every second day, that people were joining Social Credit.

The second theme: he had to move the party to the left to capture the Liberal vote and, most importantly, the centre of the political spectrum. Social Credit would be a centre-right party, not a right-of-centre party. He needed a target so that he could measure the party's progress against the time left before the next election. He would speak to Grace about this, but thought around forty thousand to fifty thousand new members would be sufficient.

The other side of the coin was the branding of the NDP. His father had run for thirty years on describing them as faceless, godless socialists. "The socialists are at the gates, my friends!" Dave Barrett had done a lot to defuse this charge. He was glib and funny and a good speaker. A slightly overweight, self-deprecating Jewish kid from the east side of Vancouver didn't leave anyone to thinking the godless socialist at the gates was a threat; in fact, he should be let in if you wanted a good party.

Bennett's analysis of the NDP's spending to date led him to believe that here was the key. In their first year in office, they had increased spending by over 10 percent; their public promises would require the second budget to increase more than double that. He had also learned that Barrett as finance minister as well as premier had done nothing to ensure financial discipline in the budget process.

As a person who had grown up in the Interior, Bennett knew the cyclical financial swings that B.C.'s reliance on commodities brought to communities dependent on forestry and mining. Any kind of downturn in the economy, and the NDP's profligate spending would result in a deficit.

One thing W.A.C. had driven into the B.C. public's psyche as the measure of political success was a balanced budget. He had argued that the NDP couldn't manage a peanut stand. Bill Bennett would focus on financial mismanagement as the symbol of overall poor management. The caucus would need to find issues that spoke to poor management broadening the base of financial mismanagement. These two themes would, in effect, be one: the NDP are poor managers. The godless, faceless socialist bogeyman would be replaced by a new threat: "The NDP are incompetent managers of your hard-earned tax dollars." Bennett would take this to caucus after New Year's and get their views, but he thought he was right.

The third theme was equally simple. The NDP had been elected with 39 percent of the popular vote. Social Credit, the Liberals and the Conservatives had polled over 60 percent. Beating the leader of the Conservative Party in the by-election had only been the first step. Bennett must also contend with the well-meaning but politically naïve enthusiasts who were trying to create a coalition on the right called the Majority Movement. His father's experience had taught him that "coalition" governments fail.

He, and everyone else in the province, knew that neither Social Credit, the Liberals nor the Conservatives could win if the three parties of roughly equal strength split the centre-right vote. Bennett had to destroy the other two parties by poaching away their strength.

First, he had to ensure that no one in his caucus bolted to form a new party. Second, he had to resist the call sweeping the province to form a new party. Third, he had to create the impression that Social Credit was the biggest, best organized and consequently the only alternative. Fourth, he had to convince the MLAs from the other non-NDP parties to desert their party and join Social Credit. All easier said than done.

It was time to return home, spend a quiet evening and then a few more days with Audrey, the kids and some friends. After New Year's he had work to do.

DAVE BROUSSON, the MLA for North Vancouver–Capilano, resigned his seat, citing business pressures. The by-election held to fill his seat on February 5, 1974, presented an opportunity for a unite-the-right campaign. But the more shrewd political analysts realized this was *not* the case to be used to unite the right. The NDP had garnered under 20 percent of the popular vote in the last election. The chances of the other right-of-centre parties splitting the vote and letting them in was non-existent.

The Liberals, still smarting from a dismal and disappointing fourth-place finish in the Kelowna by-election, argued that they had received 40 percent of the vote last time and that their candidate, Gordon Gibson, was the one to rally behind. David Anderson, the Liberal leader, speaking to UBC law students, called the Majority Movement "Fascist in content."

The new Conservative leader, Dr. Scott Wallace, refused any form of co-operation. He supported Peter Hyndman as the best and most able candidate.

Social Credit nominated Mayor Ron Andrews and ran with one of the successful slogans from the Kelowna by-election—"Unity!"

The Majority Movement plunged ahead without the support of the three parties. Gibson squeaked home with a fifty-seven-vote victory over Andrews. Bennett was not upset. He knew he had won more than he had lost: "What it took for me to be elected premier, it took a by-election in North Vancouver and for Peter Hyndman to run for the Conservatives and lose. Before it was over, the best thing that ever happened was we lost that election to Gordon [Gibson]."

The Majority Movement's last hurrah came in June. It had decided to arrange a gathering on the legislature steps to protest Bill 31, the Mineral Royalties Act. This ill-conceived legislation would have had the effect of raising royalties on mining activities, in some cases, to over 100 percent of profits. It eventually drove the mining industry to its knees. The only thing you could do if you were in the mining business in B.C. was learn Spanish and go south.

Only four MLAs attended—two Liberals and two Conservatives. More important was who did not attend—Socreds.

Bennett had held the caucus. The one-size-fits-all, single-issue Majority Movement was dead.

IN BENNETT'S VIEW, a coalition was a non-starter. He had learned by watching his father's experience that coalitions were the Antichrist. What he would build was a new party, not a coalition on the centre-right. He explains:

> Coalitions break up. I watched the coalition between the Liberals and the Conservatives break up. As soon as it served their partisan interests to break up, they did. So they couldn't work to the full good of the province with complete trust in each other in government. Social Credit isn't a coalition. You have to buy a membership and you have to make a commitment. You are a British Columbia Social Credit member. It really is a party.
>
> A coalition implies a multiplicity of leadership. A party can only have one leader. You may not like your leader—then you change him. But you can only have one. Coalitions of convenience always break up because they have a number of leaders, each with their own game plan, each with their own set of priorities. And it's always bargaining, bargaining, bargaining.
>
> The political process itself is bargaining—but not from a preconceived set of positions from which trade-offs are achieved. I've viewed Social Credit as a political vehicle that can change with the times without sacrificing its basic philosophy, without requiring great political shifts and heaves. It can be a political vehicle that can make changes within itself.

BILL BENNETT had stuck to his guns and continued to tour the province non-stop, visiting every town, every city. Speaking to large groups and small coffee klatches. Nine months after the leadership race, party membership reached critical mass, ten thousand and growing. Grace McCarthy recalls: "By this time the memberships were flowing in like crazy. The NDP were helping us greatly, and they were coming in like mad. We'd get mail, I'm not exaggerating, it would cover the whole table, it was amazing. And it was so much fun to open up all these envelopes that were memberships."

Two marketing schemes were put in place. One, created by Grace, was the "seagull" brochure, which was mailed to every household. In a time when the book *Jonathan Livingston Seagull* was hugely popular, a young volunteer promoted a Socred version of the story in pamphlet form, incorporating the seagull as a symbol of freedom. Bennett had to intervene for Grace with his bagman Austin Taylor for funding, but the brochure was mailed to every household in the province and generated thousands of memberships, financial contributions and volunteers.

The second initiative was the previously mentioned announcements every day or every few days of a new recruit for Social Credit—one day an alderman, the next day a school trustee. A well-known person upcountry here, and a notable opinion leader there. Like water torture for the other parties, a slow but relentless dripping out of new members.

Occasionally a major announcement. Peter Hyndman left the Conservatives and joined the Socreds. The mayor of Surrey, Bill Vander Zalm, who had run against David Anderson for the leadership of the Liberal Party, joined. Importantly in the legislature, Conservative MLA Hugh Curtis left his party for Social Credit. The floodgates were opening.

By the spring session of 1975 the dynamics changed again. It was clear that Social Credit was continuing to grow and that it had a real chance to defeat the government. The door was opened to hold discussions between the Liberals and Bill Bennett to see if an accommodation could be made with the centre-right. On April 22, Bennett hosted all five Liberal MLAs for dinner and said he would welcome them into the party. He told them of the state of the party machinery. When they compared it with the state of their own party, they could only shake their heads. They asked for fixed election dates, they asked for a change of party name to attract Liberal voters. Bennett told them he would not promise them anything. No cabinet posts, nothing. But they should know that he held them in high regard.

Allan Williams comments: "Before I made the decision I had a meeting in my house with senior Liberals from West Vancouver and the North Shore and they urged me to go. They said, 'Allan, there's no sense in butting your head against a brick wall. Join with Bill Bennett and get this province back on its feet.' And with George Van Rogen leading the charge, they said, 'Do it. Make the move.' And we did."

SO, ON SEPTEMBER 30, 1975, the heart of the Liberal caucus in the provincial legislature walked out on the stage with Bill Bennett and joined Social Credit. Former Liberal leader Pat McGeer and his colleagues Garde Gardom and Allan Williams left current leader David Anderson and leader-in-waiting Gordon Gibson as the only two Liberals sitting in the legislature.

The Liberals were eviscerated. Bill Bennett had won. There was one centre-right party in B.C., and it was ready and willing to take on the NDP.

WHAT CAUSED Dave Barrett to call the election for December 1975 will always be a mystery. In his book *Barrett: A Passionate Political Life,* he describes the decision in this way:

> I had to make a decision about where we were headed. We had instituted numerous changes, but they were largely misunderstood and therefore perceived as threatening. We had failed to win recognition from labour over the price freeze, and we had further alienated business. The revitalized Social Credit Party could raise all the money it needed, and the Liberal defection had ruled out any possibility of a split vote...
>
> We were in for a difficult time no matter what course we took. But the call, ultimately, was mine alone.

Barrett had just completed an extensive provincial fall tour. In the middle of it, on October 14, the federal government had announced wage and price controls, which every provincial premier had endorsed in Ottawa.

And on October 24 the province announced an order-in-council freezing prices in the province.

The rural cabinet ministers had watched Barrett out on the stump speaking to enthusiastic crowds, and they were for an early election. The Lower Mainland ministers saw none of this and argued against calling the election. The premier took further advice from two sources: the powerful Bob Williams, who said "Go!", and Marc Eliesen, who had been recruited from Manitoba as the premier's deputy minister the year before, and who also offered the view that sooner was better than later.

Tuesday, November 3, 1975, was an overcast, rainy day with gale-force winds and snow forecast for the north. That morning the premier decided to call the election for Thursday, December 11. While not known for his long-term strategic views, Barrett rationalized his election call in this way:

> I remember sitting alone after supper one night, musing that even if we lost we could probably hang on to a substantial number of seats and a reasonably high percentage of the vote...Four years hence, people would have a much better understanding, and appreciation, of what we had done in government. If we lost this time around, I hoped we could win then, before too much damage had been done.

He made the announcement at a morning news conference in his office in Victoria, after visiting Lieutenant Governor Walter Owen. His public rationale was his need for broad support to fight against inflation:

> British Columbians have been asked to accept some difficult decisions in the past few weeks, Bill 146 [the back-to-work legislation] and the price freeze on food and essential services.
>
> I am determined to find the fairest way to deal with the problems, but that also means I need continued support in implementing these decisions...
>
> I am determined to make the fight against inflation work, but for the next three years I can only help make it work if I have the necessary support to fight to make it fair to all and favours to none.

> Big business can be heard; big labour can be heard, but the voiceless majority must also be represented.

Bill Bennett's view of why Dave Barrett called the election is quite different:

> One reason was the financial situation in the country turning soft. And in B.C. you're always hit because of the resource industry vulnerability to commodity swings.
>
> But, you know, he had many things in mind. My guess is he thought I still didn't have enough experience to run against him, and he's a better debater, and they would win on the hustings.
>
> Not only that, Barrett had gone to the federal–provincial conference that Trudeau called. They were going to freeze wages, and he agreed, as the other premiers did. I don't think that he wanted to have to implement it when he got back, because he would have to deal with labour.

Bennett's Social Credit Party was ready for the election. Grace McCarthy, as president, had rolled up her sleeves, worked twelve-hour days and recruited help wherever she could. She had gone to see Vancouver businessman Jack Diamond and convinced him to give her an office. A contractor friend had done the necessary renovations. Another had provided carpet. From nothing, Grace built a professional organization.

An architect friend had laid out every poll in every riding in the province. Each poll had a poll captain and a list of volunteers who would knock on doors and record the voting intentions of each family member. Every constituency had an office ready for the campaign.

Grace McCarthy tells this story:

> I remember I had to meet [*Vancouver Sun* reporter] Margie Nichols one day. She wanted to come and see the office and what we were doing. We had every single poll completed, we had the whole 150 polls, with a captain in every poll, and sheets that they had to report on and bring back to us. They had to do that three times so that we would absolutely know

> where our vote was and where the NDP was. We didn't only do it in Vancouver, we did it in beautiful downtown Telkwa. We did it in the Okanagan, we did it in the north, everywhere...
>
> So Margie comes up and sees all this going on. They didn't know we were working so hard, 'cause we'd never worked hard before. All their memory of the Socred organization was, you put W.A.C. Bennett on the podium and you get elected.
>
> She said, "I can't believe what you are doing. The NDP have no idea you're this organized." And I said, "You're not going to tell them, are you?" She looked at me and she said, "I just can't believe it: those guys are toast. Those guys are toast!"

Bennett also knew that while people had joined for many reasons, perhaps the greatest one was to throw out the government. Allan Fotheringham described one long-time Liberal's plan for election day: "I intend to get up, have a good stiff drink of gin, go to the polls, vote Social Credit, come home, spend two hours washing my hands and then finish off the bottle!"

The branding of the New Democrats was completed in the spring of 1975. As the spring legislative session approached March 31, the end of the fiscal year, the government moved to introduce Interim Supply. This practice is normal and is done regularly by every government. But Bennett, seeing an opportunity, rose from his seat in the legislature and tried to block the passage. The opposition had run out of allocated debating days on the government's $3.2 billion budget, so Bennett tried to bend the rules to allow more time.

"Not a dime without debate!" was the rallying cry.

He was on his feet in the legislature, challenging the government again and again, until the Speaker threw him out. Just what Bennett wanted. In the media scrum he would not be denied. He vowed to abandon his seat to take the campaign against government spending without debate to the public.

A province-wide tour was arranged, and Bill was off to every nook and cranny in the province. The crowds were enthusiastic, and the "Not a dime without debate" slogan was heard, and began to appear, everywhere. People were outraged.

Even when Bennett cracked a vertebra at a rodeo horse-bucking contest in Quesnel towards the end of his province-wide tour and was in hospital for a week, the message did not stop. He taped a message from his hospital bed that was to be played at the continuing town hall meetings.

Obviously the public did not understand the legislative convention, nor could the government explain it in a simple sound bite. But Bennett could get people on their feet and angry about the NDP's fiscal mismanagement with the bumper-sticker simplicity of five words.

WHEN THE 1975 election was called, the media caught Bill Bennett at home in Kelowna. Seeing another opening, he attacked the timing of the election call: "People in the North and the Interior will have difficulty going to the polls in mid-December... We have to wonder about the premier's ethics and whether his concern was for British Columbians or for the NDP party and the future of David Barrett."

He outlined the issues he would campaign on: "Unemployment, inflation, cutbacks in funds for education, health services and the NDP government's failure to keep B.C. in the lead in providing the highest pensions in Canada for senior citizens. We will hammer away at the heavy ICBC deficits, ferry deficits, transit losses and the government record of mismanagement of Crown corporations."

Dave Barrett ran on his innovative legislative record but faced deep underlying problems that were of concern to everyone, from doctors to Joe Lunch Bucket: the appearance of administrative sloppiness, and the threat that the budget would not balance.

Three other variables made the difference. The destruction of the opposition parties saw the Conservatives run only 29 candidates in 55 ridings, and the Liberals only 49 in the 55. Then there was the relative election readiness of the two parties. Social Credit was ready in every community. Eighty thousand campaign-ready members, anxious to throw out the government, provided a distinct advantage.

The NDP, on the other hand, had a problem with both the party and its members. It ran deeper than the problem of organized labour being angry over the back-to-work legislation. As Lorne Kavic and Garry Brian Nixon relate in their book *The 1200 Days, A Shattered Dream:*

> When Dave Barrett the Premier called the '75 election, Dave Barrett the Leader discovered he had a problem. For three years the Premier had eclipsed the Leader. Pale and weak from the years in the shadow, the Leader soon found that the party was equally out of condition.
>
> Barrett appears to have caught Neophyte's Disease, a malady characterized by excessive enthusiasm, unbounded faith, acute distortion of the priorities, and terminal shortness of sight. Seeing only programs and legislation, he had ignored his own party. The party in turn began to weaken from this neglect...
>
> What was more natural, then, than to assume that the party would maintain the blithe enthusiasm he himself felt? What more reasonable than to assume that his own people would automatically understand and approve his policies and programmes? And what more fatal than to make those assumptions?

Barrett made a mistake many first-term premiers make: he forgot he was leader of his party as well as premier of the province.

The Socreds out-organized the NDP, a feat people even a few years earlier believed was impossible. The NDP leadership always felt that their people would rally behind them during an election campaign. After all, their voters had nowhere else to go. They were wrong: many of their most dedicated members, and many union members, voted with their feet. They went home and stayed there.

The third factor was money. Having united the centre-right or free-enterprise vote, the issue of money was not a problem for Social Credit. The business community got behind them.

The mother's milk of politics is money, and in sufficient amounts it can effect outcomes.

Liberal leader Gordon Gibson raised enough money to run and win narrowly. The Liberals were able to fund and run campaigns in Victoria, Cowichan and Alberni, and in these seats they stole enough votes from the Socreds to elect the NDP.

About 40 percent of the Conservatives' spending was concentrated in three ridings. Oak Bay led the way to enable their leader, Scott Wallace, to win easily.

In two ridings, Atlin and North Vancouver–Seymour, the NDP spent more than the Socreds. In every other riding the Social Credit candidate outspent the NDP candidate. In the nine ridings the Socreds won by under 1,300 votes—Coquitlam, Esquimalt, Shuswap, Burnaby–Edmonds, Skeena, Kootenay, Yale–Lillooet, Victoria and Burnaby–Willingdon—they spent over $340,000, double the spending of the NDP, at $146,000.

In total, Social Credit spent $1,693,182, the NDP spent $939,997, the Liberals $167,689 and the Conservatives only $107,471.

These three factors combined with the most important one—a public that had decided it was time to get rid of the government.

THE CAMPAIGN itself had a few unexpected twists and turns.

Barrett started out by claiming to be the underdog and running on a slogan of "Don't let them take it away."

Bennett ran with "Build with Bill."

Barrett played to enthusiastic crowds with his shirt sleeves rolled up, giving impassioned speeches. Funny, sarcastic, charming, he charged in every direction, defending his record.

Bennett gave one stock speech over and over again. He hit the same themes everywhere he went.

Both leaders travelled everywhere in the province. Sometimes conditions were not the best, for winters in northern B.C. can be unforgiving. Don Phillips recalls those conditions:

> Bill had to borrow airplanes to get around. Often small planes, little prop planes. And he was flying up to Dawson Creek—remember, it's December.

I had a big rally, and there's a huge snowstorm. And the pilot says, "I can't land in this." He tells us on the ground that it is bad everywhere and he is turning back.

I got on the speaker from the tower and told that pilot all sorts of things, and probably not too quietly, but that he had to get that plane in here. I told him, "I've got five hundred people here to see the next premier and he better just damn land that plane!"

Well, of course they slipped off the runway. Everybody was scared to death, thought we had lost Bill. But he came in and gave a hell of a speech.

Barrett got out of the gate quickly, but within a week he ran into his first snag. Frank Calder, whom he had fired as a minister, quit the NDP and the next day joined Social Credit, becoming their candidate in Atlin. In leaving he accused the NDP of being "anti-Indian, anti-labour and anti-North."

Calder said he made the move after meeting with the Nishga (now Nisga'a) tribal council in his riding at the Nass River village of Greenville. The council had told him that the Nishgas would not vote for him as an NDP candidate because the NDP government refused to negotiate their land claims. Barrett shrugged this off and downplayed it, but the issue had his own workers questioning him, and it hurt morale.

The one opportunity Barrett wanted was a live TV debate, and BCTV agreed to stage the event. The Liberal and Conservative leaders immediately agreed to participate. Barrett eagerly accepted, and Bennett said he would debate if his campaign manager could fit the event into his schedule.

Every proposal for a date that BCTV put forward did not fit into Bennett's schedule. The media were frustrated.

By the November 28 deadline set by BCTV, it became clear that Bennett was not going to debate. The great debate that Barrett had wanted and counted on was not going to happen. BCTV tried to make a political issue of the Bennett refusal, but this soon fizzled. A Vancouver *Province* editorial put it into perspective:

Social Credit leader Bill Bennett is under fire for his announcement that he will not join the other party leaders in a televised debate. The NDP,

> Conservatives and Liberal parties have accused him of chickening out and Mr. Bennett's non-appearance in the Great TV Debate threatens to become an issue in the December 11 election... We think it's the Great Non-Issue... If anything, the public is merely being deprived of a piece of circus that means nothing.

Bennett could not see the benefit in a debate: "You have everything to lose. When you want one, and when you keep asking for one is when you are behind or when you are a third party..."

Both leaders criss-crossed the province. Shirley Barrett travelled with her husband Dave, and Audrey went with Bill. It was Audrey's first campaign, and she wasn't always enamoured: "There were times during the campaign when I felt like punching people in the nose, yes, when they'd make cracks about Bill's five-o'clock shadow, about his not showing up for some meetings or about his not debating with Dave Barrett."

British Columbians woke up on December 8 to front-page headlines created by MacMillan Bloedel president Denis Timmis stating, while appearing before the Royal Commission on Forest Resources, that "there is an atmosphere of confrontation and distrust between the provincial government and the forest industry, and the future prosperity of the industry is at stake."

Unfortunately this kind of public announcement is often more damaging than helpful. Bennett commented: "I wish he hadn't done it. I didn't want it, because he tried to knock us into his camp. I was trying to be broader than that. I think these things hurt."

Bennett ended his campaign with large rallies in Prince George, where 3,300 attended, and in Vancouver, where more than five thousand came out. The Vancouver event wasn't without its drama or comedy. Bob McClelland tells it this way:

> I told Hugh Harris I wanted to bring an elephant, and my troops out in Langley were excited about it. Hugh Harris said to me, "What would happen if the elephant panics and kills a bunch of people?" I said, "She won't, she's too gentle. She's from a game farm."

> We compromised. I couldn't let all those people down, so I thought I'd just poke the nose of the elephant in the building and then turn around and go out. Of course, as soon as she showed up, the people started cheering like crazy. So we looked around and said "Let's go!" We rode through the whole place, and poor Bill and Hugh were up on the stage, shaking their heads.
>
> It was wonderful. It got front-page headlines all across Canada.

Clearly the winds of change were blowing, and the camel, errr, elephant, had its nose in the tent and was planning to move in.

BILL BENNETT and the Social Credit Party won a clear majority of the seats in the 1975 election, with 49.25 percent of the vote. Barrett's NDP won 39 percent, about the same as in 1972. The Liberals fell from 16 percent to 7 percent, and the Conservatives from 11 percent to 4 percent.

Dave Barrett lost his seat to a little-known car dealer. His party lost seats everywhere. The 1,200 days of NDP rule in B.C. were over. A new Bennett was premier.

5

STEERING, NOT ROWING

"You didn't get to know him terribly well. His dad once said that you can't become friends with your ministers, as you might have to fire them one day. And I think Bill felt the same way."

JIM NIELSEN

FROM DECEMBER 11, 1975, the day he won the election, until December 22, the day he was sworn in as premier, Bill Bennett thought about all that was required to get his new government off on the right foot. There were several tasks.

One, pick his cabinet and assign the cabinet portfolios.

Two, prepare the administrative procedures that would become the machinery of government.

Three, complete the branding of the opposition as incompetent managers.

BENNETT'S NEW Social Credit, now a modern centre-right amalgamation, which by membership and policy attracted both provincial and federal members of the Liberal and Conservative parties, had to present a public face that reflected this new reality.

The premier had to consider this new reality as well as the normal cabinet-making considerations of geography and occupational representation. Ability was the prime requirement, followed by an earned reputation for hard work. He knew that not all the ministers would be equal in political or intellectual ability. The strength of his government would come from managing a team of strange bedfellows.

Bob McClelland, who had run against Bennett for the leadership, was confident but uncertain: "You never know. There's a lot of reasons why a person is chosen for cabinet, it's not just ability. That helps, but premiers have a lot of things to take into consideration—the area you come from and the demographics of your area have to come into the making of a cabinet. But I was hopeful, and I certainly was beside my phone."

Bennett set up shop in the Harbour Towers Hotel in Victoria, which he had moved into while in opposition and where he would stay until he left office. He describes how he chose this first cabinet.

> Some people that I wanted had a certain touch. I knew Allan Williams, and I knew he wanted to be attorney general, but I said, "I need you to be minister of labour, because you are in control, you can remain calm and deliberate. You are not a hothead." And he was our first minister of labour. Therefore I could make Garde Gardom attorney general.
>
> Then Evan Wolfe—he was good, no trouble. The thing I told him was to not let Gerry Bryson run it, because he had been deputy minister of finance for my dad as well as Barrett.
>
> Others you just put in, Alex Fraser, highways, a natural. Pat McGeer, he wanted finance but got education, again a natural fit. Don Phillips, economic development—but I wanted to double-up some portfolios so that in six months or so I could reward some backbenchers—also got agriculture. Bob McClelland went to health because he always struck me as strong; he had a firm hand and health needed that.
>
> Grace McCarthy went to provincial secretary. I created a deputy premier's job and she also got that. It was a reward for having been in the

party and working so hard. It was an honorary position that did not carry any responsibility except to chair cabinet in my absences.

Hugh Curtis went into municipal affairs and housing because I wanted to put Bill Vander Zalm into social services. Tom Waterland for forests and mining, because I had faith in him and he was from the right location. And Rafe Mair went to consumer affairs.

Bennett also created the province's first Ministry of the Environment. A rookie and the youngest member of cabinet at thirty-seven, Jim Nielsen was made the minister. The premier had a practical view:

I come from the Interior, and the environment is more than a talking point. Out there—where there are ranchers and farmers and a lot of land—it is important. The streams, the rivers, all of that is an important part of their daily lives. And this was an area of growing concern. You don't want to be left behind, and you don't want to be dictated to by various pressure groups. You want to create your own agenda and put somebody into it that is strong.

Nielsen was new, but I had spent some time with him when we were looking for candidates, and he was always very plausible. He was one of those guys who did grasp government quickly. He was probably the best student of legislation, where the loopholes were and where they weren't. He was also a very bright and gifted guy.

Nielsen, an open-line radio show host on CJOR, was media savvy but stepped in it on day one. He explains:

It was a new ministry, and we didn't have all the component parts put together yet, whether parks and recreation would be part of it or water, land, air and all that. The big question was, whether parks and recreation would be part of it or whether that would go to something else.

After we were sworn in, the *Vancouver Sun* reporter asked, "What do you know about the ministry?" And I said, "Well, not that much, it's brand new."

The story the next day was, "What do you know about the environment?"…"Not much, it's brand new."

That stayed with me forever. It was an object lesson that Bennett would use once in a while in caucus or elsewhere about what to avoid.

Some government MLAs had sat by the phone anxiously waiting for a call that never came. Jim Chabot was one of those who had run against Bennett for the leadership and had been in W.A.C.'s cabinet. However, his work ethic was questioned by Bennett, who sent Don Phillips to explain to him that what was needed was more work and that he might be appointed down the road. Chabot changed, and joined the cabinet at the next swearing-in.

Bennett knew where he wanted Phillips, but he always enjoyed his friend's turn of phrase, so he asked Phillips what he wanted. Don didn't disappoint:

> I said, there is only one thing I can do. I know business, but if you give me labour there will be a strike. If you give me education there will be a strike, if you give me health there will be a strike.
>
> I walked into the Harbour Towers, the restaurant on the bottom floor, and Dan Campbell was sitting there with Bill, now the premier, and they gave me a sheet of legislation and said, "You're the minister of economic development, so go home and start studying."

Newcomer Rafe Mair had a different experience, recalled in his book, *Rafe: A Memoir*:

> After I was nominated, I met with Bennett in Victoria and he introduced me to the House, but when we went for a drink afterwards, he—rather brusquely, I thought—made it clear that no one was being promised anything, much less a cabinet seat. To be truthful, I was more than a bit scared of him—and I was by no means alone in this feeling, as I was to find out in later discussions with colleagues.
>
> So there I was, knees shaking, as I went into Bill's room, where I was told in about thirty seconds flat that I was to be his minister of consumer

services, the smallest of all the ministries, that I was to tell no one, not even my wife, and that if news leaked out, I might find myself out of a job! But for all my discomfort at that moment, I still felt very attracted to this man and felt he was a leader I could follow.

Bennett treated each minister differently and would continue to do so, particularly with regard to the amount of oversight they required. Cookie-cutter leadership does not work with sophisticated political players. Cabinet is not a military organization; diversity is a strength, and it must be rewarded. Not everyone is or should be a rocket scientist, but everyone is there to make a contribution. Bennett comments on one cabinet pick:

> He learned, he worked hard. He's what I would consider the essential, hard-working, non-politic. He didn't understand politics, given the way he thought he would get elected, but he knew what he wanted to do, he knew why he was there, he knew what he wanted to do for his province. He's a pretty good example of what I call the ordinary guy who really wants to help his province be better.

Ministers learnt under Bennett that they could express their views openly. Don Phillips comments:

> Everytime something is brought up under discussion, you have eighteen, nineteen different views on it. That is where Bill shone: he was able to narrow it down so that you focused on the issue instead of trying to prove how smart you were and how much you knew about the rest of the world. He could focus the discussion.

One last disgruntled non-appointee to cabinet was Ed Smith, the member from North Peace. Bennett was not certain about him and felt he might cause trouble: "I knew he would be pissed off if he didn't get into cabinet. You determine your trouble spots and you make them Speaker—that's what my Dad once told me, and I listened."

THERE WAS A profound difference between Dave Barrett's approach to running government and Bill Bennett's approach. Bennett's background demanded an organized, analytical approach. Business was to be done in a businesslike way. Government business was to be no different.

In her book *Mark My Words,* Marjorie Nichols describes Bennett's obsession with absorbing financial information: "The man who unabashedly confessed that he had been too busy making money to read books became a voracious reader— mostly of government documents. He was a detail man, a reader of footnotes and a checker of addition and subtraction. He was, in the manner of a small-town businessman who could tell what kind of day he had by the weight of the night deposit bag, a nitpicker."

At their first meeting, cabinet was presented with a document that described how cabinet documents would be prepared, and in what detail. The opening question was: "What decision do you want cabinet to make?" It was followed by objective, background, options, discussion, financial implications, legislative implications and recommendations. Length: 5 to 6 pages.

Two new cabinet committees, one for social policy and one for economic development, were created, and all cabinet documents flowed to cabinet through them. Every minister was on one committee or the other; a few were on both.

The Treasury Board itself was also given the task of reviewing all submissions, after the cabinet committees had recommended them, if they had financial impacts. It was also responsible for developing, overseeing and reviewing ministries' estimates preparations. In today's governments this is standard procedure, but in 1975, in British Columbia, it was revolutionary.

Cabinet's agenda was controlled from the premier's office. Ministers phoned the premier's secretary and asked for items to be included. He decided on the agenda. "Other Business" was the place to talk politics—the last agenda item.

During discussions of particular items, deputy ministers and other senior staff were invited into cabinet when their agenda item was under discussion. They were routinely asked to explain the technical aspects and to give their views about impacts. As people became more accustomed to the process, the more seasoned and skilled staff would provide impact analysis that was in effect non-partisan political advice. Once the "technical" discussions were over, staff left and the ministers turned to discuss the partisan political issues and come to a decision. Cabinet was clearly in charge.

Bennett knew that he had to build not only a new modern party, but a new modern government. He recognized that his agenda, the new government's agenda, was based on new policies. These policies had to be worked up and developed to be presented to the public in a way that would lead to their being accepted, and ultimately to his party being re-elected. He believed that good management and organization would make this possible.

To correct the legislation problem, he created the Cabinet Committee on Legislation, which reviewed in detail the drafting of every bill, ensuring that the language in the draft bill matched the prose in the approved cabinet submission. The committee then recommended the bill to cabinet prior to it being presented to the legislature.

The premier also knew that the effective control of public monies was essential, for three reasons. First, he was given the trust of managing other people's money, and that fiduciary responsibility weighed heavily upon him. Second, he understood that new government spending occurs at the margin, and therefore freeing up discretionary resources through firmer management created spending room for new priorities. Sloppy financial control leaves little room for anything other than incremental program growth—an unappealing consequence for most politicians, who prefer to initiate new programs and take bold actions.

Finally, he wanted his trademark to be good financial management. Just like he wanted to brand the NDP as terrible financial stewards of the public's money. Social Credit's brand would be strong financial managers, guarding the taxpayer's money as if it were their own, and spending it prudently.

THE DAY AFTER Bennett's election win, December 12, he announced that the government would carry out a full review of the province's finances.

Six days later, and prior to Bennett being sworn in, NDP Finance Minister Dave Stupich and Premier Dave Barrett called a press conference to present their view of the state of finances for British Columbia. Revenues originally estimated at $3.223 billion had dropped to an estimate of $3.065 billion. Expenditures of $3.222 billion were now estimated to be $3.105 billion. A surplus projected at $0.5 million was now forecast to be a deficit of $40 million.

Bennett shot back the same day: "I refuse to accept as gospel the statement on provincial finances issued Thursday by the outgoing NDP government. I suggest that the NDP statement is based more on speculation than on fact. The new government will be making statements not from speculation but from actual fact." British Columbians did not have to wait long. On December 21, Bennett's cabinet's first move was to appoint national accountants Clarkson Gordon to review the books.

The request from cabinet was for Clarkson Gordon to coordinate the production of unaudited financial information from government accounts, Crown corporations and agencies for the year ending March 31, 1976, and to produce a summary report of the province's overall financial position. The report was to be written in simple English to enable public distribution. And it was to be done quickly.

On February 18, 1976, the report was completed and delivered to the government. Two days later, Bennett went public on province-wide TV. He indicated that while direct taxes on people were growing, taxes from forestry, mining and other resources were in decline. The overall impact was that "instead of receiving as government the $3.2 billion in cash that was estimated in the former government's budget, we can expect to take in only $2.9 billion, a shortfall of over $300 million."

He then turned to the expenditure side: "So, while receiving less than it expected, the previous government committed us to spend more. Major programs were initiated, for which no provision was made in last spring's budget. For Crown corporations, more money than ever before was required. As a result there has been a serious, unexpected cash drain from general revenues. The budget will be overspent by about $200 million."

Bennett went on to highlight the reported spending mismanagement in excruciating detail:

> For the first time since 1958, our tax dollars will have to go to pay for the cost of borrowed money.

> Your government will have to pass a bill at the coming session of the legislature to allow for the borrowing of $400 million. As a result, we will have $40 million of interest to pay next year alone. We will continue to bear this burden as long as we have the debt.
>
> The point that concerns me, as it must concern you, is that these debt dollars will have to come out of your taxes. Dollars that should have been available to be spent on services to people. Dollars that should be going into housing, transit, pensions and health care.

Bennett had got what he wanted: good baseline financial data, and the public reaction. The NDP were branded as incompetent managers of public monies. Bennett saw it this way:

> I told cabinet this was my plan. Get into the finances, find the extent of the problem, get an auditing firm that's credible, one of the major ones, and do it. Don't do it through your own resources; the public won't believe you.
>
> This was the first time it had been done in Canada, but people have done it since. My idea was that this was just good business, it was common sense. It was a practice of good financial management: Get your house in order.
>
> It may have seemed to be politically successful—and it was—but financially it was the right thing to do.

Was the NDP's last budget balanced or not? The NDP said it could have been. The Socreds said it was in deficit. In their book *The Reins of Power: Governing British Columbia,* Professors Morley, Ruff, Swainson, Wilson and Young state: "The estimate of a budgetary deficit of $541 million for the fiscal year 1975–76, drawn from an audit especially commissioned from Clarkson, Gordon & Company, and the actual cash deficit later shown in the public accounts for that year as $261 million, were designed to reinforce the image of mismanagement."

There was a deficit in a province that had grown up seeing balanced budgets as a measure of government success. The NDP had not balanced.

As Bennett noted, this was the first time in Canadian history that outside auditors had been called in to check the books. It wouldn't be the last. And it would not be the last time Bennett recognized the advantage that television provided. By going province-wide for important addresses, he went over the heads of the press gallery to pitch his message straight at the voters. It was a message that stuck, and a technique that other premiers across Canada picked up.

BENNETT'S YEARS IN power were characterized by one given: weekends were spent in Kelowna. Staff knew it and scheduled accordingly.

Being premier doesn't allow many free weekends. External events, like constitutional discussions, can find the premiers, their ministers and their staff in Ottawa. International travel also takes them away from home, but at least in that instance their spouses can travel with them.

But home was where Bill's heart was—with his family. Audrey remembers, "In the winter, I'd pick him up at the plane. I'd have the car all packed, and we'd head up to the ski hill with the kids. Spend the weekend there, and come back Sunday night. To Westbank. That was enough. He didn't need to be downtown, he just needed to be with his family."

BY AND LARGE, Premier Bennett ran a laissez-faire cabinet. He allowed his ministers great latitude to get on with their mandates. He insisted on a complete ministerial review of all programs within each ministry. This allowed strong ministers to drive their agendas, and they did. Weaker ministers tended to sit on their hands and let the government agenda be driven elsewhere.

Pat McGeer was a strong education minister who knew where he wanted to go and got on with it. With Bennett's approval, the deputy brought in his old pal, Dr. Walter Hardwick, a brilliant UBC geographer and city councillor in Vancouver, to remake education policy. By the fall of 1976 they moved. On November 1, McGeer released "A Program for Performance in the Educational System of British Columbia," in which he stated: "I believe the content of our school programs should fall into three categories: that which *must be learned,* that which *should be learned,* and that which *may be learned.* With these three categories in mind, I am today announcing a program for improving the performance of public school education in this province." A core curriculum. The *Province* newspaper heralded: "3 R's to make comeback in new schools curriculum."

McGeer and his deputy never suffered fools gladly, and while his relationships with some in the school system, particularly teachers, deteriorated, he never lost sight of the objective of constantly improving classroom outcomes for students. The Independent Schools Act passed, providing, for the first time, funding for private schools. This had been a long-time goal of Bennett as both a sign of moving to the centre of the political landscape and as an expression of a personal belief in the appropriateness of providing support. It was also a long-held view of McGeer and his colleagues, one that had resided in the Liberal caucus and one of the signals that eased the transition to Social Credit.

Also in their first year in office, McGeer and Labour Minister Allan Williams announced the Commission on Vocational, Technical and Trades Training, which came to be known as the Goard Commission after its chairman Dean Goard, founding president of BCIT. They followed the adage of good public policy, "Never appoint an independent public inquiry unless you know what they are going to recommend." The last thing you want in government is an independent inquiry that actually behaves independently.

The upshot: college enrolments rose from 36,389 to 46,798 during the four years of the their first term—a 30 percent increase.

A busy first term of government saw education spending rise from $750 million in the last year of the NDP government to over a billion dollars in the last year of Bennett's first term—a 39 percent increase. Minister McGeer showed how a strong minister with clear ideas could push ahead with his change agenda. There was no specific blueprint, other than funding for independent schools, or party policy. But the ideas McGeer proposed to cabinet were clearly in alignment with the views of the premier and the other cabinet members.

It is notable that in all the media coverage of these events Bennett's name does not occur. This was deliberate; he wanted his ministers front and centre, for several reasons.

First, his management style was clear: he steered the fleet, and the ministers saw that the boats were rowed in formation. In addition, he wanted to be seen as the head of a powerful team of powerful ministers. In the end his government would get the overall credit, but the team members had to be seen as competent and decisive in their own right.

Further, he knew that a one-man band draws too much of the flak. If every decision landed at the feet of the premier, he would eventually be weakened and become unpopular and ineffective.

In addition, Bennett's ego did not demand the immediate gratification that some leaders demand as their right to be front and centre in all announcements. The ministers were required to set the stage for their announcements and then follow up with a consistent message to ensure that the policy was thoroughly explained.

Bennett also recognized that if he insisted on being front and centre on every issue, the ministers would soon begin to delegate up. Upwards delegation of responsibility negates effective management, stifles creativity and weakens accountability. Only those ministers that required very close watching were subject to greater oversight.

Finally, Bennett left himself room for what his father called the famous "second look." If something got too far off course, he could always step in and fix it. It left him room, and he did not do this often, but the principle, known in bargaining as "pinnacling," leaves the leader as the final step in the decision-making process.

Bob McClelland's opinion of his leader was echoed often by his ministers: "Bennett was a joy to work for. As long as you did your job—unless there was some kind of priority in terms of politics or something—he just let you do your job. He never once undermined me or gave me anything but support."

Ministers such as Bill Vander Zalm, however, required more watching. Vander Zalm had been the mayor of Surrey for many years. His one foray into provincial politics had occurred in 1972, when he ran for and lost the leadership of the provincial Liberal Party against David Anderson.

Always considered a colourful character and an excellent speaker, Vander Zalm leapt onto the provincial scene during the Liberal leadership campaign. His right-wing populist views were no secret; on talk shows he talked about driving hippies out of the province. About family values. About work for welfare.

In his nomination speech in the leadership race against David Anderson, while the Liberal crowd sweltered in the hot confines of the Peach Bowl in Penticton, Vander Zalm announced that he would "whiplash drug pushers, cut off welfare deadbeats, update education and crack down on wife deserters" as well as expel hippies from the province by forcing them to accept one-way bus tickets to Edmonton. Senator John Nichol, the godfather of the B.C. Liberals, walked out of the hall, remarking to David Anderson's campaign director: "I thought they shot that son of a bitch in Georgia last week"—a reference to the recent assassination attempt on George Wallace, the segregationist southern governor then running for U.S. president.

Vander Zalm started to drive an agenda of welfare reform. He commented that he would hand out shovels rather than welfare cheques to get people back to work. He announced, "If anybody is able to work but refuses to pick up a shovel, we will find ways of dealing with him."

The social activists went wild. Rather than backing down, Vander Zalm became more aggressive. He had lapel pins made up of little shovels. At charity auctions he would provide a shovel and beam a magnetic smile to raise money. He was hugely popular.

Bennett watched this with a wary eye. Not only would Vander Zalm talk to the press at every opportunity about his program responsibilities, but he could not keep himself from talking to the media about other government policy. The contrast between the charismatic, readily available minister of human resources and the premier was distinct. But Bennett gave Vander Zalm his time in the sun and enough rope to either keep skipping or hang himself.

Other ministers led their own quiet charges. In 1975, the previous government had picked Dr. Peter Pearse to head the Royal Commission on Forest Resources. Pearse's report was received by Forests Minister Tom Waterland, and by May 1978 he was ready to introduce a new Forests Act. Pearse had called for greater diversity in the industry through giving smaller firms increased opportunities, changing the term of tenures to evergreen contracts more resembling private ownership and restructuring the forest ministry. Waterland was "firmly in agreement with University of B.C. economist Dr. Peter Pearse."

The *Vancouver Sun* on May 13, 1978, reported that this was "the first major rewrite of forest legislation since 1912 and was the culmination of attempts to alter management of forests through at least two governments and the intensive review of the past four years."

Finance Minister Evan Wolfe left immediately after the swearing-in ceremony with Labour Minister Allan Williams and Consumer Affairs Minister Rafe Mair and their deputies for Ottawa to meet federal officials to discuss B.C.'s role in the anti-inflation fight. In Bennett's view, Dave Barrett's federal performance, and indeed Bennett's father's performance, had been lacking. He wanted to send a clear and early signal that it was not business as usual in B.C.

The new cabinet settled in, and controversy was never far away as eager ministers talked straight and tough. With varying results. Minister McGeer, also responsible for the Insurance Corporation of British Columbia (ICBC), put the Crown corporation on a firm footing but created anger that lasted until the next election with his blunt talk. He said, for example, "If you can afford a car, you can afford insurance for it. If you can't afford insurance for it, sell it." Consumer Affairs Minister Rafe Mair, on completing the review of programs in his ministry, decided to close a program providing personal financial advice: "I think one of the character builders of this world is to allow people to take the initiative and get kicked in the ass until they learn to take their lumps."

The media made hay of these pronouncements, the opposition went crazy and ministers were learning that it is tougher to govern than it looks from the benches to the left of the Speaker. Most soon learned that instead of attacking problems head on and getting their noses bloody by being "refreshingly outspoken," they should begin to solve problems through skilled interventions at the margins and from angles.

There was also good news. Attorney General Garde Gardom brought forward the "Counter Attack" program to fight drinking and driving.

Taking the ideas and advice of his assistant deputy minister Mark Krasnick, Gardom became the champion of sober driving.

The pattern repeats itself. Bennett managed his ministers in a common cause and in a direction set by a collective cabinet who stood together. Grace McCarthy compares his management style with his father's:

> It was the same difference as the eras that they represented. W.A.C. Bennett was there through the building, the infrastructure building and had great foresight. Think about the energy plan he had—it was unbelievably courageous and clever. And the bridges and roads. To put that kind of money into the hinterland where nobody was living at the time was courageous...
>
> Bill had a different management style. His style was of the young executives of the day. He was a workaholic, not like his dad. I know Bill read at night, because he was very knowledgeable about world finances. His dad worked hard, but he would go to lunch at noon for lunch with some cabinet minister at the Union Club and come back at 1:30 and leave at five and go home.
>
> Contrast that with Bill Bennett, who says we're having a cabinet meeting at seven in the morning. Seven, like that means you have to get up at 5:30, and then he would say, well we didn't get through it all, we'll meet again at six this evening and have sandwiches or lasagna brought in. And we would work until eleven at night, with a legislative session in between. It was just killing.

Bennett recognized he had one problem. He always thought in a "big picture" way but admits he had difficulty communicating it:

> The ability to take the big picture, which I thought I understood so well, and make it understandable to the average person quickly, so we could bring the public along in supporting us—I wasn't able to do that. I did not do it well. And I should have. And, yet, in time the public did come along and support what we were doing. But it was one of my weaknesses. Along with the work plan, I never put as much attention into the public

> information plan. I felt a sense of urgency that couldn't wait. That was a weakness of mine as a leader.

He settled into a routine. A lonely life lived in the Harbour Towers when he was in town, and home to Kelowna for the weekends every chance he got. He got up, ran or played tennis, worked, read at night and went to bed. Day after day. Jim Nielsen recalls: "You didn't get to know him terribly well. His dad once said that you can't become friends with your ministers, as you might have to fire them one day. And I think Bill felt the same way."

A self-admitted loner, Bennett had a management style to match:

> You can't be having a cup of coffee, or playing cards, or socializing evening after evening with colleagues and still maintain that leadership role. You wouldn't do it in the private sector. In government, leadership is a lonely role inasmuch as my view of it is that you pick a cabinet team, and for them to work well you have to be their leader. You have to ensure that they all have equal access, that there aren't favourites.
>
> I am not cut out for the cocktail party circuit or a lot of receptions. I would do them as part of my work. But I liked the work. In the evenings, I would take my work home if I wasn't scheduled to speak or to travel or be at a dinner. I would go home and take all of my reading, because I wanted to know as much as I could. And I would read it that night. If I had a night off, I would go to bed as early as I could and wake up at four thirty or five o'clock in the morning, and that's when I'd do my reading. Maybe it was me. Maybe some other premier could have done the job in an eight-hour day. I couldn't.

6

WORK TO LEARN

"He covered his weaknesses by building a team of experts to give him advice, and he soaked that up like a sponge."

DAVID EMERSON

THE SHOUTING IN the hallway lasted only a few minutes before the cabinet doors were pushed open by the screaming mob of welfare protesters. It was January 15, 1976, and they were crashing the newly elected Social Credit government's third cabinet meeting. Bill Bennett had been listening to Minister of Human Resources Bill Vander Zalm talk about radical welfare reform. Education Minister Pat McGeer, also in charge of ICBC, had been arguing the need to raise ICBC rates to get the corporation onto a firm fiscal footing.

Two protests, one over welfare reform led by Bruce Eriksen, president of the Vancouver based Downtown Eastside Residents Association, and another led by Victoria native Sharon McBain protesting ICBC rate hikes, joined forces on the lawn in a group of about two hundred protesters. The ICBC protest was relatively peaceful, but the jobless and welfare protest became an angry affair when Vander Zalm would not come out to meet the protesters.

About seventy-five of them had surged into the legislative buildings, up the stairs to the cabinet offices and into the cabinet meeting. The event was best described by *Vancouver Sun* writer Bill Bachop on the front page of the paper on January 16, 1976, under the banner headline "Bennett the Peacemaker Quells Protest":

> The crowd—protesting a lack of jobs, higher auto-insurance rates and what they considered derogatory statements about welfare recipients by Human Resources Minister Bill Vander Zalm—burst in on the ministers about 2 P.M.
>
> They swaggered in, helped themselves to coffee from the cabinet room coffee pot, sat down beside ministers, lit cigarettes and made themselves at home.
>
> Then for more than 45 minutes, in what at times was a tense confrontation, they shouted, jeered, heckled and presented demands to a shirt-sleeved Bennett and his cabinet colleagues.
>
> But Bennett remained cool throughout. It was Bennett who took the initiative when the angry demonstrators roared and ranted at his ministers and compared his new government to the Socred regime that was defeated by the NDP.
>
> It was Bennett, casually donning his jacket—shucked for a lengthy cabinet meeting—who manoeuvred a small group of the invaders into a closed-door discussion in the quiet of his office with Vander Zalm.
>
> And it was Bennett who managed not only to pacify them, but also to send them away reasonably happy...
>
> After the hour-long meeting in the premier's office the majority of the delegates announced they were "satisfied" with Bennett's response to their complaints...

The *Vancouver Sun* editorial the same day expressed the surprise many in the province felt: "They demonstrated that we have a cool, collected premier who, faced with a hostile crowd, possessed not only a sophisticated sense of tactics but unexpected charm... [I]t is pretty clear who the winner was: Bill Bennett."

Bennett's reaction and assessment were quite revealing: "There were only a couple of real crazies in that group, and of course they were carrying shovels. So we just let them talk, and once we got a couple down in my office we just talked to them. Security finally showed up, but it was a good chance for me to watch my cabinet to see who's got the guts to keep cool and not pass out or faint..."

The caucus also met often in the first year, far more than in years to come. During this time every member was able to see who could grasp the points and make reasonable political judgements and who could not. Although newly minted as premier, Bennett waited to add to his cabinet until all the backbenchers could see the cream rising to the top. Then it was much easier to bring in newly elected first-time members, like Harvey Schroeder, as well as an old-timer like Jim Chabot.

FRIDAY AFTERNOONS were a quiet time in the legislative buildings. The House, if in session, would rise around noon and ministers would be on their way home by 12:30.

The one o'clock B.C. Ferries sailing would be filled with backbenchers and opposition members heading home to the Lower Mainland for the weekend. Looking up, they could see government jets taking ministers home. Some of these ministers used to joke that their offices must be bugged, because the premier always knew what was going on in their departments. He didn't meddle, but he knew what was going on.

On Friday afternoons the premier, armed with his coffee cup, would wander around the legislative buildings. (He would catch the five o'clock flight home.) One of his destinations was caucus research. There he would sit and chat with the bright, eccentric George Guibault. A strange-looking man, with large bald head, awkward gait; a brilliant analyzer of polls. And, importantly for the premier, his finger was on the pulse of what was going on in caucus. What research was being carried out? What was the mood?

Bill and George never told anyone of these chats.

The other stops varied in specifics but had one underlying feature. Bennett remained the best harmless flirter in the province. He would just drop into ministers' offices and chat up the secretaries. Get his coffee cup refilled. He loved doing it, they loved him doing it and he came away with lots of interesting tidbits. Bud Smith comments on Bennett's strategy:

> He was the most skilled management-by-wandering-around-people I've ever had the pleasure of being around. He recognized people's skills and drew from a whole variety of people. He had a habit of bringing around himself people who he judged in certain areas to be much smarter than him.
>
> Around the legislature, he spoke frequently with the secretaries to the ministers. He wouldn't have them squealing on the ministers, but he would have a chat with them, and they would inevitably disclose things that were going on.
>
> He also would spend time with the caucus research people. He would discern what subjects were getting researched, both by backbenchers and by cabinet ministers. And that would give him a sense of some of the issues that were on their mind.

BENNETT WAS NOT trying to set up a business, but rather to set up government to run in a businesslike manner. In government decision-making at the cabinet level, the options considered are only bottom-line-driven by their incremental impact on budgets, up or down. Many proposals are approved and the relevant ministry is told to get on with the job, but within existing resources. This leads to governments doing many things poorly, as resources are stretched too far.

The problem is caused by ministers wearing two hats, one to expand programs to meet citizens' demands, the other to control and keep down expenditures. One of the more novel experiences for a deputy minister is to present a new program idea to a cabinet committee, where it is heartily endorsed, and then proceed to Treasury Board, where the same ministers wearing different hats turn it down.

Bennett sports a "Build with Bill" button. The slogan was used in Bennett's by-election win in Kelowna in August 1973. (HANS GIESEN OF BRITISH COLUMBIA LTD., COURTESY MELDY HARRIS)

Bennett wins the leadership of the B.C. Social Credit Party in the fall of 1975. He celebrates here with his wife, Audrey, and their boys. (CROTON STUDIOS LTD., COURTESY MELDY HARRIS)

The Socred caucus in opposition, 1974 (*left to right*): Don Phillips, Jim Chabot, Frank Richter, Bill Bennett, Newell Morrison, Ed Smith, Pat Jordan, Bob McClelland, Alex Fraser, Harvey Schroeder. (COURTESY DON PHILLIPS)

The Bill Bennett campaign team, 1975: Winnebago'ing the way to power. (PAUL PONICH STUDIOS, COURTESY MELDY HARRIS)

The Socreds' long march back to power began in earnest at the Hotel Vancouver in November 1975, when Grace McCarthy was elected party president and Bill Bennett was chosen as party leader. (ROYAL BRITISH COLUMBIA MUSEUM, PROVINCIAL ARCHIVES # I-68023)

Tina trumpets a change in government as Bob McClelland rides her into the Agridome for the large end of a campaign rally in 1975. This photo appeared in newspapers across North America. (COURTESY BOB McCLELLAND)

Bill Bennett in full flight, getting his hands around a problem and into an explanation in 1976. (ROYAL BRITISH COLUMBIA MUSEUM, PROVINCIAL ARCHIVES # I-68024)

Demonstrators storm into the cabinet chamber in January 1976, protesting welfare reform and ICBC rate hikes shortly after Social Credit was elected.
(STEVE BOSCH, *VANCOUVER SUN*)

"Follow the Leader": Bill and Audrey Bennett at a Social Credit convention in the late 1970s. (COURTESY MELDY HARRIS)

Bennett in a media scrum on an ice field in the north. (COURTESY DON PHILLIPS)

"Bill, circle the wagons and shoot out, not in!" Bennett with his good friend and campaign adviser Hugh Harris. (COURTESY MELDY HARRIS)

Dynamiter: Bill Bennett sets the first charge on the Coquihalla highway. (COURTESY MELDY HARRIS)

An official photograph of the Honourable W. R. Bennett, premier of the province of British Columbia, 1975–1986. (ROYAL BRITISH COLUMBIA MUSEUM, PROVINCIAL ARCHIVES # I-68026)

Bennett's model was to funnel all this information into cabinet, where a government, not a ministry, decision could be taken. Once decisions were made in cabinet they were government decisions, and a cabinet member's choice was to fully accept this fact or leave. If you took something to cabinet and never received approval, you could not traipse back to your senior staff executive and blame cabinet. You could only blame yourself for not selling it properly or explaining how the idea must be positioned differently. There were no ministerial decisions, only government decisions based on ministry input. Bennett recalls:

> The immense flow of paper. We would have the various committees, and time frames. It would go through the steps so when it finally came to cabinet we could decide. And that really brought discipline. Eventually what happened is that in committee before coming to general cabinet, you had different ministers going after their colleagues, where they disagreed with where it was going. It forced coordination. It worked very well.
>
> The only time it exploded was when Bill Vander Zalm tried to bring his stuff straight to cabinet.
>
> But it worked, and with fine tuning it worked over time. We made some adjustments over time, but basically the cabinet committee system worked.

He had promised two things in this regard. An ombudsman to protect people from arbitrary decision making, and an auditor general to provide independent oversight of government spending.

ON MAY 21, 1976, the following headline appeared on page 1 of the *Vancouver Sun:* "Gov't introduces legislation to establish auditor general." The story shared the front page with two other lead stories: "VGH employees refuse to return as new row flares over rehiring" and "Work to rule on ferries delays holiday sailings." The remaining space on the front page was taken up with: "Essential services" and "B.C. Gov't plans to curb strikes." Public-sector strikes were, as usual, a hot topic.

But the business of running government went on. Bennett had turned the auditor general file for implementation over to Finance Minister Evan Wolfe. When ready, the minister proceeded with the legislation. Bennett did not speak to it in the House.

Before the Auditor General Act of 1976, there had been no real separation of audit functions from other internal accounting functions of government. It is the objectivity and independence from government direction and operational responsibility that are the distinguishing features of a truly independent modern auditing and legislative reporting function. Independence is the key. The new Act provided for an external auditor. No longer could the government audit its own books.

Finance Minister Wolfe put it this way:

> The major innovation presented in Bill 45 is the appointment of an auditor general through the unanimous recommendation of a special committee of the Legislative Assembly...
>
> Among Canadian jurisdictions, only Quebec has a provision in any way similar to this. In that province two-thirds of the National Assembly must agree upon an auditor general before he is appointed. By requiring unanimous recommendation of a special committee of this assembly we feel sure that it will be clear to all that we regard the auditor general as being above any hint of partisanship. The auditor general's independence is his most valuable asset.

Bill 45 received speedy passage in the House. Everyone wanted to share the good idea. In a similar fashion, the Ombudsman Act passed into law. Bennett explains:

> I felt financing was getting too close to government itself. People felt that it was hidden, that there wasn't any authority controlling the government. Although I knew that Barrett didn't want it, and my dad didn't want it, I felt for the public's good, and for discipline on the cabinet and the government itself, the position was important. Similarly with the ombudsman. Alberta had one acting as a watchdog, and it seemed to be working.

> They can come back to haunt you, and the bureaucrats may hate them from time to time, but that's what they're there for. It's the discipline on the government itself.

BENNETT THEN TURNED his attention to two longer-term items: improving relations with Ottawa and arranging the sale of the province's NDP-acquired private-sector assets to set the stage for the next election.

Federal–provincial relations is a glacial process. Agreement requires unanimity among all ten provinces. (In the 1970s, the Yukon and the Northwest Territories were still fighting for a place at the table and Nunavut did not exist.) To reach consensus, the highest principles often sink to the lowest common denominator. Once consensus has been reached by the provinces in their preparatory meetings, they try to hold a position and indeed enhance it. However, the more complicated the position, the more likely it is to break down. This is why a lot of federal–provincial meetings fail. It is easier for the provinces to be critical of the feds than to find creative common-ground solutions. Often, all they can agree upon is how to criticize Ottawa.

This problem is exacerbated by the fact that a province will break away from the others if it can cut a bilateral deal with Ottawa to its benefit. Any province looking for a special funding favour will trade off a provincial consensus in a minute to get its priority concerns taken care of.

The federal government is of course very skilled at the game. Highly skilled federal bureaucrats with years of experience often face new premiers and their new staffs. Many of the disagreements between Ottawa and the provinces occur in provincial areas of jurisdiction, where the feds move in through their spending power. Since the Great Depression, the hot issues have been those in provincial jurisdiction: health, education and social services. The feds have the cash, they set the rules of encounter. And playing one province off the next is the sport.

This is all dressed up in the need for national standards and for a common level of services in social-issue areas. And when Ottawa faces a fiscal crisis it cuts funding to the provinces, looks as though it has its house in order and criticizes the provinces for whining. As long as no one is responsible, no one is accountable. Blame the other guy and get re-elected.

Prime ministers win elections promising to improve federal–provincial relations by improving the dialogue between jurisdictions, and their victory leads to holding at least one First Ministers Conference. The bloom soon goes off the rose, as they quickly tire of being the kicking boy of the provinces. They stop holding the conferences. In the next election the same promises are made, because the dialogue has again broken down, and the cycle repeats itself.

Into this quagmire walked the newly elected Premier Bill Bennett. He thought that Barrett's approach had been wrong. His experience in Kelowna working with the federal government had been positive. He felt that hard work, preparation and logical arguments would win out. Therefore, when the recently re-elected Prime Minister Trudeau decided to host a First Ministers Conference on the economy, Premier Bennett began to get prepared in the only way he knew—hard, disciplined work.

He did not turn to the Ministry of Finance to prepare the work because he recognized it did not have the internal capacity. This was to be a conference on the economy, and therefore the Ministry of Economic Development should carry the ball.

The deputy minister, Sandy Peel, had started to build a real economic development ministry based on the federal model. This required a strong policy arm. He had hired away an economics professor from UBC, Dr. Jim Rae, who recruited bright young professionals like Dr. David Emerson.

A B.C. economic hothouse blossomed at the ministry. Ideas flew, arguments went on late into the night over differing economic views and correcting Canada's problems of high unemployment and high inflation in a B.C. context. Once the group had reached as much agreement as can be expected from a group of economists—not much—they met with the premier to review positions and options. Bennett added the common sense that is needed to give these think-tank propositions reality. David Emerson explains it this way:

> Bennett was long on street smarts and very sharp. He covered his weaknesses by building a team of experts to give him advice, and he soaked that up like a sponge. And he would go elsewhere for advice, and come back and challenge our assumptions.
>
> I remember our neo-conservative view that marketing boards were only a vehicle to subsidize farmers. The premier took our paper and shared it with his father, W.A.C. He came back and said his father had argued that the marketing boards were the farmers' trade union.
>
> He had also read John Kenneth Galbraith's book *Countervailing Powers* and said that what his father had put his finger on was that these boards acted as a countervailing power to supply the market correction and balance utilities with monopoly powers and large distributors.
>
> I changed my view of marketing boards after this discussion, and that was what it was like dealing with Bennett. He knew intuitively how to build a strong economy, the right balances to make, and we supplied the theoretical constructs to give it focus and sound theory.

The most comprehensive documents ever prepared by British Columbia, before or since, were readied for presentation to the First Ministers Conference on February 14–16, 1978. Eight background papers were written, each with a different bright-primary-coloured cover, and slickly packaged in a black pressed-cardboard box bearing the official seal of the province. A separate overview document outlined the proposals.

When it came time for him to speak at the conference, Bennett outlined his views. Out of the hundred ideas Bennett put forward, Prime Minister Trudeau commented on only one, as reported in the *Vancouver Sun* on February 14, 1978:

> It is worthwhile to examine whether direct income supplementation for low-wage workers would not accomplish the same social objectives as the minimum wage with less distortion in the economy... One could equally ask whether income supplementation is not a more effective social and economic measure than directly controlling prices, whether

> by subsidy as we do by oil or by direct regulation as is done with rental accommodation.
>
> Indeed should we not be questioning the concept of universality in some of our social programs? Is there good reason, for example, why those Canadians with high incomes should receive an oil subsidy…
>
> If we can devise programs that can provide support to those who truly need support, without bureaucratic intervention, then we could serve our social objectives while reducing government expenditures, market interference and bureaucratic intervention.

Trudeau asked Bennett for further information and clarification, but completely ignored the other ideas.

Other premiers, like Quebec Premier René Lévesque, supported B.C.'s idea of a First Ministers coordinating institution but disagreed with the social policy. Support for cancelling the Department of Regional Economic Expansion (DREE) was warm at first. Quebec Finance Minister Jacques Parizeau described DREE as "a sausage machine…a bureaucratic tangle that is not making economic recovery any easier."

But federal Finance Minister Jean Chrétien defended DREE and pointed out that over $100 million of DREE monies had flowed to Montreal in new programs. The Atlantic region premiers came back after lunch having spoken with Chrétien, and the DREE proposal was effectively destroyed.

Ontario put forward a ten-point plan aimed at improving jobless Canadians' chances for employment that included a "Buy Canadian" program, a youth employment program, a tax credit initiative, accelerated investments in energy, an incentive program for the automotive industry and reducing red tape.

The premiers had wanted the conference to be held in public. Trudeau had agreed. With the media present, they soon turned to public posturing. This inevitably led to a private session followed by media scrums, and finally to dinner at 24 Sussex Drive to try and agree to a communiqué.

Over a meal of lobster, duck and white wine, the leaders failed to reach agreement. Bennett had not realized that he would be a majority of one when he wanted to follow where logic led. Not because of any mean-spirited conspiracy against good ideas, but rather the forum itself could not accommodate one premier, any premier, coming with a package of ideas, no matter how well thought out, and seeing them accepted.

Bennett was frustrated: "I don't think anyone read our policy research papers... We are not voicing opinions grabbed out of thin air." He accomplished only two significant things. First, he caused the participants to note that for the first time in memory B.C. came to a federal–provincial First Ministers Conference fully prepared and ready to debate. The era of writing B.C. off as the flaky province was over, at least under this premier. Bennett thinks that "it helped in a way that we were not seen as just not a bunch of dummies coming with a client list, at least trying to get that perception out of the way. We would be considered experienced, not there to whine and beg."

Also, he learned what makes these conferences tick. Upon returning home he conducted a rigorous examination of the conference, his preparation, his approach and his performance. He would learn from this experience and be ready for the next major federal–provincial go-around. "These conferences don't have the time or the ability to deal with multiple issues. But major points, they will concentrate on one, two or three at most, and that's where you put your effort... Conferences on specific issues worked better... And Pierre, he didn't want to talk about the economy. He wanted to talk Constitution. That was going to be his legacy."

PREMIER BENNETT turned off the Tuesday-night boxing program on the TV in his apartment in the Harbour Towers and looked again at the material prepared by his staff on the private-sector acquisitions the NDP had made over their short time in office. Government acquisition of private-sector companies was anathema to his political beliefs. Canadian Cellulose, Kootenay Forest Products, Panco Poultry, Ocean Falls, Plateau Mills, Westcoast Transmission and properties at Roberts Bank had all been purchased in whole or in part.

He was determined to move these private-sector entities back into the private sector. He could create a wedge issue that would highlight the difference between his free-enterprise party and the social democrats.

He also could see the risk. If the companies were sold and their values declined, his government would be seen to have dumped these assets at inflated values. If they were sold and then increased in value, he would be blamed for not getting what they were worth. He turned to his friend and Socred bagman Austin Taylor, a big, florid mountain of a man, not only a recognized expert in Canadian markets but also a chief party fundraiser.

Bennett, with Taylor's advice, set up an advisory group, code named "Project West," in March 1977. It consisted of representatives of the major brokerage firms. That month Bennett met with Project West and gave it clear instructions about what the outcome should look like:

- A holding company would carry out the privatization.
- Project West, not the government, would select the assets.
- The province would retain some share in the company.
- Foreign ownership of shares would be excluded, and limits would be placed on shareholdings of institutions and investors.
- The entire financial community would be involved in the share distribution.
- All shares would be sold to B.C. residents.

It was always clear to the participants that this initiative was a delicate combination of business and politics. Project West chose Canadian Cellulose, Kootenay Forest Products, Plateau Mills, Westcoast Transmission and the province's gas and oil exploration licences. From the beginning the major problem the advisers had was a business issue: cash flow. The advisers, as investment dealers, felt strongly that the shares which were to be sold to the public (at this time) had to pay cash dividends. Share sales were expected to generate $75 million. This would require around $6 million for dividends.

In addition, the new holding company had to pay the government for the companies it acquired, about $150 million. Money borrowed for the purchase amounted to $7 million annually. A total of $13 million was needed to effect the transaction. Where was the $13 million to come from? The problem was exacerbated by the fact that in a typical holding company the actual cash coming in, compared with the accounting earnings, is always less, often as much as 50 percent less.

Something had to give. Dividends were essential. The government controlled the sale price of the assets and had to be seen to be getting true market value. The bean counters in the Ministry of Finance and the investment dealers in Project West spent eighteen months exploring financing proposals as they struggled with this problem.

On June 9, 1977, the premier held a media conference to announce the formation of a holding company to transfer assets owned by government to the private sector. On August 23, he tabled in the House Bill 87 to create the British Columbia Resources Investment Corporation (BCRIC). The legislated entity would run in a businesslike way, independent of government.

Dave Barrett attacked the legislation, and the wedge was apparent:

> The people of this province are now being given the opportunity to sell off something to themselves that they already own. We own these assets and we are going to sell them to ourselves for the second time. What we are dealing with is the opportunity to sell to ourselves something we have already paid for once. I don't intend to stand by idle and see our company, owned by every citizen in this province, sold off to the few rich who can afford to buy that stuff up.

On September 9 the premier announced the new directors. A small elite group, all were CEOs of companies operating primarily in B.C., and all were well respected. But all of them represented companies that were at the second level in B.C. in terms of size; and more importantly, none of them had experience in or were engaged in a resource industry. David Helliwell, a chartered accountant, was hired as president and CEO. Again, he had no experience in the resource industries of B.C.

The enterprise was soon named. The irrepressible Scotsman, broadcaster and talk-show host Jack Webster, broadcasting daily at "Eleven AM, Precisely!" couldn't get his tongue around the corporation's full name when in full flight. And since full flight was a daily occurrence, he coined it "BRIC." The acronym stuck.

By the summer of 1978, all problems but one—cash flow—were solved. All the work, all the announcements, the legislation, the creation of the wedge issue were about to be for naught. The problem seemed unsolvable. A new idea was needed on how to sell the shares.

The most in-depth research into BCRIC is told in a book by Ohashi, Roth, Spinder, McMillan and Norrie, *Distributing Shares in Private and Public Enterprises.* Ohashi was a member of Project West and lived through the experience of creating this unique enterprise. He claims: "The origin of the share giveaway idea is not known precisely. However, most remember it as a suggestion from Premier Bennett... The truth is probably a combination of the two views. There was clearly a frustration level when the premier made his suggestion. At the same time, it was an inspiration which ultimately led to the success of the BCRIC exercise." Ohashi names others who had a similar idea. For example, the leader of the Liberals, Gordon Gibson, spoke about taking all the shares and giving them to the public. When Bennett was asked about the origin of the idea, he was self-effacing: "The idea came from staff, I think. We were all working on it and someone just came up with it." But Bennett handled the BCRIC file himself. This was unusual.

The giveaway solved a number of problems. It lanced the NDP argument that the citizens were being asked to buy what they already owned. It avoided any possible failure in the share offering. And giving voters fifty dollars at election time helped focus their minds on the choice between free enterprise and socialism. To drive this message home, 1.5 million British Columbians who had driver's licences received a personally addressed letter from the premier, enclosing a brochure extolling the benefits of BCRIC.

One colourful editorial quoted in the *Victoria Times*, January 13, 1979, and reproduced in Ohashi *et al.*'s book presented BCRIC this way: "It is everything the critics called it, and more—corny, deceptive, opportunistic. It is also an imaginative piece of politicking... it's a goofy, crazy idea open to all sorts of abuse but, at the same time, it just might work. At one and the same time it is more socialistic than anything the New Democratic Party or the old Socred administration ever did, while at the same time, it is the quintessence of free enterprise."

Once BCRIC was created and the board was in place to handle the administration, Bennett backed away completely. He was sincere and insistent that government be separated from the board's business decisions. The board was expected to manage the file, and he expected a high standard of business acumen and judgement.

The plan got off to a very good start. Bennett announced that five shares, "probably worth fifty dollars in total," were free upon application to any Canadian citizen resident in B.C. for one year. There was a debate about whether people would actually apply; share ownership in B.C. prior to BCRIC was only 2.5 percent of the population. David Helliwell predicted a take-up of about 65 percent. He was wrong: 87.5 percent of British Columbians took up the offer for shares.

The second debate was whether any, or many, would be sold. The board of directors sealed envelopes with their guesses, which ranged from $55 million to $210 million. Actual sales figures were $487.5 million.

Suddenly BCRIC had more shareholders than any other company in Canada, and with the exception of AT&T more than any in North America. All that remained was for the board to act wisely to manage the asset. They did not. BCRIC was soon in trouble, and shares plummetted. The honeymoon was over. The wonderful bang that was BCRIC went out with a whimper.

In March, David Helliwell announced that the cash-rich, $526 million company would invest in two ventures. First, it agreed to purchase 20 percent of the forest giant MacMillan Bloedel. Second, it would take an option for 22 percent of coal producer Kaiser Resources Ltd. The cost would drain 60 percent of BCRIC's cash reserves, a total of $324 million.

These purchases were the harbingers of future disaster. With no board experience in resource industries, and none in the president's office, the company soon found itself heading into trouble. Further, in September 1980, the media reported that Edgar Kaiser Jr., chairman and CEO of Kaiser Resources Ltd., stood to make millions on his personal shares from the sale.

The first casualty was Helliwell, who had organized the takeover of Kaiser. He was fired in November. BCRIC shares continued to fall. The company became worthless. Most people's free shares joined their high school diploma in the bottom of their underwear drawer. Of the two, the diploma was worth more. Bennett comments, in retrospect:

> These people were all CEOs and good ones in their own right. They were at that time part of a middle, younger generation. I felt they could bring a good fresh look to this. We didn't want the tired old thinking that nothing new was doable; this had to be bigger than that.
>
> I believe if they had shown patience, had they waited, let the money collect dividends, and done their research and buy when the buying was right…
>
> I was shocked at what they had done. I had sold this as independent. If I'd interfered in the first major board decision with what they said they were going to do, the whole thing would have blown up. I disagreed with their decision, but I was stuck with it.
>
> If we did it again, if I'd been running the company, I would have done it differently. I would find someone to run the company with resource experience.

WHILE BENNETT WAS busy running government, dealing with Ottawa and setting up BCRIC, he ignored an important issue. He took the Social Credit Party apparatus for granted. He had not yet understood the complex relationship between being head of government and head of a party.

7

FACEOFF '79

"No party of the extreme right or the extreme left can survive."

BILL BENNETT

BRITISH COLUMBIANS love Canada, but the sentiment "Let the eastern bastards freeze" is not far below the surface. Those "easterners" are not the Atlantic provinces, but Ontario. Toronto. And Ottawa. In some parts of B.C. there is a latent hostility towards Quebec, especially when "they" talk about a distinct society—hell, "they" are no more special or distinct than we are. But we don't feel the same animosity towards Quebecers, because they hate the same central Canadian institutions we do. Banks. Big government. Big head-office types who think they know best.

The westerners' icy response to the federal National Energy Program characterized B.C.'s feelings perfectly. Those Bay Street bankers can just go to hell. It's only three thousand miles from B.C. to Ottawa, but it's thirty thousand miles from Ottawa to B.C. If Pierre Trudeau can give the finger to the good citizens of Salmon Arm, we can send Ottawa very few Liberal members of Parliament. So the politics are good if you are a strong Canadian but can find a public reason to thrash big business or big government "back east."

Bill Bennett was given just such an opportunity over Christmas 1978. In 1975 he had coined the expression "Not a dime without debate!" after being ejected from the B.C. legislature. His province-wide tour hammering away on this theme proved vital in winning the election that year. When this opportunity knocked, he knew he had another winner.

December 27 was a cold day, cloudy but no snow on Big White—the ski hill outside Kelowna that Bennett had taken the family to after Christmas, to ski for a few days. When he wasn't challenging his kids to race down the hill—he never let them win—he was pushing himself by racing against himself. In this obsessive-compulsive way his mind was free to work over the strategy and tactics of when to call the election that everyone expected in the spring. He reviewed the past few years, trying to judge if the time was right. His father had called elections every three years. But the son preferred a four-year cycle.

Once in government in 1975, he began to modernize the machinery of government. He had commissioned Judge Lawrence Eckardt to carry out a redistribution exercise, and immediately upon receiving the report had carried it over into legislation. He had called a special pre-Christmas session to legislate back to work non-teaching staff in the West Kootenay. A new Ministry of Deregulation was created. The taxing authority of municipalities was limited by a 5 percent ceiling, putting the Socreds firmly on the side of those folks trumpeting a California Proposition 13–style tax revolt. This effectively took away the one issue in which Conservative leader Vic Stephens had been gaining traction.

And, of course, he had BCRIC. He was about to give every man and woman in the province fifty dollars worth of free shares. As he laid out the options in his mind, he stopped for a quick lunch.

Audrey, who had not been out skiing, said: "Bill, you'd better listen to the noon news. There's something you might be interested in."

On the radio he heard that Montreal-based Canadian Pacific Investments (CPI) was attempting to buy B.C.'s forest icon, MacMillan Bloedel. Bennett had not received even a courtesy "heads-up" phone call from the company. CPI was a subsidiary of Canadian Pacific. And if the banks didn't make a British Columbian mad, the railways certainly did.

He quickly arranged for a government jet to fly him to Victoria the next morning. Up at 5:30 AM, he was still annoyed at CPI's lack of courtesy in not providing a heads-up, and he had the night to work through the politics. A dangerous combination.

Fate intervened to make him testier. The pipes had frozen overnight, and he had to melt snow in order to shave. His car wouldn't start because of a dead battery. He woke his neighbour for a jump start. The Good Samaritan neighbour decided to follow him down the mountain to ensure that he did not slip off the icy roads. He didn't, but his neighbour did and had to be manhandled out. The government plane had waited the required fifteen minutes, and when Bennett did not appear left without him.

When he finally reached Victoria by commercial airlines later that afternoon and went on air, he was in no mood for compromise or negotiation. He simply stated: "B.C. is not for sale." The fight was on.

The contradiction was that a free-enterprise government and a premier who believed in the free and open marketplace should have been comfortable with the marketplace taking care of business. It would have been expected that the premier would remain silent and the leader of the opposition, Dave Barrett, would take the position of intervening in a market decision. But Bennett knew he must take the high ground and leave Barrett no room. Bennett observed: "I can win an election by campaigning against the CPR. I can lose if I don't."

His chief adversary, Ian Sinclair, president and CEO of CPR/CPI, several days later angrily proclaimed over a Shaughnessy dinner table: "I am not paid $400,000 a year to lose. I am paid to win."

Over the next two weeks Bennett coolly exploited British Columbians' deep-rooted distrust of the CPR in a high-stakes game; and he won. In an eventual face-to-face meeting with Sinclair, the premier would not move. He would block the sale by refusing to approve the transfer of the timber licences. Sinclair huffed and puffed about the damage this action would create for B.C. in world markets, but Bennett would not blink. The CPR backed down.

Allan Fotheringham got it right in his column in *Maclean's* magazine on February 12, 1979:

> The most useful weapon in politics is spurious anger...
>
> The best current example is provided by last week's cover hero, Bill Bennett, who flew into a week-long temper and blocked the big bad bear from Windsor Station, Ian Sinclair, from swallowing huge MacMillan Bloedel, thereby saving virginal little British Columbia from the terrible predators of Lower Canada...
>
> What Bill Bennett saw, actually, was not a red haze before his eyes but a way of beating the NDP in a spring election.

Most commentators agreed that the table was set for calling an election.

However, fate was to disrupt the planning when W.A.C. died in late February 1979. His father was a larger than life figure, not only for Bill Bennett, but for the province. For twenty years, between 1952 and 1972, W.A.C. had won election after election by drawing on the spectre of "socialist hordes at the gates." Yet he remarked after nationalizing the B.C. ferry system that he was "more socialist than the socialists."

It was time for Bill and Audrey to get away for a while. They headed south to have some quiet time to put into perspective Bill's father's life and legacy. The premier would have to refocus for the upcoming election.

THERE WAS NO doubt that Bill Bennett was a private person. Some even thought him aloof. They never had the opportunity to see his other side, as he remained guarded in public. Hugh Curtis describes this other side:

> I had this authentic air force helmet, a pilot's helmet. And Skylab was about to fall. There was great speculation about would it hit the ocean, would it hit on land, would it hit B.C., would it hit North Dakota? So I took it to work. And a planning and priorities committee meeting started at 8:30, nine o'clock. So I had the helmet under my arm, under a coat, and in the outer office I put it on. And I walked into Evan Wolfe's office. Bennett's in the middle saying something or somebody's talking to him. And he looked at me. He said, "Hugh? Hugh." And I said, "Premier, Skylab's falling and I just wanted to be prepared."

> Well, he fell off his chair. Now that's a joke I played. But I recall on a couple of occasions, something would happen, an ashtray would be knocked over or whatever, and he'd say, "There is a God." We saw his sense of humour, but many didn't. Most didn't.

BENNETT HAD BEEN polling. The market research carried out by the national Liberal pollster Martin Goldfarb pointed in the right direction. In what was to be his electoral pattern, he watched for the point in the mandate at which his party would bottom out and begin to trend upward. He kept these polls to himself.

He returned to finish setting the stage. First, a throne speech and a budget. Based on the $140 million surplus, some spending was in order, and the government promised a comprehensive dental care program—Denticare—and a $25 million trade and convention centre for Vancouver. A new port facility was promised for Prince Rupert. The Liberal Party's leader had just resigned. It was going to be a straight two-party race. Bennett, the man who played tennis not to relax but to win, was satisfied. It was time to go to the people.

DAVE BARRETT WAS exhausted after his election defeat in 1975. He had lost the government and he had lost his own seat in the legislature. To a car dealer, no less. His wife, Shirley, insisted they leave for a holiday. Manzanillo was exactly what he needed: lick his wounds, think about his future. He could not decide if he wanted to stay in politics, and when he and Shirley came home after two weeks, both agreed to let the caucus mood decide.

Needless to say, the caucus and the party executive had been busy navel-gazing. Much discussion, great heat, little light.

Add into this mix a rejuvenated Barrett, and the caucus—after sometimes heated and always tense meetings—realized that not only did he deserve another chance but that he was the best they had.

Barrett needed a seat. Bill King offered his Revelstoke riding, but a Vancouver kid and Revelstoke didn't work. Instead the much-respected King became interim opposition leader. In a typical Bill King gesture, he split the opposition leader stipend with Barrett fifty-fifty.

A deal was worked out with Bob Williams, the member from Vancouver East: $80,000 was paid to him by the party to step aside. Legal, but controversial.

The by-election was called for June 3, 1976. Dave Barrett was home, where he had grown up. Campaigning, sometimes with his elderly mother at his side, it was more like a love-in than hard work. On election day he won 70 percent of the vote.

Now he had to rebuild the party. First, he needed to mend fences with organized labour. A new breeze had blown into the B.C. Federation of Labour, placing the tough, articulate Jim Kinnaird into the key secretary-treasurer job. He had been an assistant deputy minister under Bill King in the labour ministry. However, he was not cut out to be a bureaucrat and left on happy terms to return to the trade union movement he loved. He was a canny Scot who realized that while Barrett might not be labour's first choice, he was the only choice. Labour was on side.

Next Barrett took a page from the Social Credit recovery revival hymn book. Recruit a couple of reliable colleagues and get out and around the province. In a second-hand Volvo he would reconnect with people at regional public meetings. They would accept briefs during the day and hold fundraisers at night. Membership grew, with many returning to the flock as well as new members angry at the Bennett government for raising auto insurance rates and ferry fares.

Bennett then turned to the party organization, not his strong point. Yvonne Cocke, wife of MLA Dennis Cocke, was the organizational genius who soon had the NDP election ready.

Barrett returned to the legislature regularly, and always when controversy loomed. So when the British Columbia Resources Investment Corporation Act was debated in the house in late August, Barrett was in full flight:

> BCRIC turned my worst nightmare into reality. BCRIC was the mother of all Socred scandals, but we who fought it were just voices in the wilderness. And the sound of our voices was lost in the stampede to buy shares.

A CONSTANT BACKDROP to B.C. politics is its turbulent labour-relations climate. In a province polarized left and right, trade union versus employer rights, a historical home to class politics, politicians exploit the issue and the media fan the conflict—strikes sell newspapers.

Two key philosophical issues establish the framework for all this unrest. Paul Weiler, chair of B.C. Labour Relations Board and one of the two creators of the labour code, explains in his book *Reconcilable Differences:*

> There are two parts of a labour code which are central to the balance of power between union and employer. One is the use of the law to facilitate growth of union representation of unorganized workers. The other is the use of the law to limit the exercise of union economic weapons (the strike and the uses of the picket line) once a collective bargaining relationship has become established. Obviously legal rules designed for the first objective (encouraging collective bargaining) help expanding unions at the expense of non-union employers. By contrast, legal rules designed for the second objective (reducing industrial conflict) hamper the established unions for the benefit of organized employers. Whatever the lawmaker chooses to do in either of these areas, it is exceedingly difficult to look neutral in doing it.

When Premier Bennett formed his cabinet in 1975, he chose Allan Williams as his minister of labour. Now, four years later, his team was ready to go to the people, and stock had to be taken of how they had performed in the labour arena. The leadership of the B.C. Federation of Labour had swung behind Barrett, and Bennett was positioned to run against both. He and Williams agreed that they would not repeal the labour code. They could change it at the margins in key areas, but they would never be foolish enough to repeal it. Never repealed, it could always be referred to as NDP legislation still on the books. The public would get that and wonder why all the fuss over amendments it did not understand in any event.

The first Bennett–Williams move was to approach Paul Weiler and tell him they wished him to stay as chair of the Labour Relations Board.

Secondly, they had no plans for major revisions to the labour code. Weiler agreed to remain.

The next step was to calmly manage the highly visible strikes the province always faces. The first was in Kitimat, where angry picketers at the Alcan aluminum smelter defied a court order, resulting in thirty-two union members being arrested. A management worker had died when an ambulance could not get through the picket lines to rescue him. The public turned against the workers, and the government acted resolutely.

Public-sector unions on strike at Vancouver General Hospital and B.C. Ferries defied back-to-work orders. B.C. Rail and West Kootenay schools were behind picket lines. Day after day, the front-page headlines treated the disputes as though they were front-line war stories.

A successful minister of labour does two things. First, he does not overreact. He is patient. And in this, Williams was naturally suited. An experienced deputy, Jim Matkin, and a supportive premier helped stay the course. The second thing is, he uses these occasions to make changes at the margins that favour the philosophy of the government without creating a public backlash. The government pushed back the right to strike by introducing essential service disputes legislation and expanding the definition of essential services beyond life, health and safety to include economic considerations.

Facing a cabinet that was far more in tune with the right-to-work movement and facing the continual lobbying of groups like the Independent Contractors and Businesses Association (ICBA), who were as right-wing in their demands as the B.C. Federation of Labour was on the left, Williams sought smaller shifts. Amendments were introduced to make organizing more difficult by increasing the degree of representation required for certification. They also provided more employer freedom of speech during union organizing drives. In these moves, seen as going way too far by the B.C. Federation of Labour and not nearly far enough by the ICBA, the government struck the right public balance.

As a result, an incensed B.C. Federation of Labour was pledging its support to any union wishing to defy the new essential services legislation, which, of course, presented the perfect target to run against in the election. Not many in the public found themselves in agreement with ferry, hospital or school strikes. On the other hand, the government now had a group of supporters in organizations like the ICBA who had nowhere to go and would continue to financially support the Socreds in hope of further amendments.

It was a delicate balancing act that paid good political dividends.

BCRIC SHARES WERE put out to offer in early April, and within days Premier Bennett called the anticipated election for May 10, 1979. The first half of the 1979 provincial election was a desultory affair. It did not seem able to attain the spark an election needs to really get going.

It started interestingly enough, with Bennett announcing the election live on the six o'clock news on television shortly after the legislature had risen for the day. Bennett, who successfully claimed scheduling conflicts as the reason to avoid a televised debate in 1975, had a new twist this time. He challenged the leader of the opposition, Dave Barrett; the head of the B.C. Federation of Labour, Jim Kinnaird; and Bob Williams to debate him. He argued that Barrett didn't really control the party, the other two did, so the debate should include all three: "I think three to one is pretty fair odds for the NDP." The media laughed it off. They knew there would be no debate, and that fact would not be an issue in the election.

Complicating the election was the fact that the federal government had also called an election at the same time. The federal election was set for May 22. For the first time since 1949, federal and provincial campaigns were fought simultaneously in B.C.

The premier's approach was unusual, for him; laid back and easy-going, until about ten days from the finish. Then he began to grow concerned. His reading of the crowds told him that something was not right. The campaign was not firing on all cylinders. There was only one thing to do—work harder.

On May 3, Bennett announced he was putting his campaign into "high gear." On that day he left Victoria and made stops in Prince George, Mackenzie, Smithers, Terrace and Vancouver. At each stop he delivered his set piece criticizing the former NDP administration and defending his record. He added a plea for more volunteers to assist local Socred candidates. This fuelled press speculation that the NDP was making gains. Since the election was only a week away, some journalists speculated that the NDP might even be able to form the government.

The NDP was now campaigning with new energy, a frantic pace. As the week progressed, rallies were held everywhere in the province. It culminated with both parties holding major rallies in the last days of the campaign.

Barrett drew eight thousand people to Memorial Arena in Victoria. Tommy Douglas, the prairie spellbinder, former premier of Saskatchewan and B.C. member of Parliament, introduced Barrett to near bedlam with the best line of the campaign: "This crowd is so big it will scare Bill Bennett out of the other half of his wits."

Bennett held his wind-up rally in Vancouver, at the Agridome. More than seven thousand people jammed into the centre, where all the Lower Mainland candidates were introduced.

On election night it was clear that Barrett had been forgiven by his traditional constituency, or that people had forgotten. His percentage of the vote shot up. Social Credit and Bill Bennett, however, had held firm and won a second term. Bennett's percentage of the popular vote fell about 1 percent to 48.23 percent and the Socreds won thirty-one seats, a net loss of four seats.

Barrett went from 40 percent to 46 percent and increased his party's representation in the legislature from eighteen to twenty-six seats.

The Liberals and Conservatives were shut out.

In the most curious result of all, Frank Calder, who had crossed the floor to join the Socreds during the 1975 election, lost his seat in Atlin to the NDP by one vote. It was later discovered that Frank and his wife had not gotten around to vote. "Landslide" Al Passeral, the victor in Atlin, took his seat and moved into the legislature (literally), only to move to Social Credit himself a few years later.

WHAT HAD GONE WRONG? Had anything gone wrong? Not according to the popular vote loss, about 1 percent. But the number of seats lost was a problem. And the eight seats the NDP picked up, more so.

Bennett never ducked problems. His goal to win had been achieved. His vote was down marginally, and Barrett's was up substantially. Bennett recognized that he had ignored the central party organization. The fact that he was not alone as a new premier in his first term ignoring the state of the party was of no comfort. One of the most important lessons a new government leader must learn is that the distractions of power inherent in being premier can take away from the different role of being the head of the party.

In the British parliamentary system the head of the government must represent all the people, irrespective of whether they vote for him. This is what Bennett did: "In my first four years less a few days we focused on governing." But he must also remain the head of his own party, and this function is totally partisan: "In the party you have to make sure the people know what they are supposed to do, and do it."

Bill Bennett had tried to keep the party active by keeping the constituencies and regions busy. He held regional policy shops in the last couple of years of his mandate. But he let the head office function that provides control, direction and guidance fall into an unorganized mess. Campaign manager Dan Campbell describes it this way: "He knew the campaign had not gone well in some areas. His own presence on the hustings had been, well, laid-back. There just was not enough oomph in the campaign, which could have made the difference between a big win and a modest one."

Faced with the problem, Bennett did what he always did. He assessed his own performance, created a plan and set about fixing the problem. The analysis started with him turning to Dan Campbell for some blunt advice:

> When we won in 1975, some of us in the premier's office and in caucus research did try to maintain organizational ties with the party office. We tried to maintain the linkage that Grace McCarthy and I had built between the legislative wing and the membership wings of the party. This we failed to do.
>
> Quickly the signs that the party headquarters apparatus was in disarray were evident. Volunteer effort began to dry up. Communications with party members became shoddily organized. I believe, at least to

> some extent, that Bill Bennett wanted it that way. Perhaps because he longed for the good old days of his father, but more likely because he did not wish to share the responsibilities of leadership with anybody else.
>
> As the deadline for the election call came, the premier came to realize that the party head office was in no shape to lead a campaign committee...
>
> However, the worst was yet to come. When the election call finally came, the field machinery of the party had been built to a measure of efficiency, but the party office was in total shambles, lacking any credibility with the field organization...

Some of those whose views were asked argued that the problem lay in calling the election during a federal election period. Bud Smith put it this way:

> I thought it was an error for the very same reason he thought it was a good idea when he did it. He did it because he thought it would divide the resources of the NDP because they had been fighting both the federal and provincial elections, so financially...they would divide the resources, which is partially true. I thought it was an error because the provincial Social Credit Party was an amalgam of federal Tories and federal Liberals. And so we were put in the ghastly position of those two groups fighting one another in one election and trying to be moulded into a team for purposes of our election. And it frankly didn't work. But I must say that Bill Bennett has correctly pointed out to me he won the election and therefore it couldn't have been too much of an error.

Bennett next looked at how the NDP had managed to capture eight more seats in the legislature and improve its vote by 6 percent. One obvious reason was their central headquarters organization. He would have to fix this problem at Socred headquarters. And, on reflection, he felt there were three other reasons.

The first was the return of organized labour to the active NDP duty roster. As Bennett cast his mind back across his four years in power, one constant was the fight with organized labour. But as he took that broad statement apart, with few exceptions, the fight had been with the relatively new public-sector unions.

The second reason was the way in which the government's policy agenda had been communicated. There were two factors in this. The part of the agenda that had been about stabilizing and improving on the financial problems the Socreds had inherited had worked well. People understood the need to restore the financial house to good order. Bennett had branded the NDP as poor managers, and this would always be a cornerstone platform. But the focus on bringing discipline to social programs had cast the government as mean-spirited. For example, in education, as a result of the province setting standards and measuring results the teachers had felt under assault. Their response was to turn more to radical politics. In social services, the public generally supported cleaning the system up and getting rid of welfare cheats, but not the radical, confrontational approach of Minister Vander Zalm. Strict financial controls would control social services spending, but there were to be no further attacks on programs. And a new minister was needed.

A more directed communication program was required. One that spoke to long-term hope and symbols that people could see and touch.

Finally, when Bennett had rebuilt Social Credit, he had attracted thousands of people who were upwardly mobile, young, family-oriented business and professional people. This constituency had been attracted by things like funding for independent schools. However, B.C. was changing and Bennett needed to change his policies to reflect this fact.

Indeed, some of the changes were directly benefiting the NDP, such as the growth of public-sector unions. As government expanded to meet the policy expectations of the core group that Bennett wanted to attract, it created large pools of workers that were natural allies of the NDP. Similarly, Bennett's aggressive approach to developing resource industries in forestry and mining with new legislation and programs led to highly unionized pockets of NDP supporters in rural B.C.

Under Bennett and Barrett, both parties appealed to the highly individualistic character of B.C. voters. Both the Social Credit and the NDP were populist parties. Both parties were dominated by members who reflected those individualistic B.C. values and leaders who understood that fact. British Columbians, more than people in any other region in Canada, emphasize direct action and grassroots involvement. Both Bennett and Barrett were able to reflect this feeling by speaking out and by being suspicious of traditional elites, whether they were big business, big unions, the professions or government. Bennett describes it this way:

> No party of the extreme right or the extreme left can survive. We are a populist party slightly to the right of centre. The NDP is a populist party slightly to the left.

The differences began with the Social Credit philosophy being driven by a business, conservative underpinning, and the NDP approach by a collective, social democratic bias. The fundamentals remained, but the rise of public-sector unionism and its fight to control the NDP was beginning, and it would have dysfunctional results for both parties.

Bennett's analysis complete, he turned his attention to the next mandate. His mind was made up about the overall strategy and the tactics that would have to be played out to position himself for the next election, four years hence. There would be four parts.

First, he would deal with and strengthen the party. He would learn. Dan Campbell observes: "1979 did produce some things that were worthwhile, to the party and to the premier. It taught Premier Bill Bennett that he must act not only as premier, but as party leader as well. It taught the non-elected members of the party that candidates are not successful if the party sits on their collective butts. Therefore, the premier did move to correct his faults of leadership between 1975 and 1979. New machinery and personnel were set up at party headquarters. The premier began to take personal responsibility for the efficiency of the organization."

Therefore, he would begin with the party apparatus.

Second, he would begin to divide the trade union movement, separating public and private interests. He recognized that he would not ever attract public-sector workers in large numbers to Social Credit. He would treat them like private-sector workers. He would also reach out to private-sector trade unionists, as they had more in common with him than with their public-sector fellow travellers.

Third, as his policies generated revenues surplus to government expenditures, he would use this surplus money to fund capital projects, providing the public with tangible examples of good financial management. British Columbia would continue to run at the front of the pack in terms of spending on social issues, but the surpluses available from robust economic growth would be directed at infrastructure.

Finally, he would strengthen the discipline on the government policy-making processes. This included revamping his communications strategy to ensure that key messages reached the voter.

BENNETT HAD A successful first term. And he learned from it.

Somehow we think that when we take people who have political ambitions off the street and put them into cabinet, they become smarter. The day after they are sworn in they are supposed to have all the answers, when most haven't learnt what questions to ask. But it goes with the territory, and the smart ones keep their powder dry while they learn—and they grow in the job.

Bennett learnt in his first term, and for his last two terms acted as a strategic premier. He had watched others, spoken to them and read about how they ran their governments. He would model his next years on approaches proven in Ottawa, Edmonton and Regina.

The party still had eighty thousand members, but the delivery mechanism—party headquarters—ran like a Model T rather than the streamlined vehicle Bennett wanted. He recruited and hired a mix of people to strengthen his party, and then his office, in three key areas: politics, policy and communications.

8

THE BEST-LAID PLANS

"Tears greet firings by 'Scrooge' Kempf."

VANCOUVER SUN

EVERY PREMIER'S best-laid plans get derailed, postponed or sidetracked by unforeseen events. How he or she deals with them is the measure of the premier. A strategic premier may get waylaid, but government goes on. Obstacles are merely bumps on the road, there to be overcome. They fall into at least three categories:

1. The bureaucracy takes action, or promotes inaction, on its own and without letting the minister know. It pays no mind to the possibly dysfunctional political consequences. Sometimes this occurs for good reasons, sometimes for not-so-good reasons. In any event, the politicians bear the fallout.
2. Scandals.
3. Someone else's agenda. In the provinces, most often that of the federal government.

The first two of these obstacles will be discussed in this chapter, the third in the next one.

CLIFFORD OLSON WAS a sociopath who killed teenagers. Exactly how many, we may never know.

The police had Olson as a suspect for several years. They could not close the case or bring charges for lack of evidence. He not only killed the kids, but he disappeared the bodies. He buried them where they would never be found, except by him.

More than a dozen teenagers had been reported missing in B.C. Police believed that some were runaways, who had nothing to do with Olson, but that others were his victims. They brought Olson in for questioning. They released him. Another child disappeared. They knew he was doing it, but they couldn't catch him.

On Wednesday, August 12, 1981, Olson left Vancouver and travelled to Victoria. He burglarized two homes in Victoria. Driving north, he picked up two teenage girls north of Nanaimo. He turned at Parksville for Port Alberni, and then on to Tofino. He pulled off the road into the bush and stopped. Beer had been flowing, and joints were passed. The kids were feeling no pain, and in minutes they would never feel anything again.

One got out of the car to pee. The police, who had been tailing Olson and listening in to the conversations, moved in quickly, convinced they had only moments to save a life. Olson was arrested on a charge of impaired driving. His belongings were searched, and a link was found in his address book to Judy Kozma, one of the missing and presumed murdered kids.

A senior police officer commented afterwards: "I'm convinced had we not intervened or been present, it would have been a first for Olson. He would have killed two persons in one incident."

The RCMP aggressively interviewed Olson again. He began to talk about a deal that would see him locked up in a psychiatric hospital instead of a prison, plus some money, in exchange for taking the police to the bodies. On August 20, Olson made the request to Corporal Fred Maile: if he cooperated and led the police to bodies or evidence, would he be guaranteed psychiatric confinement, not prison?

Olson was told that all he could get in return for his co-operation was a thirty-day psychiatric assessment. As soon as he could see the door open to a possible psychiatric plea, he jumped: "I'll give you eleven bodies for $100,000. The first one will be a freebie."

After further discussion he said he wanted the money for his wife and child, not himself. This request shocked the RCMP, but was run up the force's chain of command. It was turned down in Ottawa.

Corporal Maile moved to seek a court order for a wiretap on conversations between Olson and his wife. He attended regional Crown counsel offices on Monday, August 24. He spoke to regional Crown counsel Sean Madigan and told him of Olson's offer and the RCMP refusal. Madigan told him to sit tight and headed up to his boss's office.

Alan Filmer was the assistant deputy minister in charge of criminal justice for British Columbia. The kid from Nanaimo had received his law degree from UBC, some say majoring in bridge with a minor in law, but he loved criminal prosecution. And he was very good at it.

When he was Crown counsel in Vancouver, he had helped put away "Fats" Robertson, the first drug-prostitution-gambling crime boss in Vancouver. Filmer had a reputation for getting things done. Once, when he had taken an adjoining office space for some new staff, he found it would take the Building Corporation of B.C. a month to put in a connecting door. That weekend, he brought his power saw from home and cut his own passageway.

Now promoted to the senior criminal prosecution job as ADM, criminal justice, he went with Madigan and spoke to Maile. Maile explained Olson's offer and RCMP Ottawa's decision. Filmer was not pleased. He said: "Those goddamn feds have no balls. Of course we'll do it. Why wouldn't we? We've got nothing else on Olson."

Filmer was not used to covering his ass, but the attorney general should be told and might even overrule him. It might be controversial. It would be better to see the boss. He phoned down for an appointment and was scheduled in an hour later. The deputy and several other senior staff were with the attorney general.

The mood in the room was sour. All minds were focused on the latest constitutional proposals forwarded from Ottawa. The frustration was evident, as the feds had sent the proposals to B.C. in French.

Filmer refocused the topic in a nanosecond: "The bottom line is, Olson says he's the killer and he'll take us to the bodies if we give his wife and kid $100,000."

He told the story. Payments would be made to Olson's wife in the amount of $10,000 for every gravesite the killer would lead police to discover. "The cops say he's got himself in the nuthouse and may be trying to get himself into a not-guilty-by-reason-of-insanity kind of scenario. We don't know what he's doing, whether any of this is feasible, or whether it's bullshit. But he claims there are things about some of the bodies that he can tell us that will clearly identify him as the killer. There's some jewellery from one of the kids, *et cetera*. There will be enough to nail him cold."

Nails in the forehead was one signature Olson had used. *Et cetera* in Filmer-speak covered a lot of ground.

A total of $100,000 was expected to be paid into trust for Mrs. Olson and her infant child. It was a tricky situation. Filmer had approved the transaction. What would the AG do?

Attorney General Allan Williams listened, as he always did, with intense concentration. Filmer finished. Williams sat and looked at him, not saying anything. All Williams's staff were familiar with his habit of letting you finish, and then the silence while he thought.

A minute later, which seemed like two days to Filmer, Williams said: "Well, okay. I appreciate this is a very difficult issue that you have had to handle." He asked several questions, then said:

> Obviously this paying a serial killer's family to recover the bodies will be controversial, perhaps even with the families that will find closure.
>
> We will have to balance the families' closure, the ending of this slaughter of teenagers, against the outcry that will come from the public over these payments.
>
> One thing we will get straight right now is that I will accept the total responsibility for doing this. No one will know I did not authorize this.

> It might have been nice to know in advance, Alan, but politics will not stand in our way of doing what is right. Things are going to get messy, but we will deal with it.
>
> And I will be the public face that explains that.

Once again Williams had lived up to his reputation. He said with a sigh, "Well now, I'd better go and tell the premier."

Everyone in the room knew that legal issues were one thing, the politics another. The next day, Williams sat down with Bennett. Williams told him the story. The premier asked a few questions and then said, "You've done the right thing, stopped the killings and taken this monster off the streets. It will be controversial, messy politically. But one thing. I will take full responsibility for approving these payments. I will stand completely beside you, Allan. You are in charge. Tell me what role you want me to play, and know you have my 100 percent support."

The Olson affair took a huge toll on Williams. The public backlash was immense. Ian Mulgrew, in his entertaining and informative book *Final Payoff: The True Price of Convicting Clifford Robert Olson,* interviewed Williams: "The mail was very heavy. I think it ran 60–40 against my decision—and it got so I couldn't read the letters. Some were so vile, so vulgar. Even the staff wouldn't read them. They'd open the letters and then put them aside on the negative pile. It's amazing the emotion that that issue created."

As Mulgrew sums up: "There was no monstrous mistake made in the Olson case. Just a lot of small inconspicuous errors in judgement, sparks that ignited a forest fire. There was no clear-cut answer to the dilemma Williams faced on that rainy August morning in 1981. He was not really presented with a choice. He was handed a nightmare."

Jim Hume, the dean of the legislature media gallery, remembers: "Allan Williams aged ten years in ten months. I always thought this is why he didn't run again."

THE SCANDALS BEGAN to appear shortly after the election. Bennett's first term had been relatively free of serious political scandal, and the government was unprepared for them.

The premier had had, however, some experience with scandals when he was leader of the opposition. Frank Calder had been dropped from Dave Barrett's cabinet after Victoria police had arrested him and his female companion, both inebriated, while he was behind the wheel of a car stopped in an intersection. Calder had spent a night in jail. When Barrett asked him about it he denied the episode, but the police reports left no doubt. He was forced out, not for the episode—which Barrett recognized as a foolish mistake—but for not being honest with the premier. As recounted in his book, *Barrett: A Passionate Political Life*, Barrett said, when dismissing Calder from cabinet: "I want you to hear something very clearly, Frank. I am not firing you because of the incident. It was foolish, but I can deal with that. The reason I am asking for your resignation is that you lied to me. I cannot have any confidence in a cabinet minister who does not give me a truthful answer."

The majority of the Socred opposition caucus wanted to make a great fuss over the event. But Bennett argued, and his view prevailed, that this was just a foolish mistake and should not be raised in any malicious way for short-term political gain. This was quietly appreciated by Calder, and Bennett was to receive an unexpected bonus when Calder left the NDP to join and run for the Socreds in the first week of the 1975 election.

The second minor issue Bennett had to deal with concerned the Speaker of the House, Ed Smith. Bennett had decided not to put him in cabinet, but to take his father's advice and make him Speaker. But Smith, a married man, was smitten by his secretary, and when the affair became public it necessitated his resignation. While leading to Smith's long-term happiness, it was a lesson to Bennett about the vulnerability of people who work long hours and many miles away from home.

DURING HIS YEARS in Victoria, Bennett's daily routine did not vary much. Up early. A morning run of several miles, or an hour and half of tennis. A light breakfast, a walk over to the office, about five minutes from his penthouse in the Harbour Towers. Arrive there just after 7:00 AM.

Work until noon. Walk back to the Harbour Towers for a solitary lunch. He has had a life-long love of peanuts, and peanut butter sandwiches have always been sustenance. Bennett parlayed this well-known fact into the myth that he lived on peanut butter and sprout sandwiches. The media ate it up. With his slightly perverse sense of humour, the premier thought this was hilarious. Because he was quite a good cook, which no one, except Audrey, knew: "People would know when I came to Victoria to attend a function, but there were lots of times when I came down to Harbour Towers and no one knew I was there. I taught him to cook. He certainly managed well; I taught him to make a cheese soufflé, and he does it very well."

After lunch, he was back in the office by one, and meetings ran until well after six. On cabinet days, especially if the legislature was in session, he would not get away until close to eleven.

If the legislature was not sitting, he would watch a bit of sport on television. Boxing was a particular favourite. Then a few hours of reading, and if possible an evening tennis match. Brian Smith remembers: "I was mayor of Oak Bay, and we were both tennis players. Many nights he would phone and I would drive down to the Harbour Towers and pick him up. It would be after nine. We would play tennis. He was never a great player, but intense and competitive. Very competitive. When it was over we would sit and drink a Coke and talk politics. I learnt a lot, and he encouraged me to run."

Bennett never lunched or had dinner with colleagues in Victoria. Never a drink after work. A spartan, lonely existence. Athletics and physical activity had always been a focus for his competitive nature. This life-long interest in sport led him to establish the B.C. Winter and Summer Games.

THERE HAD BEEN two more serious incidents in the first term. In December 1977, Economic Development Minister Don Phillips was told by his executive assistant, Arthur Weeks, that he, Weeks, had purchased shares in Cheyenne Petroleum, a company whose value on the stock market improved after the government, through Phillips's ministry, had made a substantial investment in the form of a pipeline loan. Weeks refused to see that purchasing shares with this prior knowledge was insider trading.

Phillips was again blindsided when later that week his constituency secretary, Art Cameron, told him he too had purchased shares. It was time for the phone call to ask to see the premier, and then the longest walk Phillips ever took, down from the east wing of the third floor and across to the premier's office. He remembers the meeting:

> I go down to the premier's office and say, "I'd better resign. I am in this thing... My staff have bought shares."
>
> The premier said, "Have you done anything wrong?"
>
> I said, "Well, no. I have not bought any property [where the pipeline will run], I have not bought any bloody shares. I didn't know that these guys had. I sold the bloody dealership when I went into cabinet so that there would never be any conflict of interest. No, I have not done anything wrong personally, but that's not the issue, I am involved in this because I am the minister, so I will have to resign."
>
> He said, "No, you will not resign. I don't know all the ins and outs, but if you tell me that you personally have not done anything wrong, then you don't need this, but I will appoint a judicial inquiry."

But Phillips had to deal with the staff involved. Bennett had not only told Phillips to stay; he also gave other guidance. Phillips puts it this way: "I didn't have to go to anybody for help or advice. I was told by Bill Bennett to fire him [Weeks]. So I phoned him up on a Sunday night and said, 'Meet you at the office,' and I fired him... He said, 'You cannot fire me,' and I said, 'Well, you're fired. I don't know what the rules are, but you're fired.' "

Cameron soon resigned. When the investigation was completed, two other persons, a geologist and an engineer, both members of the B.C. Petroleum Corporation office, were also fired.

Bennett tried to get away with having his attorney general, Garde Gardom, conduct an internal inquiry, but once he saw the firestorm spread, he moved to snuff out the criticism. After initially stalling to gauge the opposition and media reaction, he appointed Mr. Justice Walter Kirke Smith on January 12, 1978, to hold a public inquiry.

Longevity in the premier's chair requires a delicate appreciation of when to move, and how far. Judgement and timing. As Frances Russell, a member of the *Vancouver Sun* editorial pages staff, wrote on February 16, 1978: "In dealing with scandals, he who hesitates is lost. The public wants dramatic action and the political skill is knowing when to move, and to what degree. Too little and the public, through the media, is dissatisfied. Too early and the bar is set too low. This is what political judgement and timing is about."

Jack Davis had been a Liberal member of Parliament and Canada's first minister of the environment. A Rhodes scholar, he had brought his considerable intelligence and a sterling reputation to the provincial Socreds when he joined them prior to the 1975 election. It had been reported as a major coup, and it was. Davis was rewarded with a cabinet post upon his election in 1975.

In 1978, the RCMP laid a criminal charge against Davis alleging that he had travelled regularly to Ottawa on government business, purchasing tickets to travel first class, as was his right, but that he had changed the tickets to the much cheaper economy fare and pocketed the difference.

Bennett had accepted Davis's resignation immediately upon hearing that charges were imminent. He announced this in the House on the same day, following Question Period. The RCMP took three days to actually charge Davis, and in that time the opposition roasted the premier because he would not provide any details concerning the resignation.

It is inappropriate for a minister of the Crown to comment on matters when the RCMP are involved. But that doesn't stop the opposition from having a field day. Rumour and speculation beat fact every time and make for great media coverage.

These earlier instances may have tested Bennett's mettle, but nothing could prepare him for the aftermath of the 1979 election.

THE "DIRTY TRICKS" scandal broke on September 27, 1979, the same day Bennett appointed Paul Manning to conduct a study regarding the need for a British Columbia stadium. Manning, a former newspaper reporter, aide to Prime Minister Trudeau, defeated federal Liberal candidate and expediter for the 1976 UN Habitat conference in Vancouver, was to look into types of stadiums, alternatives in design, site selection and future operating costs. Staff assistance was provided by Larry Bell from the Ministry of Lands. The report was due November 15. Manning recalls how he was hired:

> I had become close to Bill Bennett's father, W.A.C., while covering the provincial legislature for the *Province* newspaper in the late '60s. I'd then gone to Ottawa in 1970 as a speechwriter and ministerial aide, and the B.C. desk officer in Prime Minister Trudeau's office. That's how I got to know Bill Bennett.
>
> A couple of months after Joe Clark and the Tories had reduced the Liberals to two seats west of Ontario in the 1979 federal election, I met with Bennett in his Victoria office. Bennett asked if I wanted to come to work with him. I said I'd rather help the premier solve the dilemma on what to do about replacing Vancouver's ancient and dilapidated Empire Stadium: "The feds won't solve it. No municipality has the money to build one. It's going to end up in your lap, one way or the other."
>
> I went back home to Vancouver and waited. On a Wednesday, Bennett called to say he'd be in town to meet Joe Clark that Friday night and what was Manning doing Saturday morning.
>
> "I'll be out jogging," I joked.
>
> "Great. Pick me up at the hotel and we'll run around Stanley Park."
>
> "I was joking about the jogging."
>
> "I wasn't."
>
> I was in trouble. Bennett's tenacious tennis game was legend. He'd chase down every shot, however impossible. It is six miles and change around Stanley Park. I was once a jogger, but I would be dead after three. My only training in the time left was to switch from Rothmans cigarettes to the "low tar and nicotine" Vantage.
>
> I convinced him to run around Brockton Oval track, not the sea wall. We started running and after halfway round the first lap I'm panting, and Bennett said: "Okay, let's talk about the stadium."
>
> I gasped, "Can't talk and run."

So we ran and ran, lap after lap. It felt like it was never going to stop.

Finally, on the twelfth lap I knew I was going to die. He said: "I'll race you the last 220 yards."

I just stopped and watched as he sprinted away. I walked up to him, and he said: "I want you to do a stadium study for the government. Where it should be. What it should be. How much it would cost, and where the money could come from. I'll give you three months."

"It can't be done in three months."

"Fine, but that's what I'm giving you publicly. Municipal elections are in three months, and I want all those municipal politicians who say they want the new stadium in their city to declare where they stand and what they're prepared to do to get it. If you need more time, we'll extend your mandate later."

"I'll need some help, construction guy and a finance guy."

"I want you to solve the problem, not add to it. You do the study, and report directly to me."

"Okay, then the best public servant you have for this kind of thing."

"Fine, be in my office next Monday at eleven. Do you want to do a few more laps?"

"Thanks but no thanks."

I walked into Bennett's inner office at eleven and found a puzzled Larry Bell, then deputy minister of lands, parks and housing and later deputy minister of finance, standing there. Bennett had been called away for a moment. After they'd introduced themselves, Bell said: "I don't know what I'm doing here."

"I do," I said. "We're doing the stadium study for the premier."

The Manning–Bell report, released in December 1979, recommended that the province construct a covered, multi-purpose stadium on the CPR rail yards, on the north shore of False Creek in downtown Vancouver. A covered stadium could be built "for less than it cost to put the roof on Montreal's Olympic Stadium" for a "guaranteed maximum price" of roughly $125 million, and the stadium should be built as part of a world's fair, then called TRANSPO '86, which was being proposed to celebrate Vancouver's one-hundredth birthday. The report also recommended that the province and the Lower Mainland municipalities combine to build a rapid transit system.

It was typical of Bennett to reach out to people who could make things happen. He always looked for that elusive combination of brains and ability to get things done. He knew that experience combined with innovation, mixed well with loyalty and a dash of steel in the backbone, were essential to solve complicated public problems. Manning, with his Ottawa connections, had these qualities. Also, this was the final test for Bell. Again typical of Bennett, he gave his up-and-coming bureaucrats specific jobs. If they were successful, they were promoted. If they failed under fire, they disappeared. Nobody got to the top without proving themselves in difficult situations.

BUT THE STADIUM announcement, part of Bennett's plan to use capital expenditures to revitalize Vancouver, was a one-day wonder. It disappeared until the final report was presented. The media had found somewhere more interesting to feed. Their attention turned to the "dirty tricks affair."

September 18, 1979, found Socred research officer Jack Kelly speaking to the annual meeting of the Social Credit Esquimalt–Port Renfrew riding association. There were only about thirty people in the meeting, and these hard-core diehards were confidently basking in the glow of just having won government for the second time. With one exception.

Sitting quietly in the hall was Brenda Dalglish, a reporter for a small weekly, the *Goldstream Gazette,* circulation 1,200. Her report ran the following Wednesday. By sheer chance, reporter Marjorie Nichols picked up a complimentary copy of the *Goldstream Gazette* that had been delivered to the press gallery. The next day the front-page headline in the *Vancouver Sun* screamed: "Fake letters to editor penned by Socreds."

The story said that Jack Kelly and the other Socred caucus research staff had written letters favourable to the government to newspapers and signed them with names from the telephone book. Kelly went on to admit that at one time the caucus research office was using more than fifty aliases to sign letters to the editor.

The caucus chair, MLA Jack Kempf, attempted damage control by suspending Kelly immediately—a week with pay—and instructing the other staff not to speak to the media. The premier, satisfied the situation was under control, left for a business trip to Japan.

A few days later the media announced that Ron Greig, the former assistant to Bennett's communications adviser, had resigned. His name was linked to a letter sent from the premier's office to Victoria newspapers attacking a New Democratic Party MLA and bearing the name of a local NDP supporter.

The *coup de grâce* was delivered to government credibility later that week. The media reported that prior to the last election a tape recording instructing party workers "how to" write fake letters and carry out other dirty campaign tricks was made at a constituency meeting, edited and then mailed to every campaign manager and headquarters.

Bennett was forced to return from his Japan trip, and his comments appeared as the banner headline in the *Vancouver Sun* on October 17: "Cut out the cancer before it develops." He argued that "nobody in authority in the party listened to the 'dirty tricks' tapes until it was too late" and that their release was "due to a lack of coordination and cohesion in the party." This version was received with much skepticism.

A week later, party researcher Ellen MacKay, who many believed was Kelly's right hand, returned from a holiday in Europe and the ham-handed Jack Kempf tried to suspend her. She refused, turned on her heel, walked out and immediately informed the press that she was just following orders. Kempf wasn't so gentle with Kelly, who was fired.

On November 14 George Lenko, the executive assistant to Grace McCarthy and the person who organized the distribution of materials, resigned. A sigh of relief went up from the government benches. Someone had taken responsibility and resigned, and one person had been fired. Things should have quietened down.

But on December 5, Bennett opened his morning paper to read the headline: "Tears greet firings by 'Scrooge' Kempf." Unbeknownst to Bennett, the previous day caucus chair Kempf had fired the four remaining research staff, including Ellen MacKay. When asked if this was "a nice Christmas present," Kempf had replied: "I guess some of us are Scrooges."

Never put one foot in it when two will do. Some politicians never learn that when you find yourself in a hole, the first thing to do is stop digging.

BENNETT HAD INTERRUPTED his Japanese business trip to try and extinguish the dirty tricks fire. The scandal annoyed him, but the disruption of his careful plans for attracting international investment annoyed him more.

Dave Barrett had made one much-publicized trip to Japan during his term in office. Gary Lauk, Barrett's minister of economic development, had started exploratory discussions with Japanese steelmakers over the development of North East Coal. His point man was his assistant deputy minister, Jack McKeown. However, as with most of the Barrett initiatives, there was no coordinated planning or follow-up. Under Bennett, this was to change.

The first step was to put Don Phillips into the economic development portfolio. Phillips understood the B.C. economy and the need to attract international investment:

> I realized quickly what makes the province tick. We don't set the price for oil, we don't set the price for gold, for copper. We are really a pretty small player in a big field, and when people start telling you that we are giving this away or we are giving that away they don't understand. What we have to do is capitalize on the assets we have and build on them.
>
> What I wanted to do was delineate a policy, so I had some pretty scholarly assistants who would come in with these huge written documents. I said, "I don't have any education. I can only read about three or four pages. Can't we boil it down to what our strengths are?" Eventually we got a policy that said our strengths were our natural resources...
>
> We could assist manufacturing, but foreign investment has to come in. In order to have foreign investment you have to have policies that will let them spread their wings, and sometimes you have to help them.

Early initiatives started in Europe, but the province soon realized that the future for B.C. lay in the Pacific Rim. Japan, South Korea and then China became the principal targets. Missions were also aimed at Thailand, Indonesia, Singapore, Hong Kong, the Philippines and India.

The scenario would unfold. First, ADM Jack McKeown would travel, using the more skilled and helpful staff in the overseas Canadian embassies, and develop work plans. This would be followed by Minister Don Phillips leading a delegation. Then the premier would open doors that lower-level officials could not. In traditional societies like Japan and China, this hierarchical approach is understood and appreciated. For example, on the North East Coal project, McKeown would have made fifty trips, Phillips about ten and Bennett three. On a project as complicated as this one, the minister and his staff would also be dealing with Ottawa. Phillips recalls: "Back to Ottawa again. I argued: 'You develop your end, you develop the railway from Prince George.' This doesn't happen all of a sudden, but after many meetings, and gnashing of teeth, and negotiations and discussions. You develop the port at Prince Rupert, you develop the CN from Prince George. The upgrading of the railway has to be done; that's your end of the North East Coal deal. And that left the spur line."

Phillips, following McKeown, would then meet with the Japanese companies. One commitment he made was to deliver the premier to meet them in Japan. Here he had a willing partner to drive this agenda.

The Japanese also visited Victoria. The final piece had to be nailed down, and only the premier could do that. The spur line to Tumbler Ridge remained the missing piece. One morning, the major Japanese players met Bennett in his office. They explained to the premier that an agreement was possible if the spur line infrastructure was completed as part of the province's contribution to the line. No agreement was forthcoming. The Japanese left and flew by helicopter to Vancouver to catch their afternoon flight to Tokyo.

Phillips, joined by his deputy, Sandy Peel, ADM Jack McKeown, Norman Spector and the premier, were left to talk about it. Finance Minister Hugh Curtis was consulted. Everyone said their piece, for and against. When to move, when to wait. Bargaining strategy.

The room went quiet. Bennett looked over the half-glasses that he had bought—two pairs for five dollars at Woolworth's when he discovered he needed reading glasses—and focused the steely blues on each of his advisers. He got up to the window and looked out for a minute. He turned and said: "Don, I want you and Jack to immediately get on a helicopter and fly to Vancouver. Go to the airport and meet with the Japanese delegation in a private room before they board their flight. Tell them the province will pay for the spur line. Norman, talk to Curtis. Sandy, get the staff working it up and bring it to cabinet next week."

The North East Coal project became a reality, as the deal was signed shortly thereafter. This tiered approach, pushing at just the right time, also worked on other projects, such as the Toyota wheel plant in Surrey.

Bennett wanted to open one other market for British Columbia: China. The opportunity presented itself in January 1984, when Premier Zhao Ziyang travelled to Ottawa and stopped over in Vancouver. In the strange world of politics, the two leaders hit if off. At the last of the four official functions in Vancouver, Bennett was invited by the premier of China to visit. He did so in May 1984, and this was the beginning of British Columbia's, and perhaps Canada's, formal trading relationship with China.

Finally, B.C. trade offices were opened in Japan, South Korea and Hong Kong. A satellite office sponsored by the chamber of commerce so as to not offend China, but funded provincially, was opened in Taiwan. Alberta started opening offices in the area once Bennett had briefed Premier Peter Lougheed on the successes.

British Columbia, despite being more than satisfied with the service and professionalism of the Canadian embassy's efforts, opened its own trade offices. The strategy was successful. A good plan, combined with hard work, has produced long-lasting results for B.C.

RETURNING RESTED after the Christmas holidays, having recharged his batteries by spending time with the Audrey and the boys, Bennett looked forward to clear sailing in 1980. The feeling of "it's all behind us" lasted only a few days. And it came from a source that Bennett respected.

BCTV reporter Clem Chapple, experienced and even-handed, had an easy rapport with politicians on both sides of the House. Politicians wanted to talk to him because his coverage could make or break a story, or a career. Working with Vancouver BCTV reporter Russ Froese, he began to explore the workings of the Eckardt Royal Commission into electoral boundaries, particularly the events from the date of the report, June 17 until June 20, 1978, when it was tabled in the legislature. The first news report aired on January 10, 1980. It began by providing an overview of the Eckardt inquiry process.

Judge Lawrence Eckardt had headed a royal commission into electoral reform, namely redistribution of constituency boundaries to reflect population shifts. Eckardt recommended that the legislature be increased from fifty-five to fifty-seven members. To accomplish this, some constituencies disappeared and some new ones were created. When the report was delivered in late June 1978, the provincial secretary of the day, Grace McCarthy, proceeded with what is normal practice: she tabled the report in the legislature immediately and introduced legislation implementing the recommendations within twenty-four hours. This tight time line was implemented to avoid charges that the report recommendations on new electoral boundaries had been changed—gerrymandered—to suit government objectives.

McCarthy, as provincial secretary, received the report at 1:30 PM on June 20, 1978, tabled it in the legislature following Question Period at about 2:30, and had not even had time to get enough copies printed for all MLAs. They would arrive in each member's office that afternoon.

The following day she introduced Bill 38, the Constitution Amendment Act, incorporating all the recommendations for electoral boundary changes contained in the report. Two days later, on June 23, McCarthy moved second reading of the bill, and in the debate that followed the opposition aggressively attacked the bill.

It is not unusual for the opposition to protest that a report is biased and favourable to the governing party. Usually there is enough truth in the charge to make it somewhat believable; after all, the government selects the commissioner. But once the opposition is on the record, the matter proceeds quickly. The opposition know that when they are in power they will do the same thing, so one must protest, but not so much that it makes things difficult when it is their turn.

But it was noted that Eckardt was a failed Social Credit candidate and that the ridings he disappeared were held by high-profile NDPers like

Rosemary Brown and Bill King. And one irregularity was found by Vic Stephens, the leader of the Conservatives in the legislature. The western boundary of the Vancouver–Little Mountain riding was altered to include an irregularly shaped piece of land. Shaped like a finger, the riding was held by two MLAs, Grace McCarthy and Evan Wolfe, the finance minister.

Vic Stephens called it "Gracie's finger." The riding had one other remarkable feature: it voted heavily Social Credit. Dave Barrett called it political pornography. The debate spilled over into Monday, but the bill passed. McCarthy had defended it by arguing that there could be no gerrymandering because the government had accepted every recommendation exactly as put forward. The 1979 election was fought using these new electoral boundaries.

The story that BCTV went after was not about the fact that McCarthy won her seat because of the "finger," because that was not true. On January 11, 1980, the *Vancouver Sun* had reported: "While the Social Credit candidates received 53 percent of the votes in the Vancouver–Little Mountain riding as a whole in the provincial election last May, they received 77 percent in the finger. McCarthy and Wolfe would have won the riding for the Socreds even if the finger had not been added, but their margin of victory would have been narrower."

The story Clem Chapple introduced on January 10, 1980, asked: when did "Gracie's finger" appear, how did it get included and who got it included? BCTV suggested that a change had been made between the date Eckardt signed the report on June 17 and June 20, when it went to the legislature.

The next day it was revealed that McCarthy happened to be having dinner at Victoria's Laurel Point Inn on June 19 and ran into Judge Eckardt, who suggested she come upstairs and personally thank two of the support staff who were putting the finishing touches on the report. The media jumped on this as showing smoke, if not fire. McCarthy admitted she had been upstairs meeting the staff, but claimed it was for only five minutes. Evan Wolfe then announced that all the work was complete and the report was at the Queen's Printer on June 16.

However, Florence Tamoto, a typist who worked for the commission, came forward and countered, saying that she had worked all day on

Saturday, June 17, on the report in Vancouver. She was able to produce signed time sheets to prove her story. Further, she provided a sworn affidavit to the *Vancouver Sun*, who delivered it to Wolfe and Attorney General Allan Williams. In submitting the affidavits, *Vancouver Sun* publisher Clark Davey said: "The affidavit makes a most serious allegation but it is both uncorroborated and untested. Nevertheless, we believe it merits a full and responsible test."

Bennett now had no choice. An inquiry was the only route. On January 18, the attorney general ordered an investigation into allegations of interference in the drawing of electoral district boundaries. "Because of these serious questions, and the implications which may flow from them, I have turned the materials over to Deputy Attorney General Richard Vogel with the request that he take them under consideration with officials of the ministry and provide me with an opinion as to what, if any, action should be taken by me as attorney general."

The issue faded away, but sometimes the political gods are tricksters. Barely six weeks later, on March 6, 1980, the CBC six o'clock news anchor, Bill Good, Jr., opened his show with: "British Columbia's deputy attorney general has interfered with the judicial system. Tonight, a detailed report." Reporter Chris Bird alleged that Richard Vogel, the deputy AG, had intervened in three criminal cases.

The news piece was a blockbuster. It was deliberately meant to damage, and it did. The next day in the legislature, NDP House Leader Frank Howard led the charge, demanding Vogel's head, and that his office be seized and locked down. Vogel had already met with Allan Williams and told him that the allegations were not true but that he would step aside voluntarily. Williams investigated personally and in two weeks told the House that his deputy was innocent. Great damage was done, however, to Vogel.

As a footnote, in February 1982 Judge William Esson released his long decision in the case. In its 140 pages he saddled the CBC with one of the highest penalties for libel in Canadian history as well as finding its conduct to be malicious in every aspect. Bird lost his job, a CBC editor was fired and Donald Bruce, senior Crown prosecutor and Bird's "deep throat," left government.

After his reappointment, Vogel turned his attention to the Tamoto affidavit. The allegation Tamoto had sworn was that over lunch one day, commission lawyer Susan Thomson had told her that Grace McCarthy had instructed Eckardt to add what came to be called "Gracie's finger" to the Vancouver–Little Mountain riding, and that it was done on June 19.

Vogel's report, presented on August 6, concluded:

> Based on the information elicited by the extended inquiries that we had made, I can say that we have not found any fact which would support the allegation or beliefs of Miss Tamoto.
>
> There is no evidence of any communication between the Hon. Grace McCarthy or anyone on her behalf, and his Honour Judge Eckardt, or any member of his staff with respect to any part of the contents of the Interim Report on Electoral Boundaries.

Vogel recommended that no action be taken on Tamoto's allegations.

NDP member Gary Lauk found another vein a week later when he asked the attorney general why another witness, Vi Barton, who had also said she had heard of "Grace's" involvement, had not been investigated. Williams replied that the allegation had been checked out and proven false.

On August 20, Vi Barton came out swinging. She was upset by what Williams had said in the House, feeling it made her out to be a liar. She released copies of her transcripts of her interviews. This raised questions again of unwarranted influence on the commission. If not Grace McCarthy, who?

On August 21, Attorney General Allan Williams was on his feet in the legislature. Startling everyone, he announced that Dan Campbell, the premier's director of intergovernmental relations and the Socred campaign manager, had called one of the commission staff to Victoria from Vancouver and had given her a brown envelope to give to Eckardt. Williams stated that Eckardt, outraged by the action, had tossed the submission in the garbage.

This lead story on all major television and radio programs reopened the controversy, and newspapers ran detailed reviews in weekend editions. The NDP kept up the attack in the House, trying to bring enough pressure to bear to have Williams call a public inquiry. Williams, however, would not budge.

Fortunately for the Bennett government, the House then rose for the summer. The issue died over the Labour Day weekend.

BENNETT BECAME AN expert in practising political crisis management. Discredit and deflect. Gauge reactions, do not move too soon or too late. Timing is all. Be decisive when you move. But always leave yourself room for another move; for example, call an internal inquiry, leaving room for an external review later.

He also recognized that government goes on even during these rough patches, and good administration is required—perhaps more so under trying times. It was important to stay disciplined and to continue to work on your agenda. Bennett observed: "I learned something. You just ride with it, keep pushing and eventually you come back."

9

BRINGING IT HOME

"The French fact has never been a threat. So it was a very easy concession for him to make to show some goodwill to Trudeau, for whom it was the 'essence of his existence.' For Bennett it was a 'gimme,' trying to smooth the negotiations."

NORMAN SPECTOR

BRITISH COLUMBIANS would rather watch paint dry than observe constitutional discussions. They may respect the law and enjoy sausages, but they don't like to see either being made.

Premiers know this fact. There is no political gain in federal–provincial constitutional discussions. But occasionally there is no choice, and once the constitutional tar baby is picked up, you can't put it down. It takes on a life of its own.

Two events combined to give new life to the issue: the election of René Lévesque's Parti Québécois in 1979 and the ensuing referendum on sovereignty-association, and Pierre Elliott Trudeau's desire for a legacy. Bringing the Constitution home from Great Britain—or repatriation—had been an on-again and off-again issue for years. Canada's enabling constitutional law, the British North America Act, 1867, remained a British statute. The BNA Act had been little debated, slipping through Westminster following an Act to enable the control of dogs. Since Canada was an independent country, it had long been felt that having its Constitution as an Act of another nation's parliament was demeaning. This unfortunate situation was also a target of the separatists in Quebec, who portrayed Canada as a country on bended knee before the British lion.

Therefore, when Prime Minister Trudeau got the bit in his teeth as a way to demonstrate to Quebec that Canada was truly independent, both levels of government went from a slow walk to a full run. This next round of negotiations became all-consuming for Bennett and his team of ministers and senior public servants.

Canada's first federal–provincial meeting of First Ministers to discuss the Constitution occurred in 1927. The second occurred in 1931, when the Statute of Westminster was the topic. Four years passed until a discussion on procedures to amend the BNA Act, recommended by Ottawa and sponsored by Ontario, took place in 1935.

The Great Depression and a world war postponed the next round of talks until January 1950 in Ottawa and again in September in Quebec City, when once again the issue of amending the Constitution was taken up. Again, no success.

A decade would slip by until the issue of fiscal arrangements between Ottawa and the provinces brought premiers and the prime minister together in Ottawa in July 1960. Once there, they could not resist; they picked up the tar baby. Not content just to deal with equalization, they found themselves once again talking about the Constitution. Jean Lesage, premier of Quebec, raised the issue of repatriating the Constitution. Tommy Douglas, premier of Saskatchewan, became English Canada's provincial spokesperson. The prime minister, John Diefenbaker, argued not only for repatriation but also for including a Bill of Rights.

This led to a series of meetings of the attorneys general of Canada in late 1960 and early 1961, where an amending formula for the Constitution was devised that came to be known as the Fulton-Favreau formula. This document was forwarded to First Ministers at their next meeting in

August 1964 in Charlottetown, Prince Edward Island. No agreement. It was bounced back to the attorneys general in October for clarification, and on October 14–15 the First Ministers endorsed the package in Ottawa. It was published as a government White Paper, "The Amendment of the Constitution," in February 1965. It went no further.

In Canada's centennial year, 1967, Ontario convened the Confederation of Tomorrow Conference in Toronto to talk about the problems facing Canada and possible solutions, including constitutional ones. In February 1968, Ottawa hosted a meeting called by Prime Minister Lester Pearson. Agenda item 6 was a statement by Pierre Trudeau, then minister of justice and attorney general, on a constitutional charter of human rights. A comprehensive review of the Constitution was underway and meetings followed in February, June and December of 1969, September 1970 and February 1971, which led to the Victoria Conference in June 1971. Agreement was at last reached on a charter containing an amending formula.

The agreement of all the provinces and Ottawa lasted only a brief few days. Premier Robert Bourassa returned to Quebec to face intense criticism about selling out, and he caved. Quebec withdrew from the deal. It was dead.

Seven years would pass; 1978 began an intense period that slowly built through the Quebec referendum on sovereignty-association to the First Ministers meeting in February 1979. The pace accelerated. Pierre Trudeau, now prime minister, had an agenda and drove the process that would last until November 1981.

Premier Bennett played a key role. Legitimate questions remain as to why he joined in. The first reason is simple: he had no choice. Although he never ran on a platform of constitutional change and most British Columbians would have no idea what repatriation was or why it might be important, this train was leaving town and picking up speed. Once Bennett was aboard he was determined, because of what he had learned during his previous federal–provincial experiences, to play a key role.

The second reason, or rationale, was his love of this great country we call Canada. As Bennett explains it: "We were in danger of having Canada look like a bunch of foolish people who couldn't agree how to run their country, and had to beg before the Queen. The way I saw it, what we were dealing with was Canada's position in the world."

The third reason was one of chance. Every ten years, each province gets to host the annual premiers conference and therefore to act as a spokesperson for the following year. Bennett took over the chair when the file was at its hottest.

During the first term of his government, Bennett handled intergovernmental relations through his own office. Dan Campbell, former MLA and cabinet minister in W.A.C.'s government, one of the key rebuilders of the Social Credit Party, campaign manager in the 1975 and 1979 election campaigns, the premier's right-hand staffer and general all-round fixer, served as the director of intergovernmental relations. Cabinet committee responsibility also rested here.

British Columbia took its responsibilities very seriously. When Trudeau became frustrated with what he saw as provincial intransigence and began to speak of unilateral repatriation, B.C. immediately responded: repatriation was only possible with unanimous provincial support. As Bennett put it on June 3, 1976: "We feel that the repatriation of the Constitution, bringing it back to Canada, should be an act of unity, an act of bringing the country together... and that any amending formula must have unanimous consent of all provinces..."

But it was clear to Bennett that the prime minister was going to push this through: "It happened because of Pierre. It was his show; he did not want to talk about the economy or anything else, he wanted to talk Constitution. This was going to be his legacy."

British Columbia's position was simple: repatriation; no amending formula other than unanimous consent of the federal and provincial governments, or one that reflected the five regions of Canada (B.C. being the fifth); replacement of the Senate with a strengthened second chamber reflecting provincial interests; and greater provincial representation in central institutions.

In November 1976 the government published a comprehensive position paper again committing B.C. to repatriation. The following February, Bennett made a formal presentation to the Pepin–Robarts Task Force on Canadian

Unity that took the previous themes and focused them on restructuring central institutions by recognizing five regions in Canada. He established a cabinet committee on the Constitution that was co-chaired by Rafe Mair and Garde Gardom. Mair made the argument for the B.C. position on January 18, 1977:

> The proposition has been made, and very logically so, that British Columbia, the Prairie provinces, Ontario, Quebec and the Maritimes are in fact the five regions of Canada... Surely the day must pass when B.C. has only two more senators than Prince Edward Island and has eighteen less than Ontario and Quebec.

In advance of the First Ministers Conference on the Constitution in September 1978, B.C. published a more detailed and comprehensive set of proposals, which argued for:

1. A reformed Senate with members appointed by the provinces.
2. Equal regional representation from the five regions.
3. A Supreme Court appointed by the new Senate and its members balanced across the five regions.
4. Improved administrative mechanisms to replace ad hoc federal–provincial meetings.
5. Principles for restructuring the distribution of powers.
6. An amending formula based on the five regions.
7. The maintenance of the monarchy in Canada.

Following the First Ministers Conference and for the next fourteen months, until November 1979, both Mair and Gardom participated in numerous meetings of a continuing committee of ministers on the Constitution, making a concerted effort to find consensus. Attorney General Gardom responded in Question Period on April 2, 1979: "There is no way, in our view, that the Parliament of Canada can unilaterally amend the Constitution insofar as the distribution of powers is concerned, insofar as the rights and privileges of provincial governments are concerned and insofar as the rights and privileges of provincial legislatures are concerned."

However, Bennett was beginning to have doubts about the rigidity of his position. He knew that in a very short time it would be his turn to host the annual premiers conference and then to chair the Premiers Council for the following year. He felt that constitutional issues would dominate his one-year term because the file was heating up.

In Bennett's critical analysis of himself, his party and his government that occurred during the hiatus after the election of 1979 and carried on during the "dirty tricks" scandal, he knew that success on the constitutional front would require more than preparing position papers. He had learned his lesson on the economic front, where B.C.'s well-thought-out research papers had been ignored. He accepted that B.C.'s constitutional position was logical, consistent and probably a non-starter.

His goal had to be simpler: protect B.C.'s interest and keep Canada together, as far as possible. That meant finding a deal that Canada could sign on to. On November 23, 1979, the premier created the Ministry of Intergovernmental Relations. He offered Dan Campbell the job of heading a B.C. office in Ottawa. But the "dirty tricks" caught Campbell. At first he accepted, then turned down the job and retired. The new ministry had Garde Gardom move from attorney general to intergovernmental relations and Allan Williams move from labour to attorney general. This was a much better fit for both men.

THE CABINET SHUFFLE also created a vacancy in the Ministry of Labour. Bennett filled it with Jack Heinrich, the hardest-working cabinet minister in the Bennett regime. Loved by everyone, and teased mercilessly by the media and his colleagues because he suffered from a bright mind that moved quicker than his tongue.

Less than four weeks went by before Heinrich was given his baptism by fire. B.C. Rail went on strike. It seemed to the province that every two years the railway would go down, damaging the economy of the north and B.C.'s reputation as a reliable shipper of commodities. Heinrich vowed to fix the problem.

In the weeks that followed he refused to cave, or to allow his cabinet colleagues to cave, as the strike dragged on. Every time the union or management at B.C. Rail came to his office to get him to bail them out, he refused. Behind the scenes, he and his senior staff worked night and day to assist and drive the bargaining.

With Bennett's support in cabinet, the Heinrich view prevailed and there was a settlement. He comments: "Thank heaven Bill saw some merit in my views. It is very important to have the support of the premier on something. Sometimes the votes in cabinet were 20 to 19. He had the twenty votes."

GARDE GARDOM, the large, boisterous, hail-fellow-well-met former Liberal, was well connected in Ottawa and well liked by his peers across Canada. His larger-than-life personality hid a very shrewd legal mind that focused on constitutional issues.

He brought with him from the AG's ministry his assistant deputy minister of policy, Mark Krasnick, who complemented Gardom by adding an exceptionally gifted free-thinking mind to the rather conservative cadre of constitutional advisers on staff. The staff was led by Mel Smith, QC. Mel had joined government straight from law school, practising his articles in the Ministry of Attorney General in the early 1950s, and had become the in-house expert on all things constitutional. He was adviser to W.A.C., Dave Barrett and Bill Bennett.

British Columbia's constitutional position had not changed since the 1960s. If Bennett's new approach was to succeed, he needed creative minds who could think outside the box. The most creative deputy minister in government was Jim Matkin, in the labour ministry. Bennett had worked with him on many labour disputes over the last four years and was impressed. Bennett talked to him, offered him the job and sent him down to see Gardom. Matkin accepted and took with him, at Gardom's suggestion, his executive director of policy to a newly created ADM position, secretary to cabinet for federal–provincial relations. But Gardom had not checked with Bennett about this new ADM position and the order-in-council to make it effective never proceeded. The position remained, however, and morphed into a regular staff job that was used mainly to troubleshoot and administer the administratively challenged ministry.

The new ministry had three functions:

1. Coordinate and develop strategies regarding B.C.'s relations with other governments.
2. Coordinate and develop policy on proposals to reform federalism.
3. Facilitate the functioning of the cabinet's committee system.

Bennett brought home from B.C. House in London the quintessential deputy minister, Lawrie Wallace. Since his appointment in 1956 by W.A.C. he had been one of the great public servants, who through every time, every crisis, had been there with well-seasoned professional advice. In appointing Wallace as his deputy minister, Bennett silenced all the critics who were concerned with the integrity of his office following the relentless scandals that came after the 1979 election.

However, he still needed his own in-house policy advice. He let it quietly be known that he was looking. The new secretary for federal–provincial relations was going through the ministry, meeting and informally appraising staff. He recommended to Deputy Matkin that he spend time with a secondment from the Ontario government. The story was that the secondee, Norman Spector, was a friend of Mark Krasnick and had come out from Toronto on an executive interchange, having completed his PhD. a few years earlier. He was spending a year in B.C., working a little and suntanning a lot.

Matkin adopted Norman Spector, the two great minds forming a mutual admiration society. Matkin, as the elder of the two, was mentor, but there was no doubt of his respect for the intellect of the Montreal Jewish-born, bespectacled, bearded, bilingual, outspoken scholar. He recommended Spector to Bennett, who met him and hired him as assistant deputy minister, policy, in his office. The key players on the B.C. team were now in place, and the pace began to quicken.

The Quebec government's decision to hold a referendum on sovereignty led Bennett, on May 7, 1979, to introduce a motion into the legislature, seconded by the leader of the opposition, Dave Barrett: "This House joins all Canadians in expressing to the people of Quebec our love of country, our desire for continued unity and that they continue to be, with us, a part of our great nation." This was a very rare outpouring of support from both sides of the House.

Rafe Mair had returned the previous fall from a fact-finding trip to West Germany and Switzerland with Deputy Minister Mel Smith. Their study of the federal systems in those countries enabled B.C. to speak authoritatively on the legislative nuances that led to the B.C. position on upper-house reform (as well as adding a couple of inches to their waistlines). Mair spoke eloquently in the legislature about the issues facing Canada a few days later:

> What is the threat to national unity today? Is it Premier Lévesque or Claude Morin? Is it the question of a referendum in a few weeks' time? I suppose the answer to these questions is probably yes. But surely, Mr. Speaker, only a fool would see our problems as being only the matters to which I have referred, for the truth is that many of the causes of Quebec's dissatisfaction are the same as those which underlie serious concerns in the Atlantic provinces, the Prairie provinces and British Columbia...
>
> I think the situation is as simple as this: Canada's survival as a nation depends upon more than mere resolution of the Quebec situation... We must, if we wish to stay together as a nation, address all of the problems concurrently and with equal vigour.

Mair was espousing the theme of the government, a theme of staying together to make Canada work. A week later, Premier Bennett travelled to Montreal to give what most observers called his best, most passionate speech ever. He recalls: "It was one of the few times that we had a speech prepared. When I got up to speak and looked down, only half of it was there. I just had to run with it, and I did it. I spoke from the heart and flew the flag."

The new Ministry of Intergovernmental Relations team started to send out new messages. Its first annual report noted that "British Columbia demonstrated flexibility in the interest of reaching an accord by moving from some positions previously taken." B.C.'s long-held positions were being replaced by a more pragmatic, deal-making posture.

The continuing committee of provincial ministers met for four weeks of intense meetings and found all ten provinces in agreement on many issues heading into the First Ministers Conference in September 1980. The federal government, however, rejected their agreement. Demonstrating its disregard for the provinces, on October 3 the federal government unilaterally introduced a resolution requesting the British Parliament to repatriate the Constitution.

All hell broke loose. British Columbia and other provinces took a very strong position. Part of the game moved to London, England, where B.C. and other provinces presented their views to the Foreign Affairs Committee (the Kershaw Committee). The provinces were delighted when the committee's findings supported the provincial view that provincial consent was necessary for constitutional change.

RAFE MAIR'S RESIGNATION as minister of health in 1981 required Bennett to replace him. Bennett treated every minister in cabinet differently. Some were kidded, some cajoled; some you could just have fun with. Jim Nielsen remembers his appointment as health minister:

> I was out at the airport one night to catch a 5:30 plane. It was in the fall. The dispatcher said, "The premier would like you to call him in his office." So I phoned his office and he said, "Where are you?" I said, "At the airport." He said, "I need to see you now." I said, "Okay, I'll be there in half an hour."
>
> I got back in the car and I thought, what the hell is this about? It's typical Bill Bennett. Lets you wonder what is this about for half an hour as you're driving back.
>
> So I went down to his office and sat down and he said, "Rafe Mair has resigned as minister of health. He's staying on as MLA, but he's going to take a job with Jimmy Pattison at CJOR or something, doing a talk show. So we need a new minister of health." He had a list of the cabinet; he gave me one, kept one. And he said, "I need your help. I've got to find a minister of health." So I looked at it and said, "Well, Pat McGeer would not be the right person, he's a doctor... can't have a doctor in there." And

I started checking off the people and offering my opinion as to their suitability. Finally I said, "No one's going to volunteer for it," because it was really a difficult portfolio.

And Bennett said, "I guess that leaves you." And I thought, what a dummy! I could've saved an hour here. So I said, "Well, okay." He said, "You'll be sworn in tomorrow morning at ten." It was a Friday night...

ON THE CONSTITUTIONAL front, Bennett went to the legislature in Victoria in December 1980. This time he wanted to flush out the opposition.

The federal NDP had joined with the federal Liberals in supporting the unilateral repatriation resolution. This caused a split with NDP premiers in provinces like Saskatchewan. The B.C. NDP were not interested in rising to the debate, or the bait, and the resolution condemning the federal action passed unnoticed.

Bennett then decided that his minister, Garde Gardom, should slog his way across Canada over the next few winter months to urge provinces to think through their own resolutions and counter the unilateral initiatives emanating from Ottawa. By April 16, 1981, the coalition that Gardom started forming with at first six, then seven and finally eight provinces reached agreement on a constitutional proposal. The group, later called the Gang of Eight, was to be a force in the resolution of the issue and included all the provinces except Ontario and New Brunswick.

Trudeau had once again grown tired of the meetings with the provinces and decided to change tack again by submitting a reference to the Supreme Court. He asked the court if he could proceed unilaterally. If he won, then he would happily go to Westminster and unilaterally repatriate. If he lost—and he was confident he would not lose—he could always walk away, ending the process. But what he did not want was more endless First Ministers meetings in which the provinces ganged up and kicked the hell out of him and his government.

The provinces acted to counter his move. Brian Smith recalls:

> One of Bill's finest moments was as the chairman of the provinces and spokesman, which coincided with the repatriation of the Constitution.

When Trudeau decided to proceed unilaterally, the fight switched to London. He sent me to see what I could do.

I phoned my pal Jim Horsman, my counterpart in Alberta, and we went over to London to see the right sort of people who would be influential. No provincial delegation could get in to see the British ministers and Lords without help [laughing] from the Canadian High Commission. Trudeau was trying to block us that way. We found a way. Through contacts we would go out the night before to a club with this minister or that one and have a good dinner and wine, and a cigar. The civilized way to discuss issues of great import. We would tell them about the feds ramming through a Constitution against the wishes of the provinces and wanting to include a Charter of Rights. And we would tell them what it was all about and give them lists of questions to ask.

Then the next day we would go in to see them in their official offices to talk about education issues with the toady from the High Commission along, and for twenty minutes we would sip tea and ask questions. Shake hands politely and leave. The feds were happy we were under control, and we were making headway at the real meetings privately.

In any event, we and the other provinces who were doing similar things got the report we wanted.

Bennett was also watchful of the current chair of the premiers, Sterling Lyon from Manitoba. He liked him—"a straight arrow"—but found him rigid in his anti-Trudeau stand. A Conservative, Lyon took his objections to Trudeau and Trudeau's policies personally, and this manifested itself as aggressive antagonism towards the prime minister.

Bennett was fairly neutral in his views of Trudeau. He recognized that the Constitution repatriation and Canadian Charter of Rights and Freedoms were meant to be Trudeau's legacy. He also felt that as part of the Gang of Eight he had come to understand the other main protagonist, René Lévesque.

Shortly after Lévesque's recent election victory in Quebec, the Gang of Eight were poised to take out full-page ads in all Canada's major newspapers outlining their views, accompanied by all eight signatures.

At the final meeting prior to publication, Lévesque refused to sign. He and Bennett went toe to toe. Lévesque argued that he couldn't sign, for political reasons. Bennett responded that Lévesque would never be in a stronger position, because he had just won re-election.

After a heated argument Lévesque glared at Bennett, snatched up the pen and signed. He turned angrily to Bennett, punched him sharply in the shoulder and said, "Okay?"

Bennett nodded, smiled and replied: "Okay." His understanding of Lévesque and of how he would act had just increased exponentially, in exchange for a bee sting to the shoulder.

Bennett was not passionately opposed to a Charter of Rights, as was Sterling Lyon. Once he had made up his mind to be flexible in finding a solution, the legal niceties took a back seat. British Columbia's interests must not be compromised, but the rest was process. Bennett felt that if all the lawyers around the table could agree, then his contribution in the area would be minimal. He could focus on finding a deal and getting people to start paying attention to the economy.

He was beginning to move into business mode. Analyze the problem. Think through options and find a pragmatic solution. No more rhetoric. He had a goal in mind, now just bend the process to the desired outcome. With the formation of the Gang of Eight, Bennett had moved towards the premiers in the more entrenched provinces, like Lougheed in Alberta and Lévesque in Quebec. Now it was time to move towards Ottawa.

He spoke with Jim Matkin, deputy of intergovernmental relations, and Norman Spector about finding an opportunity to inform the feds of B.C.'s changing view. In June, only six weeks after signing the accord with the Gang of Eight, the first opportunity arose. Allan Gotlieb, undersecretary for external affairs, came to Vancouver on business.

Jim Matkin and Allan Gotlieb had worked together when Allan was deputy at the federal Ministry of Manpower and Immigration and Jim was deputy in the B.C. Ministry of Labour. Matkin asked to meet. He knew Gotlieb was among the inside group of deputies in Ottawa. Matkin told him that he was not happy with the April accord and asked if there was any room for compromise. Gotlieb, a seasoned player, knew Jim would not be saying these things without clearance from Bennett. He said he thought there was room, but could not commit. Message sent and received.

In August, the Canadian Bar Association's annual meeting was in Vancouver and the federal deputy minister, Roger Tassé, was in attendance. The provincial deputy minister, Richard Vogel, invited him to lunch with Matkin.

Matkin moved the ball a little further. He had reported to Bennett after meeting Gotlieb and had received another nod to proceed. Matkin told Tassé that the April accord was a mistake. The eight premiers should at least have signalled that they would consider some entrenched rights.

Matkin was in his element carrying these messages. In over one hundred labour disputes he had learned the "how to" of sending and receiving these oblique signals. And on major disputes Bennett had been kept in the loop and understood from his business experience how this world worked. It was always clear to Matkin that he had Bennett's support, but Bennett always had room to move, being one step away.

Tassé, another inner-circle bureaucrat and a top-level player in this kind of ritual dance, responded he would not be surprised that if the provinces moved on the Charter, the powers that be in Ottawa might move on the amending formula. When Bennett heard back from Matkin, he was even more eager to assume the chair of the Premiers Council and become their spokesman. An amending formula that treated B.C. fairly in the future, combined with repatriation, had become his central goal.

As this world works, Tassé was not back in Ottawa a week when Matkin's phone rang. It was the prime minister's chief adviser, Michael Kirby. Some very important federal–provincial pension coordination issue had just come up (a week later, no one remembered what it was) and this required him to come to Victoria. Would Jim and a few of the B.C. folks be able to join him and a couple of staff for dinner at some private location for an off-the-record, unofficial chat?

On a hot August evening on the second floor of a harbour fish house, the same ground that Matkin and Tassé had ploughed was revisited with Kirby. Matkin had Spector, Smith and the secretary for federal–provincial relations with him. The trade-offs were again discussed. No commitments were made, but the message was clear from both sides. It might be possible to reopen discussions, depending on the Supreme Court finding.

Shortly thereafter, Bennett hosted the annual premiers conference and became the official spokesperson for the premiers. Within a week, Kirby was back to meet with Spector to arrange a meeting between Trudeau and Bennett.

They met on September 24 at 24 Sussex Drive, the prime minister's residence. In attendance: Trudeau and Kirby, Bennett and Spector. Trudeau opened with a rant about how he was tired of First Ministers Conferences that led nowhere except to opportunities for the provinces to fed-bash.

Bennett was pleased with this opening. He felt the same way. Indeed, his father too had felt the same way and had responded by leaving early or not attending the conferences. Bennett turned the discussion to how the leaders must find positive outcomes to strive towards and reach them. But first they needed to find a reason to get back together.

Bennett went on to suggest to Trudeau that since the prime minister was going to Australia for a Commonwealth meeting and would be absent when the Supreme Court handed down its decision, the premiers could use this opportunity to have Bennett canvass the provinces to see if there was any willingness to move forward by compromising. Trudeau and Bennett agreed there were only three scenarios possible: federal clear win, provinces clear win, undecided. They reviewed what might be possible in each case.

Trudeau wanted to know if the more flexible members of the Gang of Eight could sway the others. Was a compromise possible? He mused about a possible referendum on the issue. Bennett did not react, but his reading of the situation was that there was a deal if a smaller Charter of Rights were to be proposed by the federal government.

They agreed on only one thing, a subtle signal, after the thirty-minute chat on constitutional issues. Once the Supreme Court handed down its decision, if either side indicated in its public statement that the decision was unclear, this would signal an interest in reopening discussions. If both parties sent the same signal, then it would lead back to the table.

From the date of the Supreme Court decision and for the following five weeks, Canada experienced the most intense period of constitutional discussions in its history. In their book *The National Deal,* Robert Sheppard and Michael Valpy call the thirty-three days that followed the Supreme Court decision a scherzo interlude and quite accurately trace the hectic events of those days as recalled by the major B.C. players. They recall that the prime minister had spent a night in Seoul, South Korea, on his way to Australia. He went to the Korean Broadcast facility and made his public comments on the decision.

Waiting in Ottawa were Bennett, Spector, Matkin, some other ministers and staff. Various ministers from other jurisdictions were scattered around Ottawa, awaiting the prime minister's pronouncement. Since the court's decision had been broadcast live, a first in Canadian history, it had been a tense and worrisome time for Bennett. In his view the decision, read out by Chief Justice Bora Laskin, had been mixed.

The federal government had won, 7–2, on the simple question of whether it could legally act unilaterally. However, the court split in the provinces' favour 6–3 on whether existing conventions would be violated if the feds moved unilaterally. In simple terms, a convention is a non-statutory rule but historically precedent-setting act that takes on, through tradition, something like the force of law. In other words, the federal government could proceed, but to do so would violate the history and traditions of the country. The court found that the plan put forward by the federal government was "unconstitutional in the conventional sense."

The federal government, as typified by Justice Minister Jean Chrétien, felt it had clearly won. The provincial leaders, such as Alberta's Peter Lougheed, felt they had won.

René Lévesque did not wait for Bennett to act as the provinces' spokesman. He pre-empted the process by calling his own press conference in Quebec City and announcing that the verdict was a clear win for the anti-Ottawa side. Joey Smallwood in Newfoundland called the outcome "as clear as mud."

None of this mattered to Bennett. He waited on Trudeau. Early in the afternoon he went down in the elevator from the fifth-floor offices of B.C.

House in Ottawa and gave a non-committal answer as the official spokesman, saying: "I will wait for the prime minister's comments before making any official comment."

The ball rested in the prime minister's court, and full attention was paid when he started to speak from Seoul:

> While I have not read the entire judgment of the Supreme Court of Canada, it seems that it confirms what we have held all along—namely that the federal Parliament has the legal authority to ask Westminster to enact the constitutional measure now before the Senate and the House of Commons—though there is in Canada a political convention or practice that such a request not be made without the agreement of the provincial governments... We are, therefore, in the same situation we were in before the matter went to the Supreme Court...

B.C. House erupted when Trudeau spoke those words. The prime minister had sent the signal to the premier, and it had been received. Another round of meetings was back on.

Later, in the media conference, when Trudeau answered a reporter's question indicating that he had not ruled out the possibility of meeting the provinces to hear their views, the reaction was more restrained. But huge smiles, including one on Bennett's face, appeared all around.

Five minutes later, Bennett rode down the elevator again. Standing before the cameras, he took a softer line than the one reporters had grown used to hearing from the spokesman for the premiers. He first moved to support his provincial colleagues by indicating it was a win for the provinces. He then changed tack by saying that he appreciated the prime minister's view that he might wish to listen to the provinces and announced that he would leave tomorrow on a tour of all the provincial capitals to obtain each premier's view. No rhetoric, no chest beating, just a calm, businesslike approach.

Before Bennett's jet left Ottawa the next day, Michael Kirby asked to see Matkin and Spector. This testy meeting was not the celebration the two provincial boys thought it would be. Kirby was firm: Trudeau did not mean that he would not proceed unilaterally, only that he would "live with it." The twosome from B.C. pushed back strongly. They left convinced that Kirby was bargaining, trying to gain some room for the next round of talks that were, in their view, inevitable.

Kirby was equally alarmed at what was reported back to him from the provinces that Bennett was visiting as he flew from capital city to capital city. Kirby felt Bennett was going too far. To counter this, he briefed his contacts in each provincial capital with a much tougher version of what Trudeau was prepared to consider.

This type of situation is not unusual. The provinces might fight tooth and nail in challenging the authority of the federal government in the media and the Supreme Court. Yet the same people would feed to the federal government what was being said in their private meetings with other provinces. Such is the way of federal–provincial relations in Canada.

Every senior official in every government, federal and provincial, has a contact in every other province and in the federal government. These contacts speak constantly to each other, off the record. They share secrets and spin disinformation. Premiers encourage—indeed, they expect—their ministers and their senior staff to develop contacts and to form friendships with their federal and provincial counterparts. There are no secrets, there are no surprises. The channels are used for information, and disinformation. The federal purse is used to grease the skids. Ottawa plays one off against the other, the provinces play each other and the most sophisticated players are the ones with the most developed networks.

During the negotiations, Ottawa worked hard to discredit Bennett's optimism in order to ensure that the prime minister was left with room to move. Bennett crossed and criss-crossed the country. In every airport and public place, people would come up to him, shake his hand, thank him and encourage him to find a solution. But that feeling of goodwill ended as soon as he and his staff set foot in another premier's office.

Simply put, the premiers did not believe him. Or they felt he was overstating Trudeau's position. This view was encouraged. At every stop a senior official in each premier's office, brought in for the pre-briefing just prior to meeting Bennett, would say that he had just got off the phone from Kirby or some other federal senior official who "knew" that Bennett had misread the prime minister.

Kirby did not want anyone to believe that Trudeau was at all weakened by the decision of the Supreme Court. If it appeared he was, then the "hawk" premiers would come to Ottawa to feast on the carcass. Bennett, on the other hand, wanted to get the premiers back to the table in Ottawa because he saw a deal that would meet his interests: an amending formula, repatriation and a limited Charter.

Bennett also knew what kind of tightrope he was walking: chair of the premiers annual conference and therefore spokesperson for all ten premiers. This included speaking for the federal supporters in Ontario and New Brunswick, but also for the Gang of Eight. He wore both those hats, plus a third: he had to stand up for B.C.'s interests.

In their book *Canada... Notwithstanding,* Roy Romanow, John Whyte and Howard Leeson describe, from Saskatchewan's point of view, Bennett's role, dilemma and actions:

> British Columbia's premier, Bill Bennett, had assumed the chairmanship of the premiers' annual conference in August. It was generally understood by the premiers of the eight dissenting provinces that he would also serve as chairman of their group. Obviously, the two positions conflicted since Ontario and New Brunswick both supported the initiatives of the federal government and were members of the premiers conference. Bennett would have to walk a fine line between the interests of the eight dissenting provinces and the interests of all ten...
>
> In his visits Bennett told the premiers that, as a result of his private conversations with Trudeau, he was convinced that the prime minister was now prepared to strike a bargain on the Constitution. According to Bennett, the prime minister made an offer of sorts to him. The offer, only generally explained, was immediate patriation with the entrenchment of the provisions on language and mobility rights, equalization, resources, and fundamental and democratic rights. With respect to the amending formula, the unanimity rule would be enforced for a two-year period... a referendum would decide the nature of the amending

> formula if the governments failed to agree... In a later meeting between Jean Chrétien and Roy Romanow, Chrétien disputed this version of the meeting...
>
> As well, many were skeptical that Trudeau was really prepared to compromise the basic federal plan to an extent satisfactory to the majority of the eight dissenting provinces. Nevertheless, after each provincial visit, Bennett expressed to the press his optimism that a solution was possible, and urged the governments to find a compromise. Quebec was increasingly apprehensive...
>
> Nevertheless, his unwavering stance that there was room for negotiation, even if not supported by clear evidence of change, nurtured the incipient mood for compromise and prevented an immediate recommitment to the original opposing positions. A more strident supporter of the inviolability of the position of the dissenting provinces might have greatly worsened the crisis.

Bennett was already worried about the direction the economy was taking. He knew the cyclical nature of his province's economy and that tough times were on their way. Commodity prices were falling, interest rates were moving up well into double digits. He felt that B.C. was likely to be first in and perhaps last out of a coming recession. This was unusual; B.C. was more likely to be last in, last out, but Bennett felt this time was going to be different.

It was apparent that in the acrimonious federal–provincial climate that had developed over the last few years as the constitutional discussions had dragged on, there would be no possibility of concerted federal–provincial action unless the repatriation/amending formula/Charter of Rights issue was settled.

Bennett's cross-country junket had had mixed results. The hard-liners who thought the court decision was a clear provincial win, Lougheed and Lévesque, wanted to hold firm. They were concerned that Bennett was creating cracks in the Gang of Eight wall.

Saskatchewan also began to feel that the Gang of Eight solidarity was waning. Premier Allan Blakeney phoned Bennett, Ontario's William

Davis—one of the two provincial leaders who supported Trudeau—and Nova Scotia's John Buchanan, who he thought was also wavering, and received a mandate to get officials together to discuss new negotiations. This was also Bennett's objective, and he readily agreed. So did the others.

Bennett was now off to Ottawa for an October 13 meeting with Trudeau. On the government jet flying across Canada, Matkin, Spector and Bennett reviewed hundreds of strategies and tactics. What to do if Trudeau agreed, what to do if Trudeau disagreed. They discussed what to say to the media and how to approach the other premiers. Matkin raised the idea of a "no author" text and recalled that they had used it successfully in the past, in the Skagit Valley settlement. All of it directed to finding a solution.

The meeting started easily, but soon hard discussions were under way. Kirby and Spector were the only staff in attendance. The meeting, a hard one, lasted three hours. Trudeau wanted Bennett to explain where the provinces were willing to compromise. If no compromise, why go to the table? He was skeptical.

Bennett argued that the provinces would be agreeable and would react positively to a reasonable compromise. He had no mandate; Trudeau was reluctant to show any cards. Finally, all they could agree on was that to find a deal, both sides must compromise. That was enough for Bennett, because he then argued that to do this they had to meet again. Trudeau reluctantly agreed, but was fearful of a setup. They would meet again, and the bargaining would focus on the Charter of Rights.

Bennett got what he wanted, and wasn't overly concerned what the compromises would be around the Charter of Rights, one way or the other. He wasn't a lawyer; his objective was a deal. On the plane home, he directed Matkin and Spector to meet with Saskatchewan and speak with Ontario. They were to begin to put together a no-author text combining what was on the table in a way that consolidated and rationalized existing texts. Matkin and Mark Krasnick immediately began to draft the text.

The three of them were pleased. They were right where they thought they, and B.C., should be at this point. They were swinging the discussions into a settlement framework they were very familiar with.

On October 18 all ten premiers, their constitutional ministers and staff met in Montreal. Quebec, now very concerned about B.C. and the rumoured no-author text, made sure that the Quebec and B.C. delegations shared a floor so that Quebec could keep an eye on their activities.

Jim Matkin, aware he was being watched, came out of his room with a copy of the no-author text under his jacket. He stepped onto the elevator. Premier Blakeney was already riding down, looking straight ahead. Matkin removed the brown unmarked envelope and passed it to the Saskatchewan premier, who slipped it under his suit coat. Not a word was spoken.

Norman Spector had gone off to meet with Don Stevenson, Ontario's deputy intergovernmental affairs minister, who presented him with a chart that looked like a teeter-totter. The more Charter the federal government needed, the more flexibility the provinces needed in the amending formula, and vice versa.

It was key to Bennett's strategy in his conflicted position as spokesperson for all ten premiers as well as the Gang of Eight that no settlement papers be distributed as B.C. papers. Nothing must signal the B.C. position or B.C.'s interests. That was the genius of the no-author text. It was not B.C.'s, although it went to the province's interests; it was, well, no one's.

The meeting of all ten provinces in Montreal soon got down to brass tacks, so Ontario's Bill Davis and New Brunswick's Richard Hatfield had to leave. Davis left with his normal grace; Hatfield, in one of his emotional outbursts, where tears were never far away, whined to the press.

Quebec's minister, Claude Morin, tried his best to isolate B.C. and stiffen the resolve of the other premiers. He attacked B.C., accusing it of selling out and double-dealing with the feds. Bennett stayed cool, remained silent. This sent an affirmative signal to everyone, but committed to nothing. Bennett's silence and the agenda, mainly a report from Alberta on London activities, did not lend themselves to Morin's plans. Although the meeting attempted to plan next moves, it drifted because no one was able to articulate a clear direction.

On the flight home in the little Citation Learjet, the B.C. delegation reviewed where they were and how to move forward. They had the basic no-author text. They had the revisions to it from Saskatchewan, and the "teeter-totter" from Ontario. As well, they had the feedback from the Montreal meeting and the formal and informal discussions at that meeting. It was time to pull those threads together.

Matkin now reported on his most recent discussions with Paul Weiler, the former chair of the B.C. Labour Relations Board, who was now teaching law at Harvard. Bennett actively encouraged these types of outreach discussions. He knew and respected Weiler; several years earlier, Weiler had written a paper for the *McGill Law Journal* that introduced the idea of attaching a *non obstante* clause to some of the provisions of the Charter. This in effect would allow any province to pass its own law and to include a provision in it that exempted the law from falling under the Charter of Rights—a province could "opt out" of the Charter.

Bennett liked the idea: "If we couldn't get exactly what we wanted, we would have this one additional way. That would be our protection at the end. There have been times, and there will be in the future, that you have to have it as a weapon to control your own field of government, and the responsibility. I wouldn't have been afraid to use it." This new wrinkle might provide some premiers with just enough comfort to tip the balance. It was an interesting idea. If it worked, good; if not, it would stimulate discussion.

Bennett made it clear that there would be no paper from British Columbia. Matkin and Bennett had worked together long enough to know that there was no need for specific instruction. Bennett wanted room to be able to say, honestly, that he had not instructed anyone to prepare a B.C. position. But the staff under Matkin, supported by Spector, knew that they had free rein to expand the no-author text based on all this feedback and including the *non obstante* clause for distribution. It must not seem to be coming from B.C., but it must get out there. This was a fine line, but one the B.C. delegation had much experience walking.

To the other provinces, though, it seemed almost too textbookish. None of them were familiar with these approaches. The jargon was unknown to them; it earned the B.C. delegation the less than flattering nickname of "boy scouts." As a result, the meeting in Montreal was not constructive. The Gang of Eight was unable to fashion a united, cohesive front. Quebec's Morin rejected a leadership role for B.C. because he could see that the direction it was heading might lead to a deal. Quebec was not sure it wanted one.

Bennett knew what he wanted and felt that now it was within his grasp. The interests of B.C. were secure, the fixed positions of Ottawa and all the provinces had been challenged, and more people were now thinking of the compromises that would be required for settlement. In addition, the two sides were coming back to the table. Bennett headed to Ottawa for the big dance.

Ottawa in November. Cold, windy, some days of bright sun, but often cloudy. Ten provincial premiers, their ministers, often attorneys general, intergovernmental affairs, plus several education ministers and one health minister, the only woman, New Brunswick's Brenda Robertson. Add staff for each delegation: deputy ministers to the premiers, to ministers, special advisers on the Constitution and technical and support staff. About one hundred people, all senior, all with big egos.

Now mix in the federal delegation, led by the prime minister and minister of justice and attorney general. The rest of the federal cabinet available on call. Senior staff and deputy ministers for the mainline departments and from the PMO, FPRO and PCO. Lawyers specializing in one possible section of the proposals, technical advisers on possible implications of any option, plus support staff. Another hundred people.

The Canadian Intergovernmental Conference Secretariat provided translation and secretarial services with a staff of about one hundred. Security forces numbered in the hundreds. And, of course, more than eight hundred media personnel from every possible outlet were available to satisfy the over two million television viewers who watched the opening proceedings on the first day and the millions who read the newspapers and watched evening television. This was high drama, and even people in B.C. were paying attention. All this attention was focused on the old Union Station in downtown Ottawa, which had been converted into the national conference centre. The main station floor was set up for the opening ceremony, which was being beamed live across Canada.

Premier Bennett and his entourage arrived on Friday night. They stayed where they always did, the Four Seasons on Skinner Street, a modern hotel and a brisk five-minute walk to the "train station" as the delegates called the conference centre. Bennett walked over every morning with a couple of staff, always Spector, and occasionally a minister. The short walk lightened the mood, broke the tension with wisecracks and witticisms. Bennett bandied about lines he might use when facing the inevitable scrum he would push through on his way in, key messages for a thirty-second voice clip that would be heard on the drive-to-work news back in B.C. The three-hour time difference made it possible for Bennett to provide messages at day's end, around 5 PM in Ottawa, 2 PM in B.C. and therefore played on the drive-home radio news in B.C.

The other provinces' delegations also took floors in hotels: Ontario, Newfoundland and New Brunswick at the Four Seasons; Alberta in the Skyline hotel; the rest in the Chateau Laurier, which is connected by an underground tunnel to the conference centre and served as the nerve centre for the provinces. Lévesque stayed across the river in Quebec with the largest delegation. He kept a suite at the Chateau for convenience.

The eighty registered participants in the First Ministers Conference on the Constitution picked up their name tags, and many claimed their receivers to plug into their ears for simultaneous interpretation into both official languages. Most western delegates needed them. About half the Ontario and Atlantic delegations needed them, almost none of the Quebec contingent and none in the federal group required the service. Only one in the B.C. delegation, Spector, did not need one.

Everyone knew everyone else, as they had been sharing information for years. By the time they made the cut in their own government to be among those who attended this, the highest level of meetings in Canada, they had been to many of these sessions.

Most knew many of the national media, and all of the media from their area. Part of the game afoot here, and known by both sides, was media feeding and making sure your story went out, officially or unofficially to the folks back home or across the country. The media want to be fed so that they can look informed to their audiences, and the governments want to spin the story their way. It takes two hands clapping to make a sound.

First Ministers sat around the hollow square table, with the prime minister seated at what was deemed the head and flanked by provincial premiers in the order in which their provinces entered Canada. Quebec on the prime minister's left, Ontario on his right. Down each side of the table: Ontario, Nova Scotia, Manitoba, Prince Edward Island, Alberta on one side; Quebec, New Brunswick, British Columbia, Saskatchewan and Newfoundland on the other. The senior Canadian Conference Secretariat staff person closed the loop by sitting at the foot of the table.

Trudeau opened: "We are here to find an accord and it will only be possible if everyone is prepared to compromise."

Speaking order followed the chronological order, Ontario first, Quebec second and so on. Bennett spoke sixth. He chose this public moment to establish B.C.'s position as distinct from his role as spokesman for either the annual premiers conference or the Gang of Eight. He urged compromise and accommodation. This was the first sign that the Gang of Eight consensus had evaporated.

Saskatchewan, following B.C., took a similar stance. To ensure that no one thought the whole Gang of Eight provincial-rights team was in disarray, Lougheed from Alberta aggressively attacked, dispelling any federal legitimacy in proceeding unilaterally.

The conference adjourned for lunch, and the public session was over. After lunch it would reconvene in a smaller room upstairs, First Ministers and two advisers only. The heavy bargaining was to begin. Everyone else waited.

The next three days were filled with drama and intrigue as this clumsy vehicle called a First Ministers Conference tried to find a solution acceptable to all. Interests varied and positions were held for the broadest and narrowest of political needs. Among the premiers and other delegates were many lawyers who had extensive experience with the common law. This led them to strong views on things like the entrenchment of a Charter of Rights in the Constitution. Premiers who were lawyers could argue for hours about the pros and cons of the Charter and whether it would inherently rob provinces of jurisdiction.

The questions they debated: should provinces be able to opt out, should compensation be automatically paid upon opting out of provisions, would this lead to a checkerboard country where rights differed from province to province? What did Quebec need to survive and prosper in a Canada that had a repatriated Constitution, its own amending formula and a Charter of Rights? Canadians' broad interests were subjugated to the private views of First Ministers on obscure topics. First Ministers were used to being listened to in their own jurisdictions, in fact they were kings there, not used to having to bend to others' views.

A very few, like Peter Lougheed, had in the past actually gone head to head with the federal government and won on his terms in his fight over the National Energy Program. His view was, therefore, to dig in and eventually the feds will collapse. He was one of the few with this type of practical experience. Bennett had also fought over the energy-resource issue and had won, but the media decided that Lougheed was in the lead. Norman Spector recalls:

> I don't think anybody would accuse Lougheed of being stubborn or unable to make a deal. As we've seen in his later career he's a great Canadian in that sense, he's played a very positive role since leaving office. And Bennett, his natural inclination was to try to make a deal, I don't think he thought that the Constitution was the most important issue facing the country. Remember, the economic situation was deteriorating, which was much more significant to Bennett, both personally and as premier. And finally, I think, as chairman, he saw some responsibility to try and bridge the differences.

This difficult scenario was complicated by mistrust and dislike between some of the leaders. Being First Ministers, they also thought they were superb negotiators who knew when to hold 'em, when to fold 'em, when to move and when to stand pat, when to offer a compromise and when to be aggressive. In fact, few of them had any real experience in successful multi-party negotiation. That is not to say they did not have experience in federal–provincial meetings, but the record shows that success more often than not eluded them. Most often they were there to make political points, not to arrive at a consensus.

Bennett stood pat. His views on the Charter were held in a practical, not theoretical way, and he believed almost any compromise here would meet his needs. He stood back and let others step forward. He had never needed to be on centre stage if the agenda was moving his way. He would carefully pick which hill to die on.

Bennett also had one other factor playing on his mind, based on experience that no one but the prime minister had. The Victoria Accord had been reached under his father's watch and had been rejected by Quebec shortly thereafter. He was beginning to believe what his father had said about the settlement: Quebec politicians will never sign a deal with the other provinces because politically they just can't do it and survive.

Finally, when everyone was at the limit of their patience, an exhausted Jean Chrétien and Roy Romanow slipped away to a pantry in a small kitchen off the conference centre meeting room to try to find common ground. They began by writing down the parts of the Charter that should be subject to legislative override and those that should be entrenched. It began to come together but then they realized they needed Ontario, so Roy McMurtry was found. They soon put together the essence of an idea for settlement that combined all the disparate pieces. Eureka!

Officials gathered that night to flesh out the proposal. British Columbia was represented by Deputy Mel Smith, who stood strongly for B.C.'s interests. Every province was represented in the meeting rooms in the Chateau—except, no one thought to call across the river and advise Quebec.

An agreement was reached, typed up overnight and slipped under the doors of the sleeping premiers, who were aware of the proposal but not the details.

The next morning Bennett read the proposal, talked with his delegation and told them he found it acceptable. He had to agree to the entrenchment of minority language rights, something he believed he could sell. Also, he believed it was Trudeau's bottom line as it had been conveyed in their first one-on-one meeting. No other premier had believed that. It had the potential to be controversial in B.C., but Bennett had determined that he could still protect the province's fundamental interests and agree to it. He placed it with his position on independent schools, which he had made in his first term in office. British Columbia would accept it, he could sell it and it was Trudeau's primary goal. Spector remembers the two leaders' encounter:

> I recall the first private meeting between Bennett and Trudeau. Trudeau said: "Bill, you have to give me language rights, it's the essence of my existence"—the rest of the Charter was dispensable, but that's his bottom line.
>
> As you look at that last week in Ottawa, two proposals were developed, bridging proposals—one by Saskatchewan and one by British Columbia. The British Columbia one, if I remember correctly, had just language rights in the Charter, and the Saskatchewan one had all the rights except language rights in the Charter, and in the to-ing and froing back and forth, that was very consistent with the concept.
>
> If you look at the notwithstanding clause now, it doesn't apply to language rights. It's a very strange situation, because classically, language rights are not human rights. So here we've got a notwithstanding clause that applies to all kinds of fundamental human rights, allows legislatures to override them, but not language rights.
>
> I think that my interpretation was quite sound of what Trudeau was saying at that meeting: that language rights are not subject to the notwithstanding clause.
>
> For Bennett, I don't think he was willing for a deal at any price, but I do recall him at one of the meetings at the conference centre, that first week in November, saying he was prepared to recognize section 23 language rights. He had no problem with the concept of French-language education in British Columbia. And I don't think it was because he was desperate for a deal. I think as a guy who funded independent schools, he probably understood why parents would want to educate their kids in French. And he certainly was not in any sense an anti-French bigot or anything like that, nor was he interested in assimilating French Canadians.

> Let's face it, British Columbia's going to be an English province, maybe it's going to become a Mandarin province, but the French fact has never been a threat. So it was a very easy concession for him to make to show some goodwill to Trudeau, for whom it was "the essence of his existence." For Bennett it was a "gimme," trying to smooth the negotiations.

Next morning, the Gang of Eight premiers were breakfasting at the Chateau for their daily pre-meeting meeting. Lévesque was late, as always. When he arrived he found them discussing the new proposal. Furious, he felt he had been betrayed.

The premiers moved across to the conference centre. Brian Peckford of Newfoundland presented what became known as the November Accord. Two pages, five paragraphs, then silence. No one moved or spoke.

Trudeau broke the silence: "I do not want to be the first to speak, but would welcome other comments."

Silence.

Bennett raised his hand and his microphone was turned on. He went first, and said he was prepared to accept the deal. Lougheed followed; he too would accept the deal. And so it went, around the table, until only two, Trudeau and Lévesque, were left. Trudeau asked a few questions, and then said he would accept the deal.

Lévesque said No. It was over.

Bennett recalls: "It's my view, sitting next to René, talking with René and fighting with René, that he would not, could not sign any document. He would be signing off an independent Quebec... They did not want a Canadian Constitution, but their own Constitution."

Spector comments on the relationship between Trudeau and Bennett and the deal:

> I don't think they had any great affection for each other or great respect for each other. There wasn't an animus, but in those years British Columbia was such a polarized society and Bennett had such a thin majority that he really didn't have much flexibility. British Columbia

premiers were in such a polarized province; they were generally attacked no matter what they did. They didn't have the kind of ability to be statesmen that a Lougheed did, or to a build a consensus in their province.

So that fact and the press environment made it fairly difficult for Bennett to play a role on the national stage. For example, I think that Allan Fotheringham's continual writing about him not having a university degree played a role, and the kind of press coverage that tended to come out of British Columbia played a role. But in the final analysis the country avoided a fight in London, which would have been very messy, and we got a Constitution, a Constitution with a notwithstanding clause.

I would call it a second-best outcome. The first-best outcome would have been to wait for Quebec, but you know once that die was cast I would have to say it was a success for Bennett.

Minor changes were discussed and the agreement was brought back and signed. The leaders moved downstairs and re-signed in front of the cameras. Trudeau had regrets: Quebec was not part of the deal and there was no reference to a referendum. Lévesque was bitter and angry.

Bennett, however, had met his objectives, and he flew home. He reflects: "When I was through, after all that flying. All that tension. In the air and coming back. I was exhausted. I flew home to Audrey and the kids, and when I was in sight of Kelowna I remember a long sigh. I was home. Relax."

10

TOUGH GUY?

"The premier always said that there are two ways to make money. One is to earn more, the other is to spend less."

MIKE BAILEY

BILL BENNETT knew not to expect too much from the First Ministers Conference on the Economy in February 1982. But he had to try, for two reasons.

One, he had learned that failure was a necessary step in federal–provincial affairs. Failure set the stage for the public to understand why a province had to "go its own way." Bennett believed that B.C. would have to go its own way because the other premiers did not share his view of the seriousness of the coming recession.

Two, many of the policy instruments for dealing with a recession lay in federal hands. If the other premiers would not act now, at least Bennett would serve notice, and perhaps this would lead them not to delay further once the recession was upon Canada. He would attempt to lead the horse to water; when it drank would be another matter.

Up early as always, Bennett drank several pots of black coffee and reviewed his briefing books for the tenth time. Downstairs in the lobby, he met the three staffers with whom he would walk to the conference centre in Ottawa. The one-liners and jokes began. What line to feed the media, however, was serious business. Kibitzing was the tension breaker.

Halfway to the conference centre, one of the staff started to sniff loudly. "I smell something." Sniff. "Smells like smoke."

Norman Spector picked it up right away: "Yes, smoke. Where's it coming from?"

David Emerson put in: "Don't hear any fire engines."

"No, neither do I, but I definitely smell smoke."

The premier stopped, and burst out laughing: "This suit does not smell of smoke."

Everyone laughed, the tension was cut. Bennett was ready for the scrum. He could be stiff in front of the television cameras, but in small groups he relaxed, and this mood would carry over to the scrum. The smoke joke was the staff teasing him about never buying new suits until British Importers in Victoria had a fire in their store and put their high-quality menswear on sale at 20 to 50 percent off. Bargains suited the premier.

The First Ministers Conference on the Economy proceeded as expected. Nothing happened. The premiers rejected the hard-work agenda that had led them to agreement on the Constitution. They reverted to form: Quebec was very unhappy, and the other premiers had different agendas. There was no consensus on the problem, never mind the solution, and the meeting slipped into familiar fed-bashing. The prime minister treated the premiers with disdain.

After the morning's televised session, where premiers spoke to the constituents at home rather than to each other, they moved upstairs for the afternoon to meet in a smaller, private room. The governor of the Bank of Canada, often a guest at these functions, pronounced that things were not that bad and would get better with prudence.

Yes, inflation was running at around 13 percent per annum, unemployment was in double digits, interest rates were running ahead of inflation and home mortgage rates over 20 percent were the order of the day. But things were not so bad that Canada needed to take extraordinary measures.

The afternoon droned on. For a change, the prime minister had the premiers speak in reverse order from when they entered Confederation. This left Ontario to speak last. Just before it was Ontario's turn to speak, Premier Bill Davis stretched, stood up, leaned over and whispered to his minister of industry and tourism, Larry Grossman, that he was going out to smoke his pipe and that Larry should make Ontario's presentation. Then the easy-going Davis left, in consideration of Pierre Trudeau's dislike of tobacco smoke. In the federal cabinet, Trudeau had banished smokers to the far end of the room. But in these meetings he had no such control; in any event, the chain-smoking Quebec Premier René Lévesque was not in the mood to be conciliatory, and he sat on one side of the prime minister. On the other side sat pipe-smoking Bill Davis, always finding small ways to stroke the chairman's considerable ego.

Trudeau sat slumped in his seat. Halfway through the provinces' droning, he began playing a children's game with his glasses case. Look at someone through a small hole in the bottom of the stitched case, and the person looks large, taking up the whole of the end where the glasses are slid home. Reverse the process, look through the much larger open mouth of the case and out through the small hole in the stitching in the bottom, and the person looks minuscule. Trudeau's boredom was evident, and his judgement was demonstrated by the end through which he viewed your presentation: larger than life, or minuscule.

Having finished with minimizing Lévesque, Trudeau turned the case around when Ontario's Grossman began.

Grossman attacked. Ontario was not pleased with the federal government. Feeding off Quebec's anticipated attack rather than attempting to play Ontario's traditional role of Captain Canada (here to save the day), Grossman placed the blame for all economic problems clearly on the federal Liberals in Ottawa. The glasses case quickly turned around to enable the prime minister to look at Grossman with the open-mouth end to his eye and out through the small hole in the bottom. He was minimized.

When Grossman was finished, Trudeau put down his case and for the first time responded specifically to a provincial presentation. In the tradition of a Jesuit-trained scholar, the philosopher-king shredded Grossman's arguments. This was classic Trudeau. The room grew quiet. Grossman went red in the face.

As soon as the prime minister had finished and picked up his glasses case, Grossman came right back at him. This time the attack slipped beyond blaming the federal Liberals into a personal harangue directed at the prime minister's lack of action. Halfway through the diatribe, Trudeau tossed his glasses case on the papers in front of him and that famous icy stare appeared on his face. Contempt mixed with disbelief and arrogance.

Grossman finished and Trudeau began. For ten minutes he logically, sarcastically at times, went through Ontario's arguments and demolished them. And Grossman. After the first three minutes, the quiet smirks disappeared from the faces of the other participants. Most premiers, their one minister and the two staff allowed into the meeting room started to look down at their shoes or up at some obscure dot on the ceiling. The destruction was embarrassing.

Trudeau paused and asked if there were any other comments. None.

"Well then, let us move on to the next agenda item: comments."

At that moment the door opened into the chamber, and in sauntered Bill Davis. He walked around the table to his seat, looked down at his flushed minister's face, put his hand briefly on Grossman's shoulder, squeezed it and looked up at the prime minister. The briefest, smallest smile played across his lips as he sat down.

This was the atmosphere in which Premier Bennett attempted to convey a simple message. He had wanted this conference, and it had been one of his goals at the constitutional conference. He was not optimistic but felt that a simple message might succeed. The problem for B.C. was significant: double-digit inflation and unemployment. A recession underway in British Columbia and, Bennett argued, about to sweep across Canada. Government spending could not continue to rise by double digits every year; wage settlements averaging over 13 percent a year in the public sector were not sustainable. National, coordinated action was required because individual provinces had only limited policy levers that they could pull.

His solution was simple. Limit government spending to 6 percent per annum for two years. Hold public-sector wage and benefit increases to that same 6 percent for the same period of time. This would bring down interest rates and inflation while the First Ministers collaborated on a long-term national strategy.

His colleagues listened, and then rejected his arguments. Because Bennett had been one of the few not to fed-bash and to propose a positive, co-perative agenda, Trudeau had listened to his speech. He might not agree, but he respected the presentation. Afterwards, he went back to his glasses-case game. But, by and large, the other premiers did not believe that the world and Canada were headed into a recession. Drastic action was not needed. Many premiers felt they could spend their way to prosperity.

The meeting broke up, no one was happy and Bennett was mildly disappointed. On the plane home, he said something that was to be repeated in the future: "B.C. will just have to go its own way."

ON THE LONG flight across the country following the successful constitutional conference in November 1981, Bennett had issued instructions to Norman Spector. He was now able to move on his agenda: prepare a plan for B.C. to take what steps it could on its own. Have Larry Bell, deputy minister of finance, bring forward a fiscal framework based on the workings of the provincial economy that cabinet ministers could understand, and include recommendations on how to curtail government expenditures. Have Jim Matkin, deputy minister of intergovernmental relations, prepare a proposal on how to bring public-sector wages and benefits in line with the new fiscal reality presented by the recession in the private sector. Finally, have Bell lead an exercise in which major capital-spending ministries could propose projects that might be accelerated, thus offsetting anticipated job losses in B.C.'s resource-based industries.

Spector was to find a suitable location for a two-day cabinet retreat. This was all to be done in the next few weeks, and recognizing that the

Christmas break would intervene, by the second week in January. Spector selected Schooner Cove, just north of Parksville on Vancouver Island, for the first of what were to be four conferences over the next couple of years to deal with the province's fragile economy. The others were held at Lake Okanagan, Cowichan Bay and Whistler.

Bell's new right-hand man, also newly appointed as an assistant deputy minister, was David Emerson. His job combined two previous positions, secretary to Treasury Board and deputy of corporate policy and planning. This new approach of combining jobs at the top was initiated by Bennett to send a signal to the bureaucracy: when senior jobs come up, combine them, eliminating one position.

Just prior to the cabinet retreat the media reported the latest teacher wage settlements, which had concluded on December 31, 1981. The average wage increase for teachers was to be 17.4 percent for one year. When increments were included, the average teacher's salary was to rise about 21 percent on January 1, 1982, from what it had been on December 31, 1981. The press also noted that public-sector settlements, on average, were running ahead of private-sector settlements and ahead of inflation.

The Schooner Cove meeting went well. Emerson presented an economic framework that described B.C. as having a small, open economy: small in population, open in its dependence on exports of commodities and its imports of consumer goods. Since commodities are traded in a world market, they are differentiated only by their price. A two-by-four is the same wherever it is made, and its selling price is the only determinant of its sale. Its intrinsic qualities cannot be differentiated. This holds for coal, copper or any of the other exports that B.C. ships around the world. Therefore, to generate wealth in the province the government must keep its costs down and taxes low, or B.C. exporters will not be competitive. Emerson explains:

> You spend a dollar in B.C., and that dollar doesn't stay in B.C.—it leaks out very, very quickly. So you can't have a very big effect on the level of demand in the economy by spending domestically. The demand is affected by external forces, more specifically resource markets. So we developed our thinking about the economy as one essentially driven

by natural resource markets, meaning commodity prices in the world marketplace.

The first talk of recession coming, publicly, must have been around January or February 1982. There was a little bit of talk among forecasters that we might see a slight downturn or a slowdown in rates of growth. There wasn't a soul out there who was predicting we would have the worst recession since the Depression.

How do you run a government fiscally when your whole economy is driven by natural-resource markets?

The options were extremely limited. Seeing that the economy was going into a downturn, you could not, in fact should not, turn around and deficit spend in order to get yourself out of it, because that would dig a deeper hole.

The only way you can affect the fundamentals is by supply-side measures, cost-side measures, because we're essentially selling into a world marketplace, the demand of which we cannot affect. The only thing we can do is affect our market share, and the main way we can do that is through our costs, which means productivity, government costs, taxes, wages—that whole supply-side nexus.

So my urgings were for the government to deal with the cost-side problem. And that was going to hurt.

This simple paradigm had guided Bennett over the years of his administration. But, for the first time, it was put to cabinet in an easy and understandable presentation. Bell offered a "restraint on government" program that would rein in government spending and present some difficult funding decisions for Treasury Board ministers. But he was fortunate because he had the total support of his minister, the very able Hugh Curtis. He also outlined, for the ministers' consideration, capital projects that could be accelerated.

Matkin's presentation outlined the various options that might be available to control public-sector compensation, "compensation" being a new catchword that included not only wage costs but the total cost of any settlement once the benefits were factored in. The presentation, while rather vague in detail, set out principles.

No one at the cabinet retreat was surprised that Matkin was carrying this file. Yes, he was deputy minister of intergovernmental relations, but this was one of Bennett's management techniques—choose the right person for the job and don't let organizational structure stand in the way of desired outcomes.

The cabinet thanked the bureaucrats for their input, asked them to sit in the back of the room and got down to work, spending the next day and a half planning strategy and selecting options. Bennett would go on province-wide television and explain to the public what the economic problem was, what the risks were of doing nothing, what the proposal was for going forward and what was expected of all British Columbians.

ON FEBRUARY 18, 1982, Premier Bennett appeared on BCTV at seven o'clock, following the much-watched six o'clock news. He outlined the problems caused for British Columbia by the world recession and announced a "Restraint on Government" program. Everyone would be expected to "pull their belt in a notch," to pull together to help B.C. face these pressures. Government spending was to be drastically reduced, and public-sector wages would be restrained for two years to between 8 and 14 percent per year.

The cabinet had taken a considerable political risk. It was heading towards an election, and these decisions meant it would be running on a platform of cutting back government. Politicians like to spend money, not cut services. To run an election campaign on less government and less spending and against vocal public-sector unions had never been attempted in Canada. Many members of both the public and the media thought this was political suicide.

But Bennett knew that to be electorally successful with the restraint message, he needed a vociferous response from his opposition. His dream was realized immediately when Jim Kinnaird, president of the B.C. Federation of Labour, followed him on live TV and proclaimed that if the government proceeded, there would be "blood in the streets." The cabinet stayed the course. Ministers stood together and the government made the decisions needed to bring force and effect to the restraint framework. Being ministers, and being encouraged by their staff, they all supported the fact that the restraint program had to be applied to all the ministries—except, of course, their own, which faced special circumstances that warranted exceptions. Hugh Curtis, with Bennett's full support, would allow none of this nonsense.

When Bennett appeared on BCTV, Matkin and his team of advisers had no real idea, beyond the general principles, what the wage restraint program would look like. They decided to travel to Ottawa to speak with federal officials who had been involved in the two-year national wage and price control program in the mid-1970s. Much to their surprise, five years after the end of the federal program there still existed an office fully staffed and still winding down the operation. This would never happen in Bennett's B.C.

Ideas were always the currency spent in discussion with Jim Matkin. Shortly after he returned from Ottawa, at a staff discussion the idea was born to create a program of wage restraint that would have a legislative framework, accompanied by guidelines to cover settlements that encouraged voluntary compliance. A set of regulations that were stricter and led to lesser-valued settlements would also be designed. The parties would be forced to use the tougher regulations if voluntary settlements were not found. All public-sector contracts were to be placed into the program for a maximum of two years.

The scheme would be overseen by a commissioner and have only a few staff, led by a registrar. It provided for a special mediator to help the parties find solutions. Former Labour Relations Board vice-chair and vastly experienced labour practitioner Ed Peck was named commissioner. Retired businessman Ed Lien was named registrar, and the widely respected former union organizer Vince Ready was named mediator.

From the government's point of view the program was immensely successful. The restraint guidelines of 8 to 14 percent were lowered to 10 percent within six months as the recession deepened. Finally, this was reduced to no fixed percentage, with wage increases earned only through productivity increases.

More importantly, over the life of the two-year program, of every collective agreement settled voluntarily, not one was forced into the regulations. The regulatory gun held to negotiators' heads produced the desired public policy outcome, and "jump or be pushed" became the catchphrase that was soon brought to bear on other problems.

THE ELECTION HELD on May 5, 1983, was another hotly contested battle between Bill Bennett and Dave Barrett. The NDP were confident of victory; when the writ was dropped they were seven points ahead in the polls.

Bennett had been given advice the previous fall by his team of electoral advisers. Bud Smith, at that time the campaign "wagonmaster," explains:

> The '83 campaign actually started in the fall of '82. We were at the Delta River Inn, in a big room. And there were people who knew everything about politics, Alan Gregg and Pat Kinsella. I was there as well. And we were there to tell Premier Bennett that we recommended that he call an election. This was in, I think, September '82, because we were a few points ahead in the polls and we knew it was going to be a tight election.
>
> He came into the room. He listened to all of us, got up and thanked us for our work. We were getting ready for him to say, "We're going to drop the writ tomorrow." But he finished up his speech by saying: "Thank you very much, but there won't be an election."
>
> We were dumbfounded by that. And I think individually and collectively we drew the conclusion that this guy didn't know what the hell he was doing. How could he possibly go against the will of all these people and all this polling and sampling? The organization was ready to go. The fundraisers had already done the job, there was money in the bank, *et cetera*.
>
> Fast forward then to April 1983, and we still have a year to go. And we could wait till fall. It is exactly the same gang. We're in the same room. And the advice Premier Bennett is given is, well, we're ready to go, but, he should not... it would be very foolish to call an election because we were about four and a half, five points behind in the polls.

> He got up and he thanked us for all our efforts. And we were certain to a man that he was going to concur with us. Then he said, "I will be going to the lieutenant governor tomorrow afternoon and there will be an election on May 5."
>
> What was he thinking about? We knew for sure he was nuts.
>
> Once again he proved us, the experts, wrong.

Bennett knew the secret of success in B.C. politics: wait until you have bottomed out in the polls, run on the way up. In the fall of 1982 he was ahead but slipping. In the spring of 1983 he was behind, had bottomed out and was gradually rising. Once he had turned the corner, he would rely on his new electoral machine to make up the difference and surge ahead.

His friend Hugh Harris, now executive director of the Social Credit Party, submitted an extensive report that would change the party from a largely volunteer outfit to a professional party machine. Hugh had interviewed nearly every constituency president about what had gone wrong with the Socreds. He and Bud Smith, acting as his recorder, had travelled many miles talking to other people about what went wrong. He had also travelled to Alberta and Ontario, as well as other provinces, to learn about their electoral machinery. He had visited the Republican national convention and spent time in Washington, D.C., with the professionals. He came to like best Ontario's Conservative Party's approach, that of the "big blue machine."

Hugh and Bennett met to review the report. Hugh outlined the problem, pulled no punches. They talked it through, and Bennett bought into it. The analysis left no doubt that it was time for a dramatic change. It wouldn't be easy, but it had to be done. Bennett recalls:

> We started to build the organization and get some political expertise, and we had lots of fights with the party in trying to get them to accept this discipline. I became the referee. Various people from both sides, including Hugh, were going to quit at various times. But it had to be done.
>
> And it was done with a certain amount of pain because it was dramatic change in the party: hiring organizers, building the organization

> in the constituencies, making it work, letting everyone know why they were doing certain things and letting them know about the new campaign techniques.

Hugh recommended as a first step that Bennett shore up his office with political help. And he had the right guy in mind: Pat Kinsella, from Ontario. Kinsella remembers being recruited:

> I got a phone call from Mike Burns, the chief fundraiser at the time of the Social Credit Party. He said, "We understand that in Ontario you're about to have an election." And this was in April–May 1981; the election was actually in May. So I said, "Yes, we are," and he said, "Would you mind if we sent someone down to observe how you guys run a campaign? We're looking around to see how we might do it better here in British Columbia." So they in fact did send someone. Hugh Harris came to Ontario. I persuaded Premier Bill Davis [to let Harris observe the campaign], as I was running the campaign in those days in '81. I told him that in Ontario this job was being part of the cabinet meetings that Bill Davis had. I sat behind the ministers, and I was there to observe like a cabinet secretary. I was there to report on the party.

Harris not only observed, but on his return he recommended that Bennett hire Kinsella. They met. Bennett told Kinsella that his deputy, Lawrie Wallace, was retiring, so the only position he had was deputy minister to the premier and head of the public service. Kinsella accepted.

It wasn't long before he got into trouble. He ordered $15,000 of new custom-made furniture for his office. When Bennett heard, he cancelled. Pat hadn't quite grasped the premier's view of spending money, especially taxpayers' money. The media went after him.

Then, during the throne speech, when he was invited to sit on the floor of the legislature, he told NDP MLA Charles Barber to be quiet and quit heckling. When Barber discovered the next day that the stranger on the floor of the legislature was the new hired gun from Ontario, all hell broke loose. Again, Bennett provided administrative guidance, sending Pat up to wade through a sea of microphones and apologize to Barber. Kinsella recalls, "The premier was a little embarrassed on my behalf, and we met in his office. He asked, 'Did you really say that?' And I said, 'I couldn't help myself.' The premier replied, 'You have no choice, you're going to have to go to his office and you're going to have to apologize. And, by the way, great start.'"

Kinsella brought more than a pretty face to the office. He stopped the practice of the premier setting the cabinet agenda through choosing from the list, prepared by his secretary, of ministers' requests. He argued and won agreement that cabinet needed more discipline and fixed processes. He spoke Bennett's language, and a cabinet secretariat was established. Its first secretary, chosen for his loyalty, personality and intelligence, was David McPhee.

Bennett and Kinsella also recognized that being deputy minister and head of the public service was not Pat's forte. He needed to be on the political side. Kinsella became principal secretary, and the premier's office became an even greater force on the cabinet, the party and the business community. Norman Spector had been brought in by Bennett as assistant deputy minister and had earned his spurs. He became deputy minister and head of the public service, bringing discipline and highly tuned analytical skills to the bureaucracy. Spector and Bennett fit together like hand in glove. Adults, but somewhat like father and precocious child.

A third member of the team was Doug Heal. Also brought in from Ontario, as a specialist in communication, he analyzed the government's problems and he wrote the report on how to fix it. Cost: $24,131. Doug then joined the staff, filling perfectly the job description he wrote, and soon hired a team that brought both consistency and content to all government communications.

Dave Laundy, who succeeded Heal, describes the communications approach taken in B.C. and later copied in other provinces:

> The division was run by a professional communicator with deputy minister rank. The premier now had three key senior advisers: deputy minister in charge of the public service, principal secretary in charge

of politics and communications counsel in charge of all government communications. They had equal rank and standing, and all of them attended every cabinet meeting.

Cabinet decision making had three key components: policy discussion, political discussion and communications. Therefore, key government messages, which were factually correct and politically sensitive, were agreed upon and delivered professionally. Senior communications counsel were assigned to work with individual ministers as their politically attuned communications advisers. They knew what was going on because after every cabinet meeting my number one job was to brief them thoroughly.

Ministry communications staff, the civil service professionals, reported to their deputies. They provided the myriad of non-political communications services that every government handles daily.

Government messaging was made consistent, and the boys in GIS (Government Information Services) had no shame. Nothing was sacred. One of their first projects was to design a new licence plate for the province incorporating the "wavey flag" symbol that had been used extensively by the Social Credit Party in its election campaigns. Make the people think there is no difference between Social Credit and the government. When Laundy brought the design to cabinet for final approval, Bennett remarked: "I can hardly wait to see Dave Barrett fasten this licence plate to his car."

Norman Spector did not know the others from Ontario. He was a professional public servant, they were political operatives. Peter Ladner, writing in *Vancouver* magazine in January 1984, noted: "The Ontario Connection, however, is not as simple as the B.C. press describe it, which is why Norman Spector resisted being labelled 'the lad from Ontario' by the *Province*'s Allen Garr, and 'Ontario-born' by the *Sun*'s Victoria-in-chaos correspondent, the charming Marjorie Nichols. He sued them both, in one of those strictly PR suits, shrewdly hiring NDP leadership prospect David Vickers as lawyer."

Bennett also knew his electoral machinery was ready. When Rafe Mair resigned in 1981 to become a talk-show radio host, a by-election had been held in Kamloops. The Socreds entered the fray nineteen points behind the NDP.

Mair had resigned directly by letter to the Speaker. He thought this was how it was done. He did not realize that this automatically triggered a by-election in six months, thereby taking away any leverage the premier might have had in setting the date. He told his old friend Bud Smith, who understood the unintended consequence.

Bud phoned Bennett, told him what Rafe had done and informed him of the consequences. His advice was to have the premier invite Rafe to come to his office. Rafe did and, embarrassed, explained what he had done. Together they decided the best thing to do was hold a joint press conference, as if it had been planned all along, and this they did. A quick recovery, and nobody the wiser.

BENNETT INSISTED THAT his ministers regularly get out of Victoria and talk to the people. One way in which he formalized this was through semi-annual cabinet or cabinet committee tours. Mike Bailey had joined Bennett's office as executive director in charge of administration—mail, tours, general Mr. Fix-it. Once a cabinet tour was final, he would scurry out to the designated regions and, working with protocol staff and local government agents, organize the trips. Bailey insisted that the bureaucracy respond by preparing briefing books by city, town or village, covering any possible issue that might arise—an immense piece of work that the bureaucracy hated, as they felt no one read these pages anyway. And, with the exception of the premier and some keen ministers, few did.

The press travelled with the entourage, which helped to break the formality and "humanize" both sides. Over a scotch and water, differences mellowed. (The premier never participated.) These excursions also led to interesting insights. On a train going north of Prince George after the cabinet meeting, columnist Jim Hume stood in the narrow hallway, speaking with Don Phillips, when Bennett squeezed past.

Hume said, "Don't worry, Premier, he's only giving me the lowdown on what happened in cabinet."

Bennett replied, "That's okay. He's our official leak. We left the unofficial leak at home."

Bemused, Hume sat down and thought, who was the unofficial leak left at home? Then it occurred to him, and he chuckled: "Rafe Mair!"

THE POLITICAL MACHINE that Bennett had built using Hugh Harris's advice was ready for a test drive. In the Kamloops by-election, they had a good candidate in local radio executive Claude Richmond. For most of the by-election, Barrett was in New Zealand attending a world conference on socialism. Every weekend of the by-election Bennett was in the riding, spending day after day in the small towns that surround Kamloops. He explained the problems B.C. faced and outlined the solutions. He answered questions.

The 1975 campaign model, largely forgotten in 1979, had been refined by Hugh Harris using the most modern techniques available in North America. This approach was coupled with the efforts of thousands of volunteers, many who travelled up to the Loops for the weekend. They out-organized the NDP and worked door by door on the ground. When the election was over, Claude Richmond had won. The Socred electoral machine, now that it had been test-driven, would be applied across the province for the general election.

But tragedy struck when Harris suddenly died. It affected Bennett deeply: "He was a long-time personal friend as well as a close associate politically. We will miss him very much, as I know he will be missed by countless other people who knew him for his warmth and good humour, qualities that extended far beyond his associates in the political arena." Then Bennett couldn't help but add: "You know, if Hugh had organized the service, he would have worried about the size of the crowd. And he probably would have sent Mike Bailey out to divert the ferry traffic from Tsawwassen just to make sure there were enough people."

Jerry Lampert, who had migrated to Lotus Land from Ontario's big blue machine, was able to step in and help run the party. Bennett now clearly understood his role as premier and party leader and devoted his time and attention to fostering success. To better his odds he hired Allan Gregg, the whiz kid co-founder of the Decima polling company, who had handled Ontario's Conservative Party account. Pat Kinsella describes the first meeting between Gregg and Bennett:

> Allan is a character first and a pollster second. I'll never forget sitting in the premier's office. The premier is sitting there and Allan has done his baseline in the fall of '81, and he's looking at the numbers. He says something like this to Bill Bennett:
>
> "You're essentially fucked."
>
> Allan had this way with words that the premier wasn't used to. He said, "Unless you do some things differently you're on a downward slide here. Emerging from this poll is the fact that you've got to get a little more friendly. Bill Bennett, you've got to be seen to be out there.
>
> "You are seen as a hardass good leader. But there's got to be a softness to you. You're determined to do the right thing, but in the process there are a lot of people out there who don't quite understand it; you've got to explain it, and you've got to be softer."

The "tough guy" had to soften up his image.

DAVE BARRETT HAD a difficult time as leader of the opposition in his last term. Not that he wasn't his normal fiery self, but having suffered his second defeat at Bennett's hands in 1979, he was not certain he should stay on as leader.

On the plus side, he had led the NDP to a huge comeback in the 1979 election. More seats, popular vote up significantly. The leaders of the Liberal and Conservative parties had been defeated, and B.C. was now a true two-party province. This polarization had forced clear choices, and with the clear choice limited to the NDP and Social Credit, Barrett had shown he could do very well. An NDP victory was not out of the question.

On the negative side, Barrett had already lost twice to Bennett. He had been NDP leader for almost ten years, a long time—perhaps too long, in many people's minds.

A cabinet tour in Kimberley, in search of local colour. Mike Bailey must have forgotten to arrange for a crowd. (ROYAL BRITISH COLUMBIA MUSEUM, PROVINCIAL ARCHIVES # I-68033)

The work in the Pacific Rim pays off: Bennett opens the Toyota wheel factory in 1980 as Don Phillips, the minister in charge, looks on. (COURTESY DON PHILLIPS)

Opening the Alex Fraser Bridge: Premier Bennett and Minister of Highways Alex Fraser. (COURTESY BONNIE GAVIN)

Friends meet at the Premiers Conference, Victoria, 1981: Alberta's Peter and Jeanne Lougheed chat with B.C.'s Bill and Audrey Bennett. (ROYAL BRITISH COLUMBIA MUSEUM, PROVINCIAL ARCHIVES # I-68032)

A different dynamic at the Premiers Conference, Victoria, 1981: Quebec's René Lévesque listens to B.C.'s Bill Bennett. Lévesque's wife, Corrine Côté Lévesque, looks down; the tension is palpable. (ROYAL BRITISH COLUMBIA MUSEUM, PROVINCIAL ARCHIVES # I-68031)

Downtown Kamloops is revitalized with the announcement that the B.C. Lottery Corporation will be headquartered there. Tourism minister and local MLA Claude Richmond stands at the podium as Bennett fields a question. Provincial Secretary Jim Chabot looks on. (ROYAL BRITISH COLUMBIA MUSEUM, PROVINCIAL ARCHIVES # I-68030)

Cooking up a deal at the B.C. Pavilion, Expo 86 *(left to right)*: Patrick Read, Bill Bennett, Don Phillips and Jimmy Pattison. (COURTESY DON PHILLIPS)

Bennett accepts an invitation to sit down with Chinese Premier Zhao Ziyang in Beijing. Ideological differences aside, the two hit it off.
(COURTESY MIKE BAILEY)

B.C. Place as it looked on November 7, 1981: a hole in the ground and a dream for a new Vancouver.
(H.C. ADDINGTON, COURTESY PAUL MANNING)

The Queen invites the world to Expo 86. Her Majesty the Queen of Canada, Elizabeth II, and Premier Bill Bennett lead the procession, followed by Prince Philip, Audrey Bennett, and the Right Honourable Pierre Elliott Trudeau. (TED GRANT, COURTESY PAUL MANNING)

The Prince and Princess of Wales visit Victoria: at the B.C. legislature, on the occasion of their visit to open Expo 86. Audrey and Bill Bennett stand to the left of Diana. (COURTESY DAVE LAUNDY)

A few who gave the corner office labour relations advice. Before dinner at Le Gavroche, Vancouver, September 1986 *(left to right, back row)*: Ed Peck, Don Jordan, Bob Plecas, Jim Matkin, Vince Ready, David Emerson, Stu Hodgson; *(seated)* Norman Spector and Bill Bennett. (COURTESY BOB PLECAS)

Although he remained ambivalent, his wife, Shirley, felt he should stay. She agreed with the senior members of caucus, who felt that while they had lost, Barrett's accomplishments in bringing them this close was more like a tie than a loss. But in his gut, he knew that a tie in politics was a lot like kissing your sister.

The opposition made hay over issues like "dirty tricks" and "Gracie's finger." For the first year they seemed to be gathering momentum. But then Barrett began to travel: Israel, Germany, New Zealand. He was a much-sought-after commodity as a former social democratic premier from the wild west coast of Canada. However, this left the major fights in the legislature to be fought by other NDP members. It is flattering to speak at international conferences, but nobody in Israel, New Zealand or Germany votes here.

But the opposition NDP members were attacking effectively every day in the legislature. Charles Barber from Victoria went after Pat Jordan, arguing that she was in breach of the Constitution Act for receiving pay as a cabinet minister when the Act did not provide the authority for her appointment. Stu Leggatt led the fight against the North East Coal development.

They would get on a roll, but then internal squabbles would become irritants. Bob Williams, for example, had already accepted $80,000 for giving up his seat to Barrett after his defeat in the 1975 election. He was expected to disappear, but like something stuck to the bottom of your shoe, he and the aroma he carried as the NDP's grim reaper wouldn't go away. He decided to make a comeback and challenge Barrett's running mate, Alex MacDonald, in Vancouver East in the next election. Barrett intervened directly with Williams, asking him to stand down, to no effect. Barrett and MacDonald both won the nomination, but the fight raised questions about the leader's ability to hold the party together. Hearing rumours and rumblings, Barrett called for a caucus retreat in Nanaimo in August 1982.

Two members, Charles Barber from Victoria and Graham Lea from Prince Rupert, argued against Barrett continuing. They felt strongly that a new leader, with new ideas and energy, was needed to beat the Socreds. Vancouver Centre MLA Emery Barnes countered their arguments by suggesting that while Barrett may have had these faults, he was the best bet they had. A caucus vote went strongly in favour of the incumbent.

This seemed to forge the party back together, and the members turned to get ready for the next election. When the government introduced the restraint package, they were surprised but soon ready. It was an issue they could fight, one they saw as attacking unionized workers. They couldn't quite believe their luck; who would run on cutting back government spending? Not them; no one had ever done it. Surely the public would not stand for it.

Their analysis was not sophisticated enough to distinguish the impact of the recession on private-sector workers, unionized or not, from the perceived Bennett attacks on public-sector unionized supporters.

THE ELECTION CALLED for May 5, 1983, rolled along much as expected. Both sides fielded incredibly competent campaign machines. Neither side had money problems. The media began to suggest that Barrett was in the lead, and indeed internal Socred polls showed they were up about 4 percentage points.

As the campaign rolled along, the Socreds began to pick up momentum. The press were still skeptical but began to catch on, as Bud Smith reports:

> The very first day of the campaign after Bennett's press conference, we start off in Kamloops and go on the bus to Chase and end up in Salmon Arm for an evening rally. [laughing] And in the small downtown in Chase the van went pursuing all small businesses to literally shut down: "Put a sign on the door—Closed for today to see Bill Bennett." That was pretty good theatre. And then in Salmon Arm we had a rally. And I sat in the audience to get a feel for the speech, which I ultimately heard four times a day for thirty-two days. And afterwards I had a pint with my old pal, Marjorie Nichols.
>
> She offered the view that he was really flat, it was dull, the audience wasn't really into it and so on. So I went and talked to Bill in the evening and reported to him what I found. He said, "Give it a couple of days. I don't think they're bored. I think they're actually listening and learning and they don't know where the applause lines are yet. And after they've

heard it a few times and it's been reported a few times, that will change." And indeed, that was the case.

I think that the person who's able to be well liked and to sell hope is the one who wins. All the elections that Bill Bennett ran in were like this. When you did polls about who you'd rather go to the hockey game with, people would say they'd rather go with Dave Barrett than Bill Bennett. But when you said to them who you'd rather have looking after your money, they'd say Bill Bennett rather than Dave Barrett.

Barrett always lapsed into negativity. All his campaigns were about negativity. All of Bennett's campaigns were about where he wanted to go in the future.

And it did resonate. And it resulted ultimately in a win.

As part of a long campaign day, Bennett squeezed in a visit to Atlin, in the far northwest of the province. It was his fifty-first birthday. It was a beautiful day, a glorious start, great-to-be-alive kind of day. Oh, the slippery slopes of politics!

The riding was represented by "Landslide Al" Passeral, who had won the last election by one vote. Having lived in the legislature, this colourful outgoing member crossed the floor to join Social Credit from the NDP, just as his predecessor had. The NDP was too urban-centred for his liking. The riding covered a huge geographical area with only a few thousand voters, and a personal visit by the premier might just tip the balance.

Arriving by float plane, and with only a journalist pool because of the transport problems into the isolated area, the wagonmaster for the trip, Bud Smith, decided to disrupt the planned events, a practice greatly frowned upon by experienced "pols," and visit a film set. The pool concept meant that whatever one television crew got, all the networks would show that night.

Justis Greene, the Canadian film producer for the movie *The Clan of the Cave Bear,* had persuaded the election team to come and visit the set. The visuals were great. Wagonmaster Smith had one condition; Justis was to introduce every person working on the set by name and occupation, to give the premier an opportunity for an immediate comeback line.

This worked well: "Bill Bennett, this is Joe Smith, he is in charge of lighting, etc." Well, almost.

Having met most of the crew, Justis led Bill over to a very attractive female.

"Bill, I would like you to meet Daryl Hannah."

Justis did not mention what this woman did on set as he had for everyone else because, after all, it was Daryl Hannah. Bennett replied:

"Pleased to meet you. What do you do?"

"I'm the star. What do you do?"

"I am the premier."

"Uhh... what's that?"

And turned and walked away.

Audrey, who was standing close by, just rolled her eyes.

The media coverage out of Atlin, and the lead story on all newscasts, was: "Uhh... what's that?"

It didn't get any better. Later that day in Terrace, protesters threw eggs, disrupting the planned events and splattering Audrey.

And it got worse. Moving on to an evening event in Smithers, an inebriated aboriginal continually heckled Bennett until the exasperated premier pulled a twenty-dollar bill from his pocket and offered it to the man if he would shut up and go back to the bar. The press had a field day. They considered Bennett's actions racist at worst, condescending at best.

But the worst birthday in his life didn't end there. Taking his seat on a Vancouver-bound plane at midnight, he smashed his head into the overhead baggage compartment. Reeling back and touching his head to feel for blood, he looked at two reporters and said: "I should let the assholes have the province. I don't need this, I just don't need this."

The reporters were too stunned by this out-of-character remark, and it was never reported.

An interesting footnote to this story. After Bennett had announced that he was stepping down, he was in his Kelowna office clearing it out when he looked up to see a large, young Native man standing in front of him. The kid said: "Premier Bennett, I don't know if you remember me, but I was the guy who heckled you in Terrace and I wanted to apologize and tell you I was wrong. Here is the twenty dollars you gave me."

Bennett was so surprised and touched that he forgot to ask for the interest.

But it was Dave Barrett who made the biggest gaffe of the campaign. As he notes in *Barrett: A Passionate Politcal Life*: "The Socred restraint program was the primary issue, and I had a sense the message was sinking in... in an interview with BCTV, I said the NDP would probably scrap the restraint program because it was just scare tactics and had no economic foundation. The alarm bells sounded. The clip was played and replayed and the election turned around overnight."

The Socred campaign team disputes this theory, arguing that its internal polling showed the tide had already turned and by the time of Barrett's statement the Socreds were ahead. Whichever is true, in the public's mind this was and remains the mythical tale of how the election was won.

Bennett heard of Barrett's statement when he arrived in Cranbrook after a long bus ride. He said it was nothing new and was going to get some rest. It was mid-afternoon, and he had picked up a dogged cold that had lasted over a week. He was exhausted and not sleeping well.

Campaign manager Pat Kinsella had decided to join this leg of the trip and agreed that Bennett should rest. Kinsella, jokingly referred to as "Shoppers Drug Mart" because he always had cold pills, vitamins, decongestants, nasal sprays and various other health-related medicines in his briefcase, was called upon to produce a mild sleeping tablet, which he did. Bennett, who never takes any medication, was persuaded to ingest this to get a much-needed few hours' sleep.

Later that afternoon BCTV reporter Clem Chapple approached Kinsella with an offer to go "live" on the six o'clock news. "BCTV at Six," the largest and most influential news broadcast in the province, would uplink the first live, on-location satellite broadcasts in B.C. political history. Kinsella agreed to the offer. He remembers it this way:

> We got the word that Barrett had said, "If and when I become premier I'm going to get rid of the restraint program." And the word got up to us

on the bus and Bud reacted very quickly and efficiently. The premier was told about it, and he was going to have a speech that night. But he was having a nap in the afternoon, and Clem Chapple said we could actually get Bill Bennett live on the news at six. They installed it so they could interview Bill at 6:01. It's not on tape, it's live.

So Bill Bennett is in the bedroom of this suite having a little nap. Clem is climbing through the window installing this stuff, and Bud Smith and I haven't told the premier what we had planned because he was napping. And we had to go to Audrey with thirty minutes to go and say "Pssssst, can you get him sort of ready for this, because as you know he will at least have to shave?"

I mean, he could have shaved at four, and by six he'd have to shave again.

But he was fabulous, we did some cardboard teleprompters, and to his credit Bill Bennett got up and said, "What are we doing? Okay. Good, fine." And he had a shave and put his tie on and sat behind the desk in his suite. Bud was holding up a reminder of what Bill should say. But no one told Bill Bennett what to say. And he said he was very distressed by these comments, and of course the way it played out was perfectly.

Oh, and I think there's some truth in the rumour that Bud told Clem: "If you shoot below the waist, I'm pulling the plug."

IN GETTING THE premier dressed for live TV, Audrey hadn't quite got the pants up and zipped. But the premier focused, and delivered.

He insisted the message was not new. Barrett had said it all before, and he had reacted before, what was the big deal? But B.C. was to experience its first Marshall McLuhan moment—the medium was the message. The momentum swung dramatically towards the Socreds.

The election was won. Bennett's Socreds received 49.8 percent of the vote. Barrett, 45 percent. Social Credit won 35 seats, NDP 22.

Bennett had won a decisive victory. He had not achieved the two goals he set himself: 50 percent plus one in the popular province-wide vote and 70 percent in his constituency. His father had once obtained a 70 percent win in the constituency, and the ever-competitive son wanted to better it. He didn't, but he was back in business as premier.

He also learned a lesson: "What we found out is that the Allen Garrs of the world are completely irrelevant when it comes to an election."

THE TENT-ROOM was structured around a square set of tables, hollow in its centre, with ministers seated in no particular order around the square. Deputy ministers, and one other staff person, sat in chairs behind their minister. Bennett knew that to effect the sea change he was planning, everyone in the room, not just ministers, had to buy in.

Proceeding ministry by ministry, in alphabetical order, he called on the ministers to outline their plans. The ministers' deputies would join at the table, and they would describe what steps they were going to take to meet the 25 percent reduction in staffing directed by cabinet, as well as how they were going to hold expenditures to last year's level.

Different ministers approach these exercises in different ways. They tend to fall into five categories. One puts up straw men, believing they won't be accepted, is horrified when they are, and privately begs the premier to change and substitute other programs. The second kind of minister strongly urges cuts in other colleagues' budgets but aggressively defends his or her own as special cases.

The third kind is the tough guy, argues the cuts are not deep enough. Jim Nielsen, a tough guy, would mutter asides like: "Why is it dove shit smells so much worse than hawk shit?"

The fourth kind of minister sees the writing on the wall and simply goes along—fortunately, these are in the majority.

The last kind of minister willingly makes the cuts as part of the team but has a pet peeve. Bob McClelland, as the labour minister, quietly discussed his cuts. When he had completed his comments and just before the premier moved on, he said: "Premier, I have been thinking about the Human Rights Commission. Everyone here believes it is out of control. So I think we should cut it."

"Any comments?"

"None. Everyone in favour?"

"Yes. Done. Bob, proceed."

McClelland comments:

> I guess I was surprised. I was never a fan of the Human Rights Commission or of human rights commissions. I think that we need to be awfully careful about protecting human rights, but I don't think you can set up commissions that do it. If you look at individual rights and the need for someone to go somewhere if his rights are hampered, then that's important, but this commission took on far more than that. They became a force that can intervene; they were really almost a government sort of organization, and they forgot the little people that they were supposed to be serving: I felt that was wrong. We decided we would revamp it. It was never really destroyed, but a lot of its functions were changed.

Once this horse was out of the barn, other ministers decide to move on other programs. They got caught up in the atmosphere of the day and, on impulse, cut parts of government that many British Columbians thought were hallowed parts of the safety net. Hugh Curtis comments:

> It took on a life of its own. This was a session to cut back, cut back, cut back. Those were the priorities numbered one, two and three. And I've often thought that doing away with the Human Rights Commission then was foolish and unnecessary. Similarly with the motor vehicle testing stations because in terms of total budget, they were peanuts.

The instructions to prepare for the meeting had been concise. Prepare plans for ministry 25 percent reductions or expenditure freezes. Review service levels to determine need and relevance.

The rationale was also concise: British Columbia was in the worst recession in its modern history. Natural resource revenues were down by 50 percent. It was a small, open economy. Revenues, wealth generation and employment were cyclical because B.C. sold commodities on a world market and at fluctuating world prices. Government had a structural deficit; it was unable to balance its budget at the low points in the cycle because it had overspent in program areas that had become permanent. It must realign its expenditures, and this meant reducing program and staffing costs, to enable a balanced budget at the low point of the cycle, and when the economy swung up to use the surplus to make further non-structural expenditures. Bennett and his cabinet were determined to get the province's finances right to ensure long-term growth and wealth generation.

Doing it now, doing it once, and then living within the province's means would see the province never having to go through this exercise again. Well. Hmmm. That was the theory.

BENNETT HAD TWO tactical calls of considerable importance to make. What should be the premier's role in the next few months? Should he change his management practice of being hands-off?

He recognized that the 1983 budget and the legislative program the cabinet had planned would be controversial. Managing change is always difficult, and this dramatic restructuring would be most difficult.

His cabinet was firm in its resolve, but as in all cabinets some ministers were firmer than others. If the going got tough, some would begin to waiver. Some would go to the other extreme and toughen up. A balance would be needed.

The second tactical call was whether to place before the legislature the complete package of budget and legislative initiatives on budget day. His choice was to table the budget and a few pieces of legislation, gauge the result, then introduce a few more pieces of legislation, wait, introduce a few more and so on for a few weeks until it was all in, carefully monitoring public opinion before proceeding.

One approach was a dramatic bold move that would force the cabinet to stand together behind what they had collectively defined. If it was all in, there could not be any wavering. The other approach might spook ministers as opposition mounted, leading them to argue against proceeding or to wait until next year. The pressure from their constituents was going to be immense. Like being pecked to death by a gaggle of ducks.

The second tactical call was made first. All the legislation would be introduced on budget day.

Bennett could now consider his role. Who should be the public face of the initiative? He decided to abandon his usual strategy of staying behind the scenes, for three reasons. The first was that he did not think any one minister could stand up to the public outcry. He had to be the one to stay the course. Mike Bailey comments:

> We were discussing what internally came to be known as the restraint on government program, and the premier was speaking. It was very clear that he was thinking of taking all the soon-to-come heat on himself. I'm listening, and I said, "Premier, with respect, that's not right." He looked at me. [chuckling] And it was so logical what he said: "You know what we're going to be doing here. You have some idea of the impact of what we're going to be doing. How many of my MLAs do you think actually have the strength to go home every weekend to Main Street, British Columbia, walk down their town's main street, and be able to stay strong and stick with the message in front of their irate constituents?" And I held up my fingers as a zero. He said, "It may be that close. But I do."
>
> So all of that heat he purposely directed on himself. He wanted it because he felt that it needed to be done, but he also felt that he was the one that could take it.

His second reason for taking the heat was that he already knew he would be retiring this term. He had decided this immediately after the 1983 election. He would wait a while to discuss it with Audrey, but he knew she would be in favour. He had a few things that he wanted to ensure went forward: this one, Expo, the redevelopment of Vancouver, the Coquihalla completion, the renewal of the party, a few others and he was gone.

The third reason flowed from the second. Because he would be gone when the next election rolled around, he would absorb the criticism that would soon be forthcoming. The new leader could then distance himself or herself and, with the winds of a successful Expo blowing, sail to another Social Credit victory. Bennett knew the NDP. They would not be able to resist targeting him, and not the party, in the run-up to the next election. They had never got over their initial perception of him. When he stepped aside, their target would be gone.

This is sophisticated succession planning in politics. It requires a leader not worried about his legacy but about the success of his party. Bennett had a strategic framework in mind. He would not share it with anyone because it involved stepping down as premier, and if this got out he would be a dead duck, or at least a lame one. He recalls:

> The decision was made in '83, subject to certain things happening. That is, it was almost a prayer: "Oh God, if we can get through all of this and try to get the economy going and if we can contain government costs and show that we've stabilized the deficit, and if we get Expo working... If I can get the party cranked up and if it's really working—then I'm going." I had a dozen things that had to happen. It was a conditional decision. I had made it when I first entered politics—that it'd be two terms. And I had that decision in mind when I went into '83, but I couldn't leave then.

ONE PIECE OF legislation, the Public Sector Restraint Act, Bill 3, still did not have a sponsoring minister as budget day approached. And no one was stepping forward to handle what was expected to be a hot potato. Section 2 of the bill allowed the government, and all other public-sector employers, to fire public servants, irrespective of where they worked—in government, schools, universities, health care providers, crown corporations—without cause. This provision affected some 250,000 workers. Simply put, for whatever reason the employer decided to fire you, you were fired, irrespective of your employment rights or collective agreement rights.

Bill 3 was poorly drafted by the Legislative Council under the direction of the minister of labour with the assistance of outside consultants more ideological than skilled in sophisticated interventions. It had other tough sections; for example, it contemplated regulating and arbitrarily rolling back the pay of senior executives.

When the premier's deputy minister, Norman Spector, first saw Bill 3 it was only three days until budget day. He shook his head and knew it was going to cause much unnecessary trouble. He had looked at the whole package and knew trouble loomed on the horizon. He appealed to the premier to cancel only one bill, the proposal to abolish the human rights legislation. He was turned down.

Spector raised Bill 3 with the premier but in a different context. He told him he had shown the draft legislation to experts and they were concerned. The premier listened and agreed that he would revisit the bill once a minister was in charge. Norman pointed out that no minister wanted the responsibility. The two men reviewed their options: Hugh Curtis, no, enough on his plate; Bob McClelland, no, as minister of labour he should be seen as attempting to be neutral; not Brian Smith, the attorney general, who must stay out of the fray in his special role of cabinet minister and legal watchdog, nor any minister of an affected line ministry like health or education. Who?

They settled on Jim Chabot, the provincial secretary and minister of government services. The Government Employees Relations Bureau (GERB), which was responsible for representing the provincial government as employer in collective bargaining with its own employees, reported through him to cabinet, although in fact Chabot had little to do with them.

Chabot was a long-serving member from Invermere and had served in W.A.C. Bennett's cabinet as minister of labour for a few years in the early 1970s. A Yoda-like figure, he was a grade ten graduate, a bilingual conductor on the CNR and a tough, scrappy member of the legislature who more than held his own. He was also much liked on both sides of the House for his sense of humour and poker-playing ability. If he faced questions in debate that he did not want to answer he might switch to French, which of course is legal, leaving the opposition members shaking their heads and laughing. The television in his office was constantly on, not for the news but for the stock market ticker.

Chabot was not the kind of member who worried about the fine details of the law, so he would need sound technical advice. In areas of labour the premier's office would normally look to Jim Matkin over in the intergovernmental relations ministry, but he had left to take up a new post as president of the Business Council of B.C. They turned to Jim's right-hand guy, the secretary for federal–provincial relations.

Spector briefed him on Bill 3 and another piece of legislation, the Public Sector Labour Relations Act, Bill 2—a nasty piece of work that cleaned out of the government's collective agreement with the B.C. Government Employees' Union (BCGEU)—the sections that the government negotiators couldn't get at. Bill 2 had been put forward by Mike Davidson, the head of GERB, as the only way to knock out these provisions.

Reading section 2 of Bill 3, Spector and the secretary for federal–provincial relations agreed that the "without cause" was unnecessary and should go. Could they, in the two days remaining, convince cabinet? Spector made an appointment with the premier and several key ministers the following day after Question Period to make the pitch for changing the section. The next morning the secretary told his minister, Garde Gardom, that he had been handed another assignment by the premier's office. He was to meet the premier and a few ministers to discuss Bill 3 following Question Period that day.

That afternoon, as Question Period wound down, the secretary and Spector sat outside the premier's office waiting for the meeting. Then Jas Gandhi, the premier's secretary—who combined efficiency with a compassionate spirit—told both men that the meeting had been switched. The minister of intergovernmental relations, who was also chair of the legislative committee of cabinet, which reviews all law before tabling it in the House, had grabbed the premier on his way from the chamber and told him that the committee was meeting across the hall in the Birch Room. They could discuss Bill 3 there, as there would be a broader cross-section of cabinet in attendance. Bennett agreed.

When the secretary arrived he was asked to present his views, which ministers now understood were different from cabinet's on why the bill should be changed, and how. He did so, flying as close to the flame as possible around political ramifications. Questions flew. Answers were given. The premier listened. After twenty minutes, one minister asked the Legislative Council staff lawyers who had drafted the bill if the proposals now under discussion would allow the government to proceed with certainty.

The senior lawyer replied: "Well, not with certainty, because there might arise issues of what is called 'natural justice,' and perhaps issues of 'judicial fairness' also might see dismissals end up in court. No guarantees, but possible."

That was enough for the ministers. We will move forward. We want certainty, we have a job to get done. Firing without cause was in, and the final table was set for budget day, 1983.

11

RESTRAINT

> *"What Bennett is now trying to do is nothing short of totally redrawing the economic and social contours of his province."*
>
> MACLEAN'S

ON JULY 7, 1983, the conservatively and expensively dressed minister of finance, Hugh Curtis, rose from his seat in the legislature to deliver the budget speech of the newly elected Social Credit government. A rose was pinned to his lapel. The slight smirk on his lips may have been caused by anticipation, or nervousness. The message was a simple one: "Restraint."

When he had called the election on April 7, Bennett had run on the theme of a conservative restraint program. He argued that the public service, in all its many manifestations, must be treated no differently from the private sector, which was then suffering from a worldwide recession. This message had resonated well, leading him and his party to a resounding victory on May 5.

Now, two months later, the Socred version of restraint was unveiled. It took most people's breath away.

The media lockup that day started normally. Coffee and danish while the budget materials were handed out. By nine that morning, in the secure room, where the media and key stakeholders are always given the budget documents to review, the minister of finance and his officials began the pre-briefing. Pre-briefing allows the government to provide the technical details in the budget and to answer questions about it. It also gives the media time to digest the government spin and to gauge the reactions of the key stakeholders.

Markets can rise or fall on the basis of the interpretations of the budget when it is made public. It is essential that the budget messages are clearly understood. The spontaneous release of all the budget information in the afternoon affects marketplace decisions, and this requires the media to have enough time to digest the information. If you want to be spontaneous, you must be well organized.

The program-spending allocations in the budget were moderately conservative, the large amount of capital spending Keynesian. A small deficit, which had been widely rumoured, was evident. Spending on government programs was tightly controlled and held near zero year over year. Capital spending was accelerated to spark the economy and offset the province's 14 percent unemployment rate. The overall budget increase was twelve percent.

The real show began when Curtis finished his budget speech. Minister after minister rose to introduce legislation. This had not been part of the pre-briefing. Twenty-six major pieces of legislation were introduced and given first reading—an unprecedented amount of legislation directed at changing the social contract in B.C.

The opposition was slack-jawed, unbelieving and overwhelmed. The media could not believe the breadth and scope of the legislative package. They collectively pounced. Quickly attacking the legislation, the budget itself was forgotten. As the public began to pay attention, the media made it clear that Social Credit had gone much further than even the most ardent conservative would have thought possible. *Maclean's* magazine commented on October 17, 1983:

> Two months after his Social Credit Party won an overwhelming victory on May 5, voters were stunned by the premier's fierce determination to implement his radical measures virtually overnight. What Bennett is now trying to do is nothing short of totally redrawing the economic and social contours of his province. The heart of that revolution was a legislative program, containing 26 bills that did everything from cutting the civil service by 25 percent to eliminating the human rights commission and rent control board. Underlying the program was an almost messianic fervour. Bennett wants to virtually rewrite the postwar social contract, and change fundamentally the voters' expectations of what their government can do for them.

Simultaneous with the tabling of the budget and the legislation, more than four hundred pink slips were handed out. Some ham-handed administrators, in their cockeyed zeal, were handing out dismissal letters to temporary staff and using the RCMP to find employees who were out camping on weekend excursions to deliver the notices. The front-page headline in the *Province* on July 12 screamed: "Socred hitmen swoop on rights workers." A temporary auxiliary human-rights worker who was blind was fired, and he and his dog appeared as the poster children in most major papers.

The *Province* explained the turmoil: "Stunned and angry public service union leaders have vowed to challenge the thousands of civil service layoffs promised in the provincial budget." It went on to report: "'That's contrary to some international conventions, the Canadian Constitution and perhaps some common law,' said Art Kube, president of the B.C. Federation of Labour."

Bennett was clear in his own thinking about why B.C. was taking this action. He explained in *Maclean's:*

> The international recession caused the change. It struck the industrialized world, this country and British Columbia very hard. With our economy two-thirds export oriented we had to make some very hard decisions. Not only has our economy dropped but the growth rate we

experienced in the 1960s and 1970s is not projected for the 1980s or 1990s. So we have to make our priority decisions now...

Especially resource revenues, which dropped from a high of about $1.6 billion in 1980 to $570 million last year, reducing our total revenues in real terms. This has not happened in any other province—ever...

We're paying $180 million in interest on last year's debt. That is even with the reduced deficits we are achieving through some of our tough actions, which will make a $5 billion to $6 billion difference by 1988–89. That, in turn, will make the difference between carrying interest charges of over $1 billion and having less than half that...

The only jobs that can drive our prosperity are jobs in the private sector. To create them, we have to do everything we can to encourage business investment and broaden our international markets. And that is the program people clearly supported in the election.

No government can spend its way to prosperity. You cannot have one group of people working in the public sector immune from the recession—governments must have the ability to lay off people on the same terms and conditions as the private sector.

Unfortunately, the message couldn't fit on a bumper sticker.

Bennett's decision to have the expected criticism directed at him, rather than his ministers, got off on the wrong foot when he got off message.

"Fired B.C. workers aren't doing their jobs," he said on July 10.

By July 12 he backtracked: "It's all a mistake," he said, calling the statement "an unfortunate story," and adding: "There's no way I want to be confrontative or inflammatory." But the horse was out of the barn, and she had started to run. And run she did, like never before in British Columbia.

What was the legislative package that was so controversial?

- The Public Sector Labour Relations Act stated that no collective agreement would interfere with the government's power to establish and eliminate positions, to assign duties to positions, to establish work schedules and to determine the method of program delivery.

- The Public Sector Restraint Act permitted the government to terminate employees without cause to decrease the size and complexity of public service operations and to increase their efficiency.
- The Income Tax Amendment Act repealed the personal income tax credit and the renter tax credit.
- The Residential Tenancy Act repealed the Office of the Rentalsman and eliminated rent controls.
- The Education Interim Finance Amendment Act gave the government the power to supervise the budgets and expenditures of school districts and to fire unco-operative boards.
- The Alcohol and Drug Commission Repeal Act dissolved the Alcohol and Drug Commission.
- The Municipal Amendment Act eliminated official regional district plans as a deregulation measure.
- The Compensation Stabilization Program Amendment Act extended the wage-restraint program on all public-sector workers and embodied the concept that public-sector salaries must be based on the employer's ability to pay and that productivity increases were the prime justification for pay increases.
- The Tobacco Tax Amendment Act increased the tax rate on tobacco products.
- The Social Service Tax Amendment Act increased the general rate of sales tax from 6 percent to 7 percent and imposed a 7 percent tax on prepared meals and a 7 percent tax on long-distance calls.
- The Institute of Technology Amendment Act gave the government more power to appoint boards of governors and to control courses and programs.
- The College and Institutes Amendment Act eliminated occupational training, academic and management advisory councils and their staff.
- The Crown Corporations Reporting Repeal Act eliminated the staff of the Legislature Crown Corporations Committee.
- The Motor Vehicle Amendment Act removed the requirement that private vehicles be taken to inspection stations once a year, and closed the stations.

- The Medical Services Act gave the Medical Services Commission authority to issue and restrict practitioner billing numbers and to establish and modify payment schedules for different practitioners in different locations.
- The Harbour Board Repeal Act dissolved the B.C. Harbours Board.
- The Employment Standards Amendment Act eliminated a company officer's liability for severance pay in cases of bankruptcy and bank action.
- The Human Rights Act wiped out both the Human Rights Branch and the Human Rights Commission.

And a few other minor pieces, combined with the government's announcement that staff would be reduced by 25 percent, translated into about ten thousand anticipated pink slips. Offices were to close, programs were to be cut.

The strategy moved on two fronts: direct legislation and indirect actions. Direct legislative moves, intended to remove the cost burden from business by making it less expensive and easier to operate, included property tax breaks, less protection for unionized workers and municipal planning decisions not being subject to regional vetoes. The indirect actions that would signal investors that government costs would be kept down included a willingness to eliminate government services, a reduction in government expenditures by cutting the payroll, the introduction of efficiencies to public-sector contracts, such as reining-in public-sector salaries and benefits, and increased central control of all public-sector employers.

The signal to investors was clear: B.C. was getting its house in order and therefore was a good place to invest and create jobs. But on the ground, where government action directly affected people, all hell broke loose.

Within days, the opposition began to consolidate. The B.C. Federation of Labour established a ten-point program of action and, more importantly, put up a $1 million war chest. Rumblings of a general strike began. A new organization was started, borrowing its name from Poland: "Operation Solidarity."

Diverse community groups, religious leaders and academics also came together into a "Solidarity Coalition." They joined together into what was called "Solidarity," but in the public's mind it became and remained "Operation Solidarity." Art Kube, president of the B.C. Federation of Labour, played an inspirational and tireless role in meeting with and bringing together all the diverse groups.

For the first time in the province's history, trade union leaders, albeit mainly from the public sector, cast their lot with community activists. This combination was Solidarity's great strength. It was also its great weakness. Most swords are double-edged.

The *Vancouver Sun* reported it this way on September 28, 1983:

> Solidarity—Premier Bennett's "tyranny of the minorities"—is made up of two branches that its leaders claim represent up to 950,000 people.
>
> Operation Solidarity is a coalition of unions ranging from the B.C. Federation of Labour affiliates to the building trades to the B.C. Teachers' Federation to the B.C. Nurses Union to B.C. members of the nationalist Confederation of Canadian Unions...
>
> Solidarity Coalition is an alliance of community groups headed by an administrative committee chaired by Renate Shearer, Art Kube and Father Jim Roberts. The group also has a 30-member steering committee and 49 coalition associations across B.C....
>
> The difficulty of keeping Solidarity's parts together is exacerbated by its schizophrenic political personality. All those in the coalition are opposed to the Socred budget and its accompanying legislation. But some elements want to go slow, others want to go fast.

Right from the start, Operation Solidarity connected with the public mood and gained momentum. On July 19, BCGEU staff occupied a public-health facility in Kamloops and held it for a few weeks. The next day, six thousand people gathered in Victoria's Memorial Arena.

Even those who might be considered friends of the government entered the fray against the restraint program. On July 22, the heads of both Lower Mainland universities wrote the government protesting that Bill 3 would eliminate academic job tenure. The B.C. Hotels Association issued a release condemning the introduction of a 7 percent tax on meals over seven dollars.

Newspapers across the nation—*The Globe and Mail, Edmonton Journal, Montreal Gazette* and *Ottawa Citizen*—ran headlines such as:

> 400 fired in B.C. bill called fascist
> No redress left for discrimination in B.C.
> B.C. destroying rights: Broadbent
> B.C. reels at "cruel, fascist cutbacks"
> Ottawa offers to help rights groups fight, says Serge Joyal
> Bennett takes a chain saw to the civil service

Other provincial governments were also watching closely. Ontario treasurer Frank Miller commented: "I am watching with trepidation. If Bennett succeeds, every government will be trying the same thing in its own way. If he fails, the cause of government restraint will be set back a decade."

On July 24, twenty thousand people turned up for a rally at B.C. Place. Four days later, more than twenty-five thousand marchers protested on the lawns of the legislature.

IN THE MIDST OF the turmoil, life in the Bennett family went on. Sometimes we forget that politicians have private lives. Death threats were received while teenagers were being raised in the Bennett household. Indeed, their eldest son, Brad, was married that summer. Audrey remembers:

> The summer of 1983 with Operation Solidarity was not fun. It was difficult on my children, it was hard on them. Some teachers were not being professional. And death threats, not on the family, on me. Phone calls, that's why we had the number switched.
>
> The other thing—and this one was quite comical—is that Brad's wedding was at our house, and the police were around. Everywhere I went, they were tailing me. Here I was trying to get this wedding organized, and it's the night of the wedding. We had about 250 people out on the front lawn by the lake, and there were boats out there. We were all

shaking hands with people we didn't know, and it turned out they were all undercover police!

Death threats are never publicized. Hugh Curtis received them, and some senior staff did also. Bennett received the most, of course, and the most serious ones. Mike Bailey recalls:

> We never talked about them, but we can now. No premier really likes to think they need security. It kind of goes against the grain of being a people person.
>
> I'll give you an example. There was one case... this is just my memory. The fellow was from Quesnel. I got a call from the RCMP. What happened, as I understand it, was a woman had been laid off from one of our ministries during the restraint program. Her estranged husband and her father were having coffee, and her estranged husband makes comments to the effect that he's going to get Bill Bennett or whatever. The father-in-law took it enough to heart he thought he should tell the RCMP. This is in a time and place where obtaining guns is a lot easier than it is today—you can walk into a store and buy one. So the RCMP took it seriously. Small town, easy to track down. And indeed, he had got a gun and he left town. So I ordered a massive manhunt. They got him at about Langley, as I recall, on his way.

STAFF WERE TRYING to solve some of the problems resulting from the restraint legislation. The secretary of federal–provincial relations was assigned to report to Jim Chabot and to review the "without cause" section of Bill 3, a section that had become, in the public's mind, a symbol of what was wrong with the restraint program. It was so obviously unfair. The secretary began working closely with the Vancouver-based labour-relations lawyer Don Jordan to craft amendments to the bill. On August 5, Chabot introduced the amendments, redefining "firing without cause" as "dismissal means layoff," which would be explained more fully in regulations to come down in a few days.

Art Kube, president of B.C. Federation of Labour, pushed back: "Bill Bennett is not going to buy off the trade union movement with meaningless cosmetic changes to little parts of his legislation. It is the whole package that has to go."

A *Province* newspaper poll on August 8 found that 58 percent of respondents disapproved of the 25 percent reduction in public service; 50 percent approved of wage restraints on the public service; 60 percent disapproved of limiting items that public unions could bargain; and 54 percent supported unions, while 24 percent supported the government restraint program.

On August 10, forty thousand people turned out for a rally at Vancouver's Empire Stadium. The message was the same from Operation Solidarity. The whole package must be withdrawn. Public-sector trade union leaders, led by Art Kube, shared the stage with community activists. There was a heady feeling that they were winning. The next day, the Business Council's president, Jim Matkin, called for an end to the legislation, the conflict and the protest. "We are not happy about what is going on. It has an unsettling effect on everyone."

EVEN AMONG ALL the turmoil, there were some sectors that were functioning smoothly. This often happens in government when a minister makes a particular effort to understand and get to know personally some of the key players in the interest groups that government is dealing with. A feeling of trust and mutual agreement on the overall direction that government is taking can often overcome controversy. For example, Minister of Health Jim Nielsen got a remarkable deal with the doctors based on building relationships:

> I phoned Dr. Norman Rigby, executive director of the BCMA, and said, "I'd like to see you and your president, Dr. Bill Gorie." So they came out to my place in Richmond on a Saturday, late in the afternoon. We were good friends, so I pulled out a bottle of scotch, because I knew Norman enjoyed a shot of scotch. Half a bottle of scotch later, Dr. Gorie and Norman had agreed to a 7 percent cut in the fee schedule.
>
> And they agreed that they would send out a ballot to their members and recommend it, which they did. And the doctors agreed to a 7 per-

cent cut in the fee schedule, which that year was 31 million bucks. And I think later on, we agreed with a three-year cap on the fee schedule.

AFTER HIS FIRST public statements, the premier stayed out of the media limelight. He sat back to gauge public reaction, following the advice of his deputy, Norman Spector: "In a time of crisis, it is better to be sinned against than to sin." But by August 17, the premier felt it was time to attack on one front. The opposition was filibustering the government's legislative agenda: "Since budget day on July 7, the fifty-seven MLAs haven't completed discussion of a single bill. The NDP has steadily filibustered debate on each one the government has brought forward."

Socred backbencher John Reynolds began to advocate closure. The government, however, decided not to go there yet but to fall back on a technique much used in B.C.: if the opposition want to delay, then the legislature will sit around the clock. Legislation by exhaustion.

But filibuster was the only tool the NDP had. In their view, they had to keep the legislature tied up to enable the external forces under Art Kube's leadership to develop and thus force the government to back down. The Solidarity movement on the streets had become the real opposition.

In the House, the NDP divided itself into three teams, each consisting of an equal number of members and assigned to the floor of the legislature in four-hour shifts. If the "A team" was on the floor, then B and C teams could sleep in their offices.

The government caucus organized itself to ensure that there were always enough members in the House to guarantee a quorum. The other members napped. When the division bells rang throughout the legislature calling the members to a vote, the groggy-looking motley crew would stagger to the floor, representing both sides of the House, and vote before returning to sleep. Wrinkled clothes and unshaven faces were the order of the day. The body odours in the offices—this was August—reminded visitors of summer camp bunkhouses.

Protest marches were held in Kelowna, Kamloops and Prince George. Each attracted four or five thousand demonstrators. The wildfire spread into Socred strongholds. But cracks began to appear in Solidarity. The

Victoria chapter of Operation Solidarity tabled a counter-budget on August 24, which surprised Kube and the other leaders of the movement in Vancouver. It proposed trade-offs that no one there was prepared to make at the time. Kube was critical of the Victoria group, who he claimed were naïve and "walking in a minefield."

The Victoria spokesman, Moe Sihota, tried to repair the tactical mistake caused by his desire for publicity over good strategy: "In no way should our comments be interpreted to mean strife, discord or division with Operation Solidarity."

Voices of reason—that is, those objectively questioning the assumptions of the restraint program and its effect on people—were lost in the noise of the protest march. Sane voices went unheard. Vaughn Palmer, associate editor of the *Vancouver Sun*'s editorial pages, wrote on August 30:

> The provincial government's budget has been called some nasty names this year, most of them allusions to ugly right-wing philosophies. But the budget is decidedly un-conservative if you consider the thing that right-wingers are supposed to consider, namely the bottom line. The increase in spending (12 percent) is way ahead of inflation and the projected deficit ($1.6 billion) is the largest in B.C. history…
>
> In fact, for sheer spending power, the Social Credit plan seems weirdly similar to the economic philosophy of that well-known liberal Franklin D. Roosevelt…

But legislating by exhaustion was still not moving the legislation along quickly. The government decided to use closure.

Closure is a controversial move. In effect, it stops debate in the legislature and a vote is held on the matter under debate. Oppositions rail against the use of closure because often their only power is the power to keep debate going while the public wakes up to the issues. Since the essence of our political system is to create a place, parliament, where elected representatives of the people can debate issues on our behalf, denying that right is serious. It must be approached carefully and only as a last resort. Each parliament in the British parliamentary tradition has its own rules, and the use of closure is rare. But B.C.'s rules are simple. A member stands and informs the Speaker that he or she finds the debate tedious and repetitious and moves that the question be put: the vote must be taken immediately.

In the spring of 1975, Bennett had himself ejected from the legislature when the NDP used closure to force a vote on a budget bill and then toured the province under the slogan "Not a dime without debate." But what is good for the goose in opposition is not necessarily good for the gander in power.

The opposition cried foul every time the Socreds used closure to gain second reading of one of their bills. However, little attention was being paid the NDP in the legislature. Barrett, as leader of the opposition, decided to filibuster the second reading of Bill 3. In a creative way, he made a motion that would see the bill put aside for six months to enable consultation—a hoist motion. He told the Speaker he was the designated speaker on this hoist motion.

One of the non-controversial ways the legislature moves along legislation is by all-party agreement to use closure when it is appropriate. In B.C., existing House rules place limits on the speaking time of everyone except one member, the designated member, who can speak for as long as he or she wants.

Barrett had only started his filibuster, and the press were not interested—they knew he was doing it to get media attention, and it smacked of same old/same old. He had spoken for only three hours and twenty-six minutes. That was enough for the government. It wasn't unnoticed that the press gallery was not paying attention.

Minister of Agriculture Harvey Schroeder asked for clarification of the rules. Did the rules on a designated speaker cover motions, or just the bill itself? A bit of mischief to disrupt the filibuster.

The Speaker of the House, Walter Davidson, was out of the chair, quite normal practice, and MLA John Parks was presiding. He ruled that the rule applied only to the bill itself, not to amendments like the hoist motion.

Barrett challenged the ruling. He describes the results:

> Parks then ordered me ejected. Sergeant-at-arms staff members Dick Nicol, Bill Roach and Jack Dunn waited ten minutes, then converged on

> me seated in my chair. At first they tried to lift me in the chair, but it tipped over. I fell to the floor, arms crossed. They dragged me through the revolving doors of the legislature and deposited me on the red carpet that runs the length of the Speaker's corridor. I had become the first member in the 112-year history of the B.C. legislature to be physically tossed from the House.
>
> My dispute with Parks lasted fifty-seven minutes.

Unfortunately for Barrett, the media had decided this was not of interest. No newspaper, radio or TV coverage. No success. And because Barrett was physically ejected from the legislature, he was suspended for the remainder of the session.

Closure now became a regular practice.

The debate about getting on with the government's business and cutting off debate is one in which your position is determined by the side of the House you sit on. George MacMinn, the long-serving, wise, non-partisan clerk of the House, wrote in his book *Parliamentary Practice in British Columbia:*

> The closure rule is without doubt the most controversial rule in Parliamentary Law. The very sound of closure conjures up the "mailed fist"—the abolition of free speech and the emasculation of the Opposition.
>
> No such reverse images are created by a persistent and heated minority frustrating the business of government with endless filibusters.
>
> Much has been written about the rights of the minority, nothing has been written about the rights of the majority.

Pushing legislation through the House presented an opportunity for some of the more radical members of Operation Solidarity to up the ante. On September 22, three thousand protesters in Prince George gathered to hear Mike Kramer, secretary-treasurer of the B.C. Federation of Labour, threaten a general strike if the Socreds continued to force legislation through the House: "I suspect the trade union movement will have to look at a closure movement of its own."

The next day, the government used closure to pass the Municipal Act amendments. A *Vancouver Sun* poll the following day showed that although 51 percent of the people polled agreed with restraint, 75 percent disagreed with how the government was handling it. On September 26, the BCGEU threatened to strike if anyone was laid off when their contract expired on October 31. On September 30, Operation Solidarity attempted to gain public support by offering to bargain for a resolution.

Bennett replied that governments don't bargain with protesters. He softened the message by indicating that he was open to suggestions for change, but there would be no negotiations. The government the same day used closure for the seventh and eighth times. The next day, October 1, Bennett agreed to meet with Kube. The meeting was arranged for October 3. The B.C. Teachers' Federation announced a strike vote, to be completed by October 21.

For the meeting with the premier, Art Kube brought along Renate Shearer and Jim Roberts, the co-chairs of the Solidarity coalition. They left the meeting believing the premier was now open to consultation on the legislative package. When Bennett heard this in the media, he clarified: there would be no special treatment, they were welcome to provide input to ministers, the legislation would proceed.

Barbara McLintock, writing her column in the *Province* on October 3, 1983, recognized the inevitable:

> Operation Solidarity has suddenly realized it is coming down to the crunch—and it has nowhere to go.
>
> The rag-tag coalition of labour unionists, human rights groups, women's groups, tenants' groups and others is learning one of the most bitter lessons of B.C. politics: power is the only thing that matters.
>
> And power is the one thing they don't have.
>
> The result is that the coalition is likely soon to fall apart, with not a thing gained.

News commentary like this refreshed some ministers' and staff's resolve. Bennett paid little attention; he never let the media know about his interest or lack of interest in what they wrote. And it never influenced his long-term strategy. He might, however, use them for his own short-term purposes. Jim Hume, a lifetime member of the press gallery, often ran into Premier Bennett. Jim recalls:

> He was in power for eleven years. In that eleven years he never once, not on any occasion, ever commented on anything I had written. Whether I had done a good job, or bad job. Nothing.
>
> Never even acknowledged that he read me.
>
> In fact, the only time he referred to anything to do with my career is when he would meet me in a corridor or the bus station or wherever, and his line was always the same:
>
> "Hi Jimmy, are you still writing for the newspapers?"
>
> And that would be it. The total comment.

THE FIRST ATTEMPT AT government–labour consultation occurred on October 6. Minister Jim Chabot and his staff were instructed to meet with the BCGEU. Pushing through a huge media scrum, they met in the Rattenbury Room on the main floor of the legislature. They started an hour before Question Period, which opened the afternoon sitting of the legislature.

The BCGEU demanded that Bills 2 and 3 be withdrawn. The language was acrimonious, the atmosphere tense, the anger palatable. Chabot sat quietly, looking more like Yoda than a fierce warrior fighting the working class.

Norm Richards, the elderly president of the BCGEU, was too much of a gentleman and was in over his head. He did not raise his voice and, more importantly, did not clearly and forcefully articulate his concerns. It was left to staff member Cliff Andstein to do the heavy lifting. Chabot misread this. In his mind, if only staff were raising issues, not the elected leader, the angst they claimed to be feeling couldn't be that great. Elected leaders should talk to elected leaders.

Chabot responded: he had heard them and would think about their concerns. The BCGEU walked out into the media scrum and announced that because the government would not change its position, the union would strike on October 31. When the press asked Chabot what he thought about the union threat to strike, he shrugged, smiled and walked up one floor to the chamber. As soon as Question Period ended, he stood up and introduced Bill 2 for second reading. A few hours later, closure was used to pass second reading.

The next day, Chabot rose again immediately after Question Period and introduced a whole sheaf of amendments to Bill 3, the Public Sector Restraint Act. The policy team of advisers had now had time to craft amendments designed to take the sting out of the tail of this particular scorpion. One amendment in particular caught the media's attention, as it permitted unions to reject the entire regulatory package if they could negotiate a settlement within a year. But if no settlement was reached, the much more rigorous terms of employment standards would apply. Classic jump or be pushed. Marjorie Nichols observed in the *Vancouver Sun:* "The responsible deputy minister just smiled and refused to comment when it was suggested by a reporter that the entire package was a Machiavellian masterpiece."

OCTOBER 13 AND 14 were extraordinary days, even for B.C. It started in the premier's office, where Operation Solidarity presented Bennett with its "definitive brief" on how to solve the issues. The brief was received, but no commitment was made to act upon it.

Things really got rolling later that day in the legislative chamber, when the House resumed sitting at 2:00 PM. Chabot rose and introduced Bill 3 for third and final reading, clause by clause debate.

The House sat continually until it was forced to call a halt the next day, October 14, at 1:50 PM, to enable the House rules to be followed, in order to reopen the legislature and resume debate on Bill 3 third reading at 2:00 PM. Following Question Period, debate again returned to Bill 3.

The NDP's A, B and C teams had been rotating through the House, as planned, every four hours and continued to do so. Chabot sat through it all, leaving the chamber only twice, for brief bathroom visits and a quick smoke. Because it was third reading clause-by-clause debate, Chabot was allowed a policy adviser on the floor with him. The adviser also sat there the whole time, leaving only for Question Period, and then returning. At eight o'clock that night, Bill 3 passed third reading.

The government had used closure ten times during the thirty hours of debate. Sixty-seven divisions had been called. Don Phillips had got the closure ball rolling when he came into the House for the first time at about seven o'clock the first night. Just back from Japan on a business trip, he listened to the debate for about fifteen minutes and rose:

> Mr. Speaker, I have been here listening closely to the debate and the Opposition just repeats itself and repeats itself. They don't get it.
>
> They have no more chance of getting it than a tiger has of changing its spots.
>
> Mr. Speaker, I find the debate repetitious and tedious and move the question be put.

Closure. While not the precise language required, Don in his normal way, got the message across and closure forced a division for that section to pass.

With Bill 3 passed, Chabot left the chamber exhausted. Finance Minister Hugh Curtis jumped up and moved third reading of the Compensation Stabilization Amendment Act. The house groaned. Both sides were exhausted. The policy adviser to Chabot went to his office, retrieved a set of fresh clothes, stopped to shower in one of the building's washrooms and returned to the floor of the legislature, as he was also policy adviser to Curtis on the bill now under debate.

Five hours later, the bill passed and the House adjourned for the weekend and the Social Credit annual convention. Nowhere in the British parliamentary system had there been such a raucous thirty-six hours of debate, with an unprecedented use of divisions and closures. Lotus Land had lived up to its reputation.

On October 14, the *Vancouver Sun* began to rethink its previous editorial stance of supporting the protests. It finally recognized that the Solidarity leadership had an agenda different from the one it presented to the public: "Operation Solidarity's 'definitive brief' to Premier Bill Bennett shows that it does not seek concessions from the provincial government. It seeks only capitulation." No government would let this happen. To do so was to accept anarchy.

The Socred convention opened the next day and Bennett went on the attack, accusing Solidarity of "wanting to fight the last election over again." Again and again, to standing ovations, he said, "We will never back down." Gone was the awkward speaking style of several years ago; this was a fiery presentation by a seasoned pro.

But the "happy days are here again" spirit was soon replaced with fear among many delegates when Operation Solidarity marched on the Hotel Vancouver. Over fifty thousand angry protesters surrounded the city block, screaming insults, chanting slogans. They scared the wits out of the delegates and drowned out the proceedings. The media did not mention much about Bennett's speech. Instead, they devoted the lead stories, front pages and in-depth coverage to the largest protest rally in the province's history. The pendulum swing of support–non-support for the government continued.

Talks between GERB and the BCGEU began the following Monday at the B.C. Labour Relations Board. They were acrimonious and bitter and broke off the following day, October 18.

Bennett had had enough. He sensed an opportunity to move to the high ground and booked a province-wide television address for October 20. In his address, he argued: "You can't picket your way to prosperity." He announced the adjournment of the legislature and promised to slow down layoffs to allow for a cooling-off period. "Now is the time for consultation to prevail over confrontation. Now is the time for a cool professional approach to prevail at the bargaining table."

The BCGEU proposed to return to bargaining if LRB chair Steven Kelleher was accepted as mediator. The government agreed.

The legislature adjourned and Bennett headed south for a road trip with some buddies. Before leaving, he instructed the secretary of federal–provincial relations to attend the negotiations and "keep an eye on things, look for a way to settle, not at any price, and report back to Norman Spector."

The secretary attended the first rounds of bargaining, phoned Norman and reported. This scenario repeated itself for the next two days. There was no movement at the bargaining table. Mike Davidson, head of the government bargaining team, would not take any advice to modify his position. He told Spector that he must come to Vancouver, to the LRB, and get involved or there would be no settlement.

Spector refused. He and the premier were still deciding the next steps. If he was to come it would place the dispute too close to the premier, an impossible situation because it would back him into a corner with no room to manouevre.

Over the next twenty-four hours, Spector was phoned by his mentor Jim Matkin, now president of the B.C. Business Council; Ed Peck, chair of the Compensation Stabilization Program; Steven Kelleher, chair of the B.C. Labour Relations Board; and well-known labour mediator, Vince Ready. The message was the same: he must get involved or there would be no settlement. Spector knew who instigated the calls, but he also knew how to take advice. He decided to investigate—after all, the premier had left this call up to him.

He told the press that he would attend to get "a first-hand look at the government's critical negotiations with the BCGEU." He was in, and after a brief visit with Davidson and Kelleher, Spector knew he must stay. He and the secretary of federal–provincial relations took over the negotiations, and Davidson was sidelined. Talks began in earnest, with a meeting between the president of the BCGEU, Norm Richards; his right-hand staff man, the very able Cliff Andstein; Norman Spector; and the secretary of federal–provincial relations, under Kelleher's interest-based mediation model.

Kelleher explained that with a strike looming and critical issues of essential service levels likely to come to the LRB for resolution, he as chair had to step down as mediator. He recommended Vince Ready be asked to step in and mediate. This had been what the premier and Spector had wanted all along. It was accepted. There was, however, still a long way to go. On October 29, the BCGEU announced a strike vote, with 87 percent in favour of a strike. A seventy-two-hour strike notice was served.

The B.C. Teachers' Federation followed suit that afternoon, announcing their first-ever strike vote, with 57 percent in favour of striking. This unprecedented move was immediately branded "unprofessional" by Vancouver school board chair Kim Campbell, who said she hoped teachers "would get kicked in the ass."

The talks at the LRB now attracted a media scrum larger than the combined delegations of negotiators. Whenever Spector or Andstein left their caucus room, they were mobbed. Whenever either one spoke to the media, there was always someone from the other side listening and recording the comments for the response that was soon forthcoming. Spector would take great delight in speaking to the French-language broadcasters in perfect French because the BCGEU had no one who could translate. It drove them nuts—what's he saying?

On October 31, the BCGEU indicated that talks were stalled and that they would proceed to strike the next day. Spector phoned Bennett for his daily chat; back for a few days now, Bennett no longer chided Spector for getting personally involved in the dispute. He knew this was the only way to find a solution. For the first time at the LRB, Spector did not respond to a BCGEU announcement of strike action.

It was time to kick it up a notch. Bennett held a press conference in Victoria, asking for an extension of the strike deadline. It was time for the adversaries to talk. He asked on behalf of all the people in the province. Importantly, he would hold off on the layoffs. He was conciliatory.

The BCGEU refused Bennett's offer and went on strike. The *Province*'s Allen Garr, never a Bennett fan, put it this way: "Once over lightly and we would all agree the union plays into Bill Bennett's hands. He is sweet reason. They are brute force. He offers to talk without a strike. They want to have their cake and eat it too. The strike is on. In a time when black and white is always better than shades of grey, the union goes from dead even to dead last."

SLOWLY THE MOMENTUM was shifting to the government. The B.C. Ferries workers also had a contract expiry date of October 31. They too would be in a legal strike position, like the BCGEU, and they were also poised to walk out. Round-the-clock negotiations over two days finally produced a settlement on early Sunday morning, October 31.

They found several creative solutions regarding the issue of layoffs, replacing the language in Bill 3 and thereby enabling them to seek an exemption order from wage-restraint czar Ed Peck, the compensation stabilization commissioner. The deal had finally closed when the chair of the Ferries Board, the wily former woodworkers' union boss and former commissioner of the Northwest Territories, Stu Hodgson, rode in on his white horse to save the day by sprinkling a little money on the deal.

The deal required Peck's approval, and he was enjoying a weekend getaway in Victoria. Don Jordan, negotiating for the Ferries Corporation, tracked Peck down, and he agreed to head back to his offices in Vancouver to consider the deal. One problem was that the ferries, under the threat of strike, were backed up with overloads and a two-sailing delay. The union president and Hodgson met quietly; neither wanted a walkout. When Peck arrived at the terminal ticket booth in Swartz Bay, the seller said: "Mr. Peck, we have been waiting for you. The three o'clock ferry has just arrived and you will be the first car boarded. Drive straight on now, and, oh yeah, approve our deal." Peck did both.

Marjorie Nichols, writing in the *Vancouver Sun* on November 1, 1983, recognized the situation:

> Last night's precipitate walkout by 35,000 provincial government civil servants proves that lemmings aren't the only species given to collective self-destruction…
>
> The current situation is almost too ridiculous for words. At 4:30 P.M. yesterday, the premier announced that the government is extending until Thursday noon the deadline for the firing of 1,600 civil servants, in order to give negotiators time to work out an alternative layoff agreement…
>
> The premier was holding an ace up his sleeve…
>
> Earlier yesterday, government negotiators successfully concluded an agreement with employees of the B.C. Ferries Corporation on the same contentious issues of layoffs that has precipitated the strike of 35,000 workers.
>
> No doubt the settlement was a devastating blow…
>
> The civil service union's only club is the guarantee from the Solidarity Coalition to set in motion a general strike the moment one of those 1,600 civil servants is fired.

> Well, no civil servant has been fired...
>
> Indeed if the premier and his negotiators are as clever as they appear to be, they will again delay any firings, thus ensuring that the civil servants remain alone on the picket lines...
>
> With enemies like the BCGEU, Bill Bennett does not need any friends.

THERE WAS, HOWEVER, too much momentum to derail the Solidarity Express just yet.

Still, the fortunes of the Solidarity movement, and particularly the BCGEU, were about to take another body blow and from a very unexpected source. On November 2, Mr. Justice Allan McEachern, chief justice of the B.C. Supreme Court, issued an *ex parte* injunction banning picketing at all courthouses in the province. The BCGEU agreed to honour the injunction while an appeal was heard next Thursday. McEachern's ruling said, in part:

> It is with sadness and regret that I learned this morning that the staff of this court has withdrawn its services and the BCGEU has caused pickets to be posted at the entrances to and within the precincts of these courts of justice...
>
> The question arises whether it is proper or permissible for anyone... to interfere with the business of the courts...
>
> It is my view, however, that pickets which may be lawful in many private... settings... interfere with the courts...
>
> It is my further view that such conduct is a contempt against justice itself...
>
> I must therefore make an order restraining and enjoining all persons... picketing at or in the vicinity of... court.

BCGEU CHIEF NEGOTIATOR Cliff Andstein said afterwards that this was the moment he knew their grand protest would be ground down to dust.

Bargaining dragged on at the LRB; little or no progress was being made, even with sixteen- to twenty-hour days spent searching for solutions. Solidarity, in constant contact with BCGEU negotiators, urged a go-slow approach still believing it could bring the government to its knees. There was a major card to be played the following Tuesday, when teachers were planning to walk out in support.

At about this time, big Jack Munro, president of the International Woodworkers of America, the leading private-sector trade unionist in the province, decided he should take a look at what was going on. In his book *Union Jack* he describes what he saw:

> I had been watching this thing from afar since it got started in July, but I didn't really get active until things seemed to be getting completely out of control in November. I had my own problems. A lot of us in the private sector were up to our ears in negotiations. That was a tough year. We were all taking a beating at the bargaining table. Anyway, we had a meeting of the private-sector unions, the building trades and pulp and a whole lot of others, and we pledged support. But we never realized the magnitude of what was being created.
>
> Then we went back to our negotiation sessions, and before we knew it Operation Solidarity was growing like Topsy. There were meetings upon meetings upon meetings. It became clear that I had better take a closer look to see what the hell was really going on. I went to one meeting up at the Plaza 500, where a decision was going to be made about what we were going to do next. Every goddamn group in the country was there. Everyone had one representative, and there must have been seventy people. For example, there was a woman there from the Rural Lesbians Society sitting next to a representative from the West End Gay Community, and they were part of a decision to have a general strike.
>
> They were all well-meaning, all dedicated to their causes—and I don't want to detract from any of them—but with all due respect to their organizations, they shouldn't have been voting on whether our members were going to be out of work. We trade unionists were the moderates in all of this. These people were drunk on their own power, and I don't know what they thought the end of it was going to be except that they were going to overthrow the government. Well, at that meeting I got pretty nervous about what was happening.

> The problem was that there were all these people fighting and championing their causes, and I'm sure they never thought that they would ever have a chance of being part of voting on a general strike. This was power beyond belief. So, suddenly, we started to realize that all of us, the two officers and ten vice-presidents of the Fed, were in trouble.

Big Jack got involved. With the approval of his negotiating committee he phoned Jim Matkin. He knew, like the premier and the government negotiators, what Cliff Andstein had recognized when Supreme Court Chief Justice McEachern issued his injunction. Eventually the courts would get involved, and any party out on an illegal strike would be sued by its industries for damages. This would have bankrupted the unions, and like a bankrupt political party they would be useless.

There had to be a solution because the private-sector rank and file members were not going to go on strike. Munro explains:

> Our members weren't going to stand by and watch decisions being made by people who had no stake. They weren't going to go out on the picket line, lose wages in one of their worst recessions since the 1930s—for what? To make sure that sexual preference is written into the human rights code?...Art Kube said he could deliver. And he believed his own nonsense. But the whole thing was falling apart.

Munro met with Matkin, who phoned Spector. After talking with the premier, Munro was green-lighted to open discussions, quietly. There would be no concessions. When this was communicated back to Matkin, it was agreed that the three of them would meet at Steven Kelleher's house for off-the-record talks. They soon agreed that Matkin and Munro would host the trade-union leadership of Solidarity.

Meeting in Ed Peck's modest offices were Peck, Matkin, Vince Ready, Munro, Kube, Larry Kuehn (president of the B.C. Teachers' Federation) and Mike Kramer (secretary-treasurer of the B.C. Federation of Labour and former CUPE president). After a couple of hours it looked like a deal had been hatched, at least one that Matkin felt comfortable in taking back to Spector.

Then the least-experienced negotiator, Larry Kuehn, stood up and said: "It isn't enough." Munro asked what he meant. Kuehn demanded legislative assurance that the quality of education wouldn't suffer. The meeting had been focusing on specifics, like how do we get school boards exempted from the layoff procedures enforced by Ed Peck, as the ferry workers had been.

Munro blew up. He got mad, and as is Jack's style, he started shouting at Kuehn and swearing at him. "How in the hell do you do that? The goddamn legislature isn't even sitting. Do you have any goddamn idea what the hell we are trying to do here?"

Kuehn stormed out. He wouldn't stand up to Munro. Here Kube too made a critical mistake. Rather than staying and concluding the deal that would go forward to Spector and the premier, he walked out and joined Kuehn. Kramer followed. Solidarity would drive on with its agenda, and if a general strike was necessary, they would proceed. Munro explains: "That was Kube's death knell. By going off with Kuehn and not sticking with the IWA and the other leaders, he cut himself out of the action. In a critical way, he also divided the labour movement."

Bennett was pleased with this outcome. He had known from the start of this fight that a conclusion would be reached only if the public- and private-sector unions could be split.

Back at the LRB, progress was slowly being made under Vince Ready. He now imposed a news blackout, and this was being respected, much to the chagrin of the media scrum that now numbered over eighty. He would occasionally go out and feed the scrum. Ready, the best mediator in North America, knew the stakes were high and was using his forceful personality to drive the parties together.

He had entered the talks and met with both parties separately. He gave them his normal line: he was here to find a settlement if there was one; if there wasn't, he would book out of the dispute. He wanted to know whether the parties wanted to "fuck, fight or hold the light."

He looked at both negotiating teams to find "the man with the golden nuts." Then he began to squeeze, especially on the weaker party. He knew that Spector was not going to budge, so a great deal of pressure focused on Andstein. He also knew that Spector wanted to settle and would be willing to make decisions to find an agreement, but would only go so far as the premier had decided.

November 6 found the parties at the table for eighteen straight hours. They were trying to find a settlement to head off the teachers' strike, planned for Tuesday. Both the union and management caucus rooms now stank of stale pizza, coffee and cigarettes. On this Sunday night, as pizza had been ordered again for dinner for the management caucus, a knock came to the door. An LRB staff person asked to see the secretary of federal–provincial relations and then gave him a picnic basket. The food in the basket—freshly baked baguette, chicken paté and French gherkins—had been sent to Spector and the secretary by Barbara Gordon, owner of the exclusive restaurant La Cachette. It was like having a picnic in a garbage dump.

Leaving that night, one of the union negotiators shouted out: "Just like management, always leaving early."

The secretary of federal–provincial relations shot back across the bow: "The reason we can leave early is because we don't have to form a circle, hold hands and sing 'Solidarity Forever.' "

Back to bargaining. Spector now had two tables to attend: one with the BCGEU, one confidentially upstairs with Jack Munro. He was in constant contact with Bennett all the while.

On November 8, teachers escalated the dispute by walking off the job in Victoria, Vancouver, Cranbrook and Fort Nelson, in sufficient numbers to convince the media and the public that the rotating strike plan put out by Solidarity was working and would continue.

Spector broke the news blackout by walking out to face the media after a phone call from Bennett. He stated that there was a "hidden agenda" in the union plan to use a teachers' strike to wring concessions in wage demands of 5 percent, plus benefits, and to create chaos in the public's mind. He commented that negotiating with the BCGEU was "like nailing jelly to a tree."

However, his media conference got second billing. Art Kube had contracted pneumonia and was suffering from total exhaustion. On national television he broke down in tears, sobbing uncontrollably. He was finished. Over 120 days of non-stop meetings and eighteen-hour days had eaten him up. His doctor ordered him home, and that is where he stayed while the drama played out.

In response to the teachers' strike, school districts sought court injunctions and the vast majority of teachers returned to work on November 9. But the province was in turmoil.

On November 10, Solidarity announced that it had "solidified into an organization that intends to be around for years." It released its schedule of future strike activity. Every day in the following week a different union would strike, one following another. Seventy-five thousand workers would be on the street. Impressive. But not one private-sector union volunteered to go out on strike. Bennett refused to call the legislature back, calling the actions "just a public service strike."

The premier knew the end was in sight. The union movement was split, and bets were on the private-sector unions derailing the Operation Solidarity locomotive. Bennett also was confident that the private-sector unions would not give up their jobs to support the broader Solidarity social concerns.

Jack Munro called a meeting at his office on Hastings Street. Present were Joy Langan, vice-president of the B.C. Federation of Labour, Leif Hansen of the United Food and Commercial Workers, Jack Adams of the BCGEU, Larry Kuehn of the teachers, Roy Gautier from the building trades, Jack Gerow from the health care union, and Bill Zander of the carpenters union—all the major power-brokers in the B.C. Federation of Labour. Kube was not invited, nor could he have attended. The public-sector union officials also realized it was over; it was time to find a face-saving way out. They formed a simple proposal for settlement: kill Bill 2, grant exemptions from Bill 3, carry out no reprisals for those who walked out, keep education funding at 1983 levels, and make some changes to the human-rights and landlord–tenant legislation, followed by consultation on other social issues.

Jack Munro, a guy who cares more for B.C. than for his own aggrandizement, agreed to be the spokesman—a decision he called either the bravest or the stupidest he had ever made. He was persuaded by Jack

Adams of the BCGEU that only he could stand up to the pressure that would come when it got out that the union movement was trying to cut a deal.

November 11, Remembrance Day, found the parties back at the table for an early morning start. An hour into discussions, the secretary of federal–provincial relations was handed a note from a colleague. He read: the Honourable Grace McCarthy would like a word on the telephone.

A minister phoning for an update was very rare. Spector would speak with the premier a couple of times every day, and likewise his colleague the secretary would speak to Chabot. On a very few occasions, one of them would speak with Attorney General Brian Smith. But Grace?

The secretary phoned her right back. She said: "You know this is a very public fight, and you know this is Remembrance Day. It would be the right thing to have you and Norman go to the Cenotaph for the Remembrance celebration, to show the public that you represent a government that knows its responsibilities. I don't think you should tell the union that this is what you are doing."

He returned to the negotiating room, and at about 10:30 asked for a break in the action to enable private discussion. This was not unusual and happened regularly, and therefore no one suspected anything. Spector looked at him curiously and asked, "What's up?"

Grabbing Don Jordan, he led the two men out the back steps to Don's car. Once there, he got Don to drive downtown and explained Mrs. McCarthy's idea. They shook their heads in admiration. Amazing Grace.

Arriving at the Cenotaph, they stood quietly during the ceremony. Solemn, respectful. The TV cameras swarmed them, but not a word was spoken. When the ceremony was over, they turned and walked back to their car. They would not speak with the media. They were not there to use the ceremony to make a statement. The media would do that for them.

Back at the bargaining table, nothing had changed. As usual, the parties broke to watch the news at six, usually standing in the lobby and mingling with the press. The lead item was the Remembrance Day ceremony, and there were the pictures of the government negotiating team in attendance and the voice-over comments that during the hectic rounds of talks at the LRB at least one side, the government side, had the decency to attend the service.

The union was understandably furious, as much at themselves for forgetting to attend as with the guys on the other side of the table. They knew the process they were engaged in was as much about the fight for the hearts and minds of the average British Columbian as it was about finding a collective agreement.

The deal with Munro was conditionally completed, subject to Munro presenting it to the premier. Munro had it approved by the Operation Solidarity executive. Spector headed back downstairs to negotiate with the BCGEU. Munro put pressure on the BCGEU through his friend John Shields, the vice-president.

On November 12, the talks went round the clock, and again on the 13th. The media constantly reported that this was the critical moment. Headlines and news reports read: "B.C. holds its breath." Finally the deal with the BCGEU was made, on November 13, early in the morning. The last details were ironed out as the day slipped by.

Part of the agreement with Spector was that Munro would fly to Kelowna and meet the premier in his home. Munro was reluctant but eventually agreed when he was told that this was the only way, and that it would be the very first time any government business had ever been conducted in the very private premier's home.

Once the settlement was reached with the BCGEU and signed by both sides, the union executive pulled the pickets from the government airplane hangars, thus allowing a government jet to fly to Vancouver to pick up Spector, Munro and the B.C. Fed public-relations guy, Gerry Scott.

On arriving in Kelowna, the three headed to Bennett's home. The media beat them there, and they waded into the front door through a gaggle of reporters and live television coverage. Bennett remembers Munro as nervous: "Jack, when he first walked in, the first thing he says is, 'How about a drink of scotch?' And I said, 'Jeez, Jack, I'd like to help you but the liquor stores are on strike. You can have wine, I think I'm having coffee.' He's grumbling, 'Guy wouldn't even give me a drink.'"

Several hours of tough talk followed. On several occasions Bennett dug in and Munro had to phone back to the B.C. Fed offices to get agreement to proceed. He did this from the premier's and Audrey's bedroom, sitting uncomfortably on the bed, looking at the premier's dressing gown and slippers. Finally they reached a deal. In his words:

> After a few hours Bennett and I agreed on a package of terms. I went upstairs again and phoned Mike Kramer and ran through all the points with him. In turn, he told the Solidarity leaders what was happening. Then they took a vote. I hung up the phone and waited while they voted. The vote was unanimous that we accept the agreement.

They went outside to face the media and announced an agreement. Bennett had faced down Solidarity. There was no written deal, just a verbal one. Munro believed that this hurt him, in the end. Bennett explains why he wanted no paper:

> We would have had a hundred lawyers reinterpreting every bit. When you talk verbally you're both under the same kind of pressure of having to stay within what you agreed to, the things you talked about, and nobody wants to be the one that doesn't keep their word.
>
> You don't want other people combing over this stuff trying to get away with a little bit more here and there and putting Jack Munro in a place where he is going to face questions... How come you didn't do this? Where's that? You know, if it was on paper it would be hard for him to defend because of all the interpretations. This was our word. And he was the right one out of all of them to give his word.

The reaction across the province was an overwhelming sense of relief. The *Province* exclaimed, "The clear winner in the thirteen days of public sector strikes and marathon weekend bargaining was Premier Bill Bennett's government." Labour reporter Rod Mickleburgh commented: "Bennett budged, but he budged on his terms."

Not everyone was enthralled, and some paid a price. Jack Munro remarks:

> The most unexpected thing for me was that some of the leaders in the B.C. Fed who were at the meeting where we decided to stop Solidarity suddenly jumped on the bandwagon of opposition to the Kelowna deal and nailed me at the B.C. Fed convention a month later. It was pretty obvious by the time the convention rolled around that they had the momentum going. It was clear I was in trouble. Kube was trying to save himself at my expense...
>
> I was down and getting a lot of crap from a lot of people. As a result, the IWA was defeated at the Fed convention. I lost as first vice-president...

THERE REMAINS ONE real question: why did a B.C. government that had perfected running on the right and governing in the middle as a sure path to win election after election decide it should swing widely right?

There are several answers, all equally important.

Bennett knew from the day he won the 1983 election that this was to be his last term in office, and he felt he had to "fix" the problems caused by the recession in order to secure B.C.'s future. And while doing so, he dealt with a few pet peeves.

He wanted to change the agenda in a radical way, leading the NDP to focus on him. Since he would be leaving, they would have expended their energy on the wrong target.

Finally, hubris. The rarefied air of the cabinet chamber and electoral success got all the Socred ministers caught up in what they could do, and therefore would do. The sin of arrogant pride. Not healthy.

THE LAST OF BENNETT'S four cabinet retreats was held in Whistler. Because of the restraint program, deputy ministers had to share rooms.

When the meetings opened, a few ministers asked the premier if he would mind a "political session" being held prior to the general practice of ministers meeting with their deputies. A few had strong views that the appropriate place for deputies was in the hall, to be called if needed. Bennett went along with it.

A few appearances were put in that day, but by the end of the afternoon most deputies had headed back to Victoria. Little came out of the cabinet retreat.

But being in Whistler was itself a treat. It had a long history, and over the lunch hour the premier and cabinet made an announcement that opened the convention centre and guaranteed that the ski hill would become a world-class facility.

Whistler, Mount Washington, Hudson Bay Mountain, Silver Star, Powder King and Panorama Ridge would not be there today without the intervention of the Bennett government. Don Phillips remembers:

> When the husband of Nancy Greene Raine came to me because I was also chairman of the Economic Development Committee, he said, "Look, we would like to develop more around Whistler but the government will not release any more land, nobody can get title to land..."
>
> I said, "Let's go to work to get your land," and then of course it developed from there.
>
> I will never forget the *Vancouver Sun* headline, "Sin City Comes to Whistler," and I thought, you bloody asshole donkeys.
>
> I had Price Waterhouse do the whole analysis. We put $25 million into building the infrastructure. And the government got more than their money back because we charged for the land and included the price of the infrastructure.

HUGH CURTIS BROUGHT in seven budgets from 1979 to 1986, the most of any finance minister save W.A.C. Bennett. He will always be remembered for the "restraint" budget. But much to his credit, although not recognition, he and his deputy Larry Bell built the modern Ministry of Finance. When Curtis was appointed minister of finance, the deputy minister was long-time W.A.C. Bennett–Dave Barrett–Evan Wolfe deputy minister Gerry Bryson. It was time for retirement.

Larry Bell was brought in from the housing ministry, where he had worked with Curtis. There were four other deputies doing a variety of jobs in the ministry as well. Within two weeks there was one, Larry Bell. The others were gone.

They also discovered archaic legislation that dealt with the province's finances and arcane ways of doing business that needed drastic overhaul. Curtis explains: "In the old Act or in one of the old Acts which governed finance, there was the requirement that someone would make the deposits from the previous day in person at the Bank of Commerce at the corner of Fort and Government streets. There was some funny old stuff in there. The province desperately needed a new Financial Administration Act."

HOW SUCCESSFUL WAS Bennett's strategy in managing restraint? Answering this question involves two key considerations: should he have introduced the legislation as a package, or dribbled it in and gauged the reaction? Further, was he correct in drawing all the fire to himself?

It is certain that Bennett would never have been able to get all the restraint legislation introduced if he had done so one piece at a time. All at once was the only way to meet his legislative objectives, and most of it stuck.

We don't have a Rentalsman today. Nor an Alcohol and Drug Commission. Lifetime job security is gone for public servants. The education system is better for not having a plethora of academic and management advisory councils. The fact that these changes were not undone by later administrations is not surprising, as Jim Nielsen comments:

> You very seldom see from one government to the next a real modification of the previous government's legislation. Very little has changed, because governments are more administrations than anything else. And the difference between governments really is administrative skill.
>
> Dave Barrett brought in ICBC and the Agricultural Land Reserve. Both were very controversial, but we never changed them.
>
> We did things that were controversial. When the NDP eventually came back into power, they never changed them because after a while it just becomes part of society and it's accepted.

> A lot of people today have spent their whole life with the Agricultural Land Reserve or ICBC or tolls on the Coquihalla. W.A.C. had his twin rivers policy and taking over the Black Ball ferries. Very controversial at the time, but after a while the NDP never changed any of it, when Barrett got into power.
>
> We didn't change a lot of Barrett's stuff. Harcourt didn't change a lot of our stuff. That's the way the province is governed. You don't see great changes.

So, these great changes, some considerable structural changes, are still with us today.

The other side of that coin is the social upheaval caused by these changes. If the government had introduced them more slowly, it might have been more selective or might have backed down at some stage, before thousands upon thousands of people were marching in the streets. The province's history of polarization was not stood down; indeed, it was stepped up.

The second issue is whether Bennett's tactic of having all the attention focused on himself worked. He knew he was retiring and that this would misdirect the NDP and have them spend time and resources fighting a target that he, and he alone, knew was not going to be there on Judgement Day. The answer here is an unequivocal and resounding Yes. His strategy worked.

David Mitchell's book *Succession* describes the transfer of power between Bill Bennett and Bill Vander Zalm in this way:

> The NDP, recognizing the premier's image problem, developed a political strategy of attacking Bennett personally, capitalizing on his lack of popularity. The result was perhaps the most vindictive manifestation of the politics of personality yet witnessed in British Columbia. A confidential NDP election strategy paper distributed late in 1985 outlined the reasons for such an approach:
>
> "You will note throughout the paper that we refer to the Bennett government as opposed to the Social Credit government. Indications

are that a great many Socreds agree that the Bennett government has failed, in particular younger people who may have voted Socred in the past.

"If we focus our attack on Socreds, we make it more difficult for these former Socred voters to vote New Democrat. We want to rally them to the fact that the Bennett government has failed and that many other former Socred voters share this view and will be voting New Democrat in the next provincial election..."

The opposition party thus launched into a brutal attack on Bill Bennett. With newspaper and television ads they decried "the Bennett record of lost jobs, lost hope." They said, "Bennett's school cuts were hurting our children and our province." And "the Bennett government is killing our forests, our communities and thousands of jobs," and "the Bennett government has failed women in B.C."

Bennett recognized and planned to counteract what he knew must be the NDP strategy. He was right. But it takes a rare politician to sacrifice himself for the long-term good of his party.

12

IT ENDS WITH EXPO

"The premier's eyes hardened like two ice cubes. And he said, 'In that case, Roy, it'll be nothing.'"

BUD SMITH

TOURISM MINISTER Grace McCarthy was in London in 1978 lunching with B.C. Agent General Lawrie Wallace and Patrick Reid, president of the International Bureau of Expositions. She was casting about for ideas to celebrate Vancouver's centenary in 1986.

Japan had already won the rights for 1986, she was told. That would never stop Grace. The lobbying began, and Japan proved co-operative; 1986 was now open for a bid. Vancouver won the right to host a second-tier fair, to be called Transpo 86. Bennett at first was not too keen about the idea. He recognized that Grace considered it mainly a vehicle to get a trade and convention centre for Vancouver.

The throne speech in 1980 announced that Transpo 86 would be an $80 million exposition that would celebrate Vancouver's centennial and coincide with the one-hundredth anniversary of the CPR reaching Canada's west coast. It was to be a special-purpose fair, in which all the pavilions would be prefabricated. The land needed to build the exposition had not been acquired when the announcement was made.

Bennett had received from consultant Paul Manning his report on the feasibility of building a domed stadium in Vancouver. Manning and Larry Bell, the deputy minister of finance, had visited every dome in North America and found the blueprints for B.C. in Minneapolis. Literally. They had not only decided that the Minneapolis dome was the right one, on the basis of the city's similar population size and the dome's cost, but they had been able to sweet-talk the project managers to give them—at no cost—all the blueprints and working documents to speed construction. The construction cost was estimated at $126 million.

Bennett was distrustful of the economic boom that B.C. was riding. He knew that in a province dependent on commodity sales, the cycle was due for a downswing. It was not a question of if, but when. He thought it through and, faced with the scandals plaguing his second term, decided the timing and the politics were right to move onto more positive things.

A few problems needed to be dealt with. The first was the land for Transpo. Bennett had an idea and opened discussions with the CPR regarding the False Creek lands. He describes what happened:

> We made an interim agreement, and it helped that I knew people who worked there. They came over, and they verbally agreed on the price.
>
> We started the construction, we start clearing land and doing site preparation. Nothing was ready for official signing; lawyers were now involved. Canadian Pacific was tiffed because of a forest land issue on Vancouver Island. They began making noises about not completing the sale. I said, keep building; we had a deal. The only one who thought he could still use it as linkage was their president, Ian Sinclair. Just keep building, and eventually someone from their side agreed to a land swap.
>
> But Expo was more than just that. It was...if you think of all the things that went into Expo, we got the tunnel so that the transit system would go all the way over to the waterfront. It allowed us to finish SkyTrain in time for Expo, to really show what it was all about, because the themes were transportation and communication. The Coquihalla

> too was part of what it was about, transportation, communication. All of the things that fit together fit even more realistically, but I don't think the public was able to understand how all the things intertwined.

No one knew. Bennett took the land deal to cabinet as a done deal. He had, of course, discussed the financial implications with the minister of finance, but he knew that in this game he would do what he always did: turn to the best person available. And the best person available to put the land together and play hardball with the CPR was himself. The going had gotten tough:

> I had only one other deal with the CPR, and that was the extension of the tunnel to the waterfront. They were building a hotel and the convention centre and they wanted air rights, a horrible amount of money they felt that we had to buy their rights. We made a tentative agreement, and they came over and talked about the value of the air rights. I said I'd never heard of it.
>
> I said, "I'll tell you what: you have a choice, your interests or the benefit of the public." They replied, "It's our air rights, you know you're going to have to pay for it." That was a Friday. I said, "I'll give you the weekend to think about it. Get back to me on Monday, because if you don't agree and you want that money I will cut off the terminal for SkyTrain one block away from your hotel, and if you don't believe me, ask around."
>
> They came back on Monday and said okay.

His next move was to bring in the federal government. He met Prime Minister Trudeau in a Vancouver hotel room for a private meeting and asked for federal assistance. Trudeau had just been re-elected. In the footnote to history that was Joe Clark, the federal Tories had promised support to B.C. for the exhibition. To Trudeau, Bennett explained that the exhibition was to celebrate Vancouver's centenary, the completion of the rail link that brought B.C. into Canada and the opening of the Pacific Rim to Canadian trade.

Trudeau said no.

Bennett was surprised. After all, the Liberals were getting little support in the west, and here was a way to demonstrate that B.C. was important. It made good political and business sense.

Trudeau said no.

Bennett argued that the federal government had supported Expo 67 in Montreal, and if it could do that in the prime minister's home province, Quebec, it could and should support B.C.

Trudeau looked at Bennett and said: "The decision to support Montreal and Expo 67 was made by Prime Minister Lester Pearson. Not me. I would not have supported it then, and I will not support your fair now."

Bennett stared back: "All right, we will go it alone. We will do it. It will be successful. And we'll do it ourselves."

The meeting was over. Canada would not support or be part of the exhibition. But the practical businessman Bennett knew the financial burden of completing the exposition alone would be tremendous. Bennett needed Canada, he needed a way to deal with Trudeau.

There was one federal B.C. Liberal Bennett respected: Senator Jack Austin.

Trudeau, back in power, had to choose between two senators who would act as his "B.C." minister, Ray Perrault or Jack Austin. He chose the party favourite, Perrault, but told Austin that if nothing was moving in B.C. within a year he would reverse his decision, and he did. While Perrault would stay on in name, Jack would get the key files.

The federal government had conducted a cost–benefit analysis of various proposed B.C. projects, and Expo was the clear winner. Austin was ready to attempt a deal and travelled to Victoria to see Bennett.

They met three times. At the first meeting, Bennett painted a bleak picture of Expo, besieged on all sides by nay-saying academics and the mayor of Vancouver projecting a fair failure. He wanted federal help, but if necessary would proceed on his own. Austin agreed to help.

The second meeting got down to serious money issues. Bennett wanted at least $100 million, not including all federal costs for things like security and overseas embassy assistance. Austin, who had already reported on this as an information item to cabinet, had told the ministers he thought the total bill would be about $175 million. They were within a settlement zone. Now they had to agree on what was in—convention centre, SkyTrain hook-up, security, overseas embassy involvement—and what was out—provincial infrastructure, land acquisition and so on.

At the third meeting they put together the package. They had a deal, and Austin went back to Ottawa. Taking the agreement into the Economic Development Committee of cabinet, it was turned down. He took it to Treasury Board. Turned down. Took it to Planning and Priorities, with the tide running against him. Before the vote was taken, one that he was sure he would lose dramatically, he asked the prime minister to delay the discussion for two weeks. He gained two weeks and asked to see the prime minister privately. Waiting to go in to see Trudeau, Austin reflected on the personality of his prime minister. He remembers that "Trudeau was what I would call a 'compensatory leader.' If he was on a boat and everyone rushed over to one side, Trudeau would go to the other side."

Austin said to Trudeau:

> Thank you for seeing me, Prime Minister. And importantly, thank you for providing the two-week delay at P and P. I was getting a real rough ride in there before you arrived, as I think they are all against it. Can't see the politics out west, I guess.
>
> It is only my view, but if you are going to win seats in B.C. in the next election, if you are running—

He paused. Trudeau looked over the top of his half-glasses, staring, turning down the temperature in the room, but saying nothing. Austin continued:

> then you will not win any seats, nor will the Liberal Party win any seats for a very long time, unless you support Expo.

Trudeau was noncommittal. He would look at it. He knew his cabinet was opposed.

At the next planning and priorities meeting of cabinet, the ministers sat around waiting for Trudeau, who was running slightly late. They were taking the mickey out of Austin. There was clearly no hope for Expo. Finance Minister Marc Lalonde sat silently in his seat, not commenting. Then Trudeau entered, called the meeting and turned to the first item: Expo. He began to speak: "I have studied the file and I am in support of it, unless any minister here wishes to specifically speak out against it."

Silence. No one challenged the boss. Expo got its funding. The feds were back in the game, and the fair was on its way.

BENNETT WAS NOT satisfied with how things were proceeding at Expo itself. Further, he could see that the recession was deepening and would likely get much worse. He needed to shake up the Expo team if it was to be an agent of hope—a symbol of future prosperity in B.C. In 1981 he phoned Jimmy Pattison. He recalls:

> I phoned him in New York and asked if he would do it, and he said, "Sure, what does it entail?" I said, "About a half day a week." [laughing] I said, "You know how it goes with a board; just running a board, it's not going to take much time." He says, "I can do that." He came to Expo and then found out it was eight days a week.

As Pattison says in his book, *Jimmy:*

> I agreed to be a part-time, unpaid chairman for two years. The job grew like a bad weed as the fair ballooned into a $1.6 billion World Exposition. For thirty-six months I did nothing else.

Bennett and the staff of both B.C. Place and Expo had to deal with the lacklustre leadership emanating from city hall. The failed NDP candidate in Vancouver–Little Mountain, Mike Harcourt, had run for and won the mayor's job. One of the most likeable people ever to hold public office, he was a great conciliator but a weak leader with very limited vision. Indeed, it was worse. He actively opposed the world's fair.

When Provincial Secretary Hugh Curtis had announced the fair on June 19, 1979, and had pitched the International Bureau of Expositions for the fair, then-mayor Jack Volrich had been front and centre with him. But Mayor Harcourt was opposed. He wrote in December 1980: "As you can see, we are not committed to Transpo and it can still be cancelled." In July 1981 he briefed Vancouver city council, as the minutes show: "The mayor questioned the need for a Fair. He expressed concerns about the capacity of the City to absorb all the proposed major projects and the facilities to tolerate it." As late as the fall of 1982, Harcourt was still expressing concerns: "However, as you know, I have been a critic and skeptical of Expo" and "I have been unable to support Expo."

Bennett decided to move ahead with his plan for the Greater Vancouver Area in spite of the city's leadership. Capital spending would be accelerated to mitigate the effects of the recession and to revitalize Vancouver. His plan would include:

- The fair on 173 acres along the north shore of False Creek.
- The construction of the domed stadium, at a cost of $125 million.
- A $135 million trade and convention centre on the waterfront, to be paid for by the federal government.
- The $854 million rapid-transit system, SkyTrain, from the waterfront to New Westminster.
- The world's fair itself, Expo 86.

It was one of the great ironies of B.C. politics. The high school graduate from small-town Kelowna would drive the revitalization of B.C.'s great urban centre. Bennett puts it this way:

> I said to myself, if we're going to build a stadium and we're going to have an Expo, why not buy the whole False Creek site? The city of Vancouver had been wasting time on it, never showing any leadership. In the meantime they never would let anything positive happen there. The site was filled with sawmills, other inappropriate businesses. And this is going on in the most beautiful city in Canada, and in the heart of the city.
>
> Once I made up my mind, looked at the report that was done on the stadium, saw that it could be done, the estimates were reasonable. I said

to myself, if we're going to do that and Expo, in spite of the city, we will buy the whole thing from the CPR and do it.

And as a final stroke, with good management and political judgement, when the fair was over the 173-acre site would become one of the largest urban redevelopment sites in North America. If done properly, it would create jobs and business activity for Vancouver for the next twenty years.

By the end of 1983 Transpo had morphed into Expo 86 by adding communications to transportation and upgrading the whole exhibition. Jimmy Pattison had fulfilled his original two-year commitment and had resigned, only to be convinced by Bennett, while he entertained the governor of Alaska on Jimmy's boat, that someone who had generated much of his wealth in B.C. owed the province. Jimmy recalls the conversation: "Bill said, 'If I can't ask people like you to come and help me, people who made money and became successful in this province, who can I turn to?' I replied, 'You're absolutely right. I'll do it.'"

They built a first-class board and early in the new year announced that the exposition would now cost $800 million and would incur a deficit of $311 million, which would be paid from lottery revenues. They balanced the expenditures by revealing that an independent study by Currie, Coopers and Lybrand estimated that Expo 86 would generate $2.8 billion of economic activity in B.C. and pay taxes of about $400 million to the feds and half that to the province.

Clearly a symbol of hope for the future and a good business deal for British Columbia.

JIMMY PATTISON AND his board wanted to negotiate a project agreement with the B.C. and Yukon Building Trades Council to ensure labour peace during the construction of Expo 86. He entered into talks with the building trades president, Roy Gautier. In exchange for a no-strike agreement and union-scale wages, the Expo site would be union only.

Bennett, when he heard, vetoed the idea. All British Columbians would be allowed to bid on Expo work. Competition would determine the wage scales paid.

The reason for this was found in an earlier dust-up between the B.C. and Yukon Building Trades Council and an open-shop builder, Kerkhoff Construction. Kerkhoff had recently successfully built a courthouse in Kamloops using both union and non-union workers, or open shop, who worked side by side. This violated the union's monopoly on industrial and commercial construction as well as ringing the death knell for jurisdictional work rules.

Upcountry may be one thing, but downtown Vancouver was another, and this worksite was in False Creek, the second of two condominium complexes called Pennyfarthing, and was funded by the B.C. Central Credit Union. The first site had been built union-only, as was the practice across the province. Defending the practice, the secretary-treasurer of the building trades union, Al McMurray, said: "the unions are determined to make a stand at the [False Creek] site because an industry precedent would be set if Kerkhoff completes the project. Large union firms like Dillingham and Commonwealth would also try to set up non-union divisions."

The protest turned violent. The site was blocked by seven hundred angry union members. Ewald Rempel, a non-union concrete contractor, was pelted with a foul-smelling concoction of human waste and rotten meat as he tried to enter the site.

Police were called. Tempers flared. Lawyers for both sides went before the B.C. Labour Relations Board. A cease and desist order was issued; it was ignored. The order was filed in the B.C. Supreme Court, and that order was ignored. Finally the Supreme Court ordered the union organization to appear in court on March 29 to show why it should not be held in contempt of the court orders.

Eventually, saner heads prevailed and the project was built by Kerkhoff. But Bennett would not see this happen again: "Everybody, you know every British Columbian, should have a chance to bid. And so Pennyfarthing, although not a government project, was what set up this policy... Open shop was going to be how we built Expo." On March 17, Bennett gave Pattison ten days to reach an agreement with Gautier that would provide the unions with the lion's share of work but would also allow some non-union work.

Jimmy tried. Roy tried. An agreement was reached that saw a very limited number of non-union jobs permitted and a union wage paid. Cabinet rejected it.

The negotiations started again. At one point the discussions failed because Bennett told Pattison that he could offer the CSP average rate of increase, government lingo for the wage-restraint program's average rate of increase, and Jimmy offered Roy the CPI, or consumer price index, which was higher. Roy accepted the CPI wage increase, but cabinet rejected it because they had insisted on the lower CSP rate.

By April 10, Pattison had had enough. He travelled to Victoria to attend a cabinet meeting. He recommended that government should "cancel Expo unless a settlement that ensures construction labour peace is accepted by the Building Trades Council." He was not bluffing. In his view B.C. would be better to cut its losses now, anticipated to be around $80 million, and suffer some international embarrassment, than fail to deliver in two years and face much harsher international criticism. His proposal to cancel Expo was made public during the cabinet meeting that day.

A tidal wave of reaction rolled over the province. The majority supported the government's tough stand. People on all sides of the political equation, from the Business Council's Jim Matkin to IWA President Jack Munro, called for meetings with Bennett and pressed him to continue. One voice was missing—Vancouver's. Bennett's principal secretary explains:

> The premier opened the window from his office and called to the mayor of Vancouver, who was walking by, to come into his office. I was there. He asked him his view, and Michael Harcourt offered many views but he wouldn't give an opinion on whether Expo should go ahead or not, which was a surprise to us, given it was probably the most important thing that was going to happen to his city during his entire term of office. But he could not bring himself to give an opinion about whether it should go ahead or not. And there were many others who came in and said go ahead.

Within days, the government introduced legislation to divide the Expo site into "special enterprise zones" where, by law, both union and non-union workers would bid and work. Bennett waited while the anger against the unions built.

Again Pattison opened discussions with Gautier, and again they found a deal, only to have the Expo board vote it down after impassioned pleas by Tourism Minister Claude Richmond and Labour Minister Bob McClelland that it was not fair to all British Columbians. The legislation ground through the legislature.

One last attempt was made at negotiations. Norman Spector and Roy Gautier sat down in the offices of the new principal secretary, Bud Smith, as cabinet met upstairs, just down the hall from the premier's office. A long day of bargaining was moving frustratingly slowly. Bennett left the cabinet meeting, came down the spiral staircase and joined the meeting. Bud Smith recalls:

> Ultimately the premier's deputy, Norman Spector, began negotiations with the union: 85 percent of the work would be done union and 15 percent max would be non-union. Those meetings took place in my office. I was in and out of them from time to time, but largely it was Norman who did that. And eventually, about seven or eight o'clock in the evening, cabinet was beginning the debate whether Expo would go ahead or not. The premier came down and he said, "You've had enough time, what is it?"
>
> And Roy Gautier looked at the premier and in his best Scottish brogue said to him, "Mr. Premier, it will be all or it will be nothing."
>
> To which the premier's eyes hardened like two ice cubes. And he said, "In that case, Roy, it'll be nothing."
>
> Turned on his heel, went back up the spiral staircase to a cabinet meeting. I went with him. He went in, sat down at the head of the table and said, "Colleagues, we've reached a consensus." And everyone clapped.
>
> It wasn't until the next day that they heard the consensus. But it was agreed that it would go ahead.
>
> But the reason it went ahead was the public opinion that came into the office was absolutely, overwhelmingly supportive of going ahead.

> The only one who, of all the people we met in the office, wouldn't say "Go ahead" was Mike Harcourt. And he didn't say "Don't go ahead," he just wouldn't say anything.
>
> And, in fact, only 8 percent, if I recall, was done non-union. It was, in my view, one of the great strategic errors of the labour movement in British Columbia, because in politics symbols often are more important than reality.
>
> They got, in fact, 90 percent of the work, but to this day people still believe Expo was done largely with non-union labour. It's not true. But that opened the floodgates everywhere. If Expo could be done with an open shop, then everything else could be done with an open shop. And that decision by Gautier was a colossal strategic error. And the change in the union–non-union relationship in construction in British Columbia can be traced to that meeting.

Bennett moved quickly. He announced that Expo would go ahead. The government passed the legislation, and the orders-in-council were prepared and passed by cabinet to establish the special enterprise zones. Expo was underway and would be built on time, with construction costs $17 million under budget, and with both union (about 70–80 percent) and non-union workers employed in over nine thousand construction jobs for three years.

There is an interesting footnote to this struggle. The construction industry in B.C. has never been the same since. Prior to 1984, non-residential construction on commercial and industrial plants had been exclusively carried out by unions affiliated with the B.C. and Yukon Building Trades Council. Within ten years, about 90 percent of that construction was being undertaken by open-shop contractors, some contractors and subcontractors being union shops, others being non-union, but all working side by side on open sites. Construction, as a result, is less expensive and more competitive.

Jimmy Pattison recognized the differences in his job and Bennett's this way: "The premier, looking at the bigger provincial picture, had a different agenda. Yet, in the end, I thought that Bill Bennett did exactly the right thing for B.C. because it ushered in a whole new tone to provincial labour relations."

IN CABINET'S VIEW the timing didn't seem right to settle aboriginal land claims during the Bennett administrations. This had been Dave Barrett's position during his administration, and it persisted under Bennett. Tom Berger, writing in the spring 1983 issue of *B.C. Studies,* noted:

> Ever since British Columbia entered Confederation, the province has refused to acknowledge aboriginal rights. This has been the policy of governments of all parties: Liberal and Conservative in earlier times, Social Credit and NDP in our time. A shift in governmental attitudes and policies under both Social Credit and NDP administrations can, however, be observed within the past decade. Sometimes concessions have been made, agreements reached, even changes in governmental arrangements decided upon, which profoundly affect native communities and which serve the same purpose as native claims.

The NDP changed its position and agreed to negotiate comprehensive claims in the early 1980s, but the Socreds hung on to the province's traditional position even in the face of court case after court case finding in favour of First Nations. In 1985 Vaughn Palmer, the *Vancouver Sun* political columnist, wrote a column about the B.C. position:

> Its first position is that title never existed. The second holds that if it ever existed, it was extinguished. Then the government will argue that even if title exists it has little meaning in terms of compensation ... The next fallback is that even if the natives are entitled to substantial compensation, the federal government must provide it under the terms that brought B.C. into Confederation. And the fifth and final position, though seldom articulated, is that the public will never stand for the level of compensation expected by native leaders, and therefore little risk attaches to the efforts to defeat the claim in court.

Provincial staff who had developed the position, and defended it through successive administrations, made convincing arguments—none more so than the province's long-time deputy minister of constitutional affairs, Mel Smith. Bob Exell, the senior staff person in charge of aboriginal relations under Bennett's Social Credit government, comments: "Mel was extremely antagonistic towards Indian land claims, it's as simple as that. Mel fought it tooth and nail. I had a lot of incidents where I was with Mel, and 'antagonistic' is a kind word. He had no sympathy whatsoever." This isn't to say that ministers always take public servants' advice; they do not, nor should they. But there just didn't seem to be good politics in going the other way.

But Bennett ran a pragmatic government, so some practical and significant things got done. In 1982, B.C. awarded the Stuart–Trembleur band in northern B.C. a tree farm licence. This was the first time that a TFL had been awarded to anyone other than a forest company. Again Exell remembers: "The Stuart–Trembleur band had a smart kid named Eddie John. Eddie was a young lawyer. And I got into negotiations with Eddie and eventually we were able to get the Ministry of Forests to configure a tree farm licence tenure application in such a way that the only possible successful bidder could be the Stuart–Trembleur Lakes band. So they got their tree farm licence."

When cabinet turned down comprehensive land claims negotiations, it did green-light steps to be taken to deal with "cut-off lands." In the spring session of 1982 the government introduced legislation, the British Columbia Indian Cut-off Lands Settlement Act, which created an opportunity to deal with a long-simmering dispute between First Nations and governments.

In the late 1800s Canada had created reserve lands, and in 1913 the federal government established the McKenna–McBride Commission to examine the extent and location of the reserves. The federal government promised the bands that no land would be taken away from them without their consent. They lied.

The sizes of thirty-four reserves belonging to twenty-two B.C. bands were arbitrarily reduced, or "cut off," without the consent of the First Nations. Land "cut off," mainly on the south coast and southern Interior, was almost entirely land considered highly desirable by white farmers, ranchers, developers, speculators and municipal government officials.

Negotiations were entered into and settlements were reached. In 1982, settlements were reached with the Osoyoos Band and the Penticton Band; in 1983, with the Squamish (Ambleside) Band, West Bank and Whispering Pines/Clinton Band. Three more were settled in 1984: Chemainus, Becher Bay and Okanagan Bands.

The government presented two other legislative initiatives. One was to provide subsurface mineral and gas rights to the First Nation at Fort Nelson. The second was to pass legislation to provide for municipal-like status for the Sechelt Band. Finally, in the hurly-burly world of B.C. politics, common sense sometimes applies. And good political judgement. Bob Exell tells this story:

> Jimmy Gosnel called me up one day. He was president of the Nishga tribal council. He shot a moose out of season. They took his moose. They took his gun. You know, some eager wildlife manager. And they were going to charge him under the Wildlife Act. Allan Williams was attorney general, so I went to Williams and I said this was just ridiculous...the president of the Nishga tribal council. They took his moose, took his gun! I got his gun back for him, and Williams made sure that no charges were laid.

THE NEWS HIT CABINET like a sucker-punch to the gut, just after nine o'clock on May 22, 1986. It had been delivered by Jerry Lampert, Bud Smith's successor as principal secretary.

Premier Bennett would not be joining cabinet today. He was in Vancouver that morning, where he would announce his retirement and would be calling a leadership convention for later that summer. The ministers were stunned. Some were in tears. Bob McClelland remembers the day: "It was pretty hard on us. I was surprised...and, I must admit, a bit angry when I thought about it. I had not planned on running again, and he had come to me and convinced me to run again. So that was annoying. But what I really was, was surprised. I couldn't believe it, until I thought about it after."

The ministers attempted to reach Bennett in Vancouver before his media conference and convince him to stay. Although most knew this would not happen, at least they would be with him. The cars left the buildings immediately for the airport. Ministers were tight-lipped in front of the press as they raced to be with their premier.

Of course the reason Bennett was in Vancouver was so they wouldn't be able to stop him. By the time their planes landed in Vancouver, he was in front of the microphones announcing his decision.

NOW, BENNETT RELAXED for the first time in years. He would watch but stay out of the leadership race. He would see his pet projects, Expo and the Coquihalla highway, as his last accomplishments before leaving office.

The Coquihalla was built partly to soothe Interior nerves, which were beginning to fray because of all the money and attention being spent in Vancouver. It was built partly because Bennett realized that to open up the Kelowna–Kamloops–Merritt triangle he needed to connect them, both to each other and to the coast.

The project had been announced in the 1978 throne and budget speeches, but nothing much had happened on the project, other than preliminary engineering. This followed the old adage of never ruining a good election promise by actually doing something about it; you could always promise it again.

At the third cabinet retreat in Cowichan Bay in 1984, the assignment given the ministries was to bring forward ideas to creatively accelerate capital expenditures within existing budgets. Once again, ministers sat at a hollow square table with deputy ministers behind until it was their ministry's turn to present ideas. Then they then joined their minister at the table.

The meeting had gotten off to a rousing start when Alex Fraser, the MLA from Quesnel and minister of highways as well as one of Bennett's most trusted political advisers, arrived. While driving through the scrum of media he told them, "Piss Off! You're a bunch of dorks." The media rushed this comment onto the six o'clock radio and television news, arguing it showed a government in decline and out of control. When Fraser was asked by one deputy what he thought the outcome of his comments would be, he replied: "Get me ten thousand votes in my riding."

The next day, just before lunch, it was the highways minister's turn. His deputy joined him at the table. Bennett said: "Alex, I want the Coquihalla accelerated and opened in time for Expo."

Alex turned to his deputy minister, Al Rhodes, a long-serving, much-respected senior official who had worked his way from day labourer to deputy. Rhodes said: "Well, Premier, that is just not possible. We can get started on it, but we will not be able to be anywhere near completing it."

Bennett fastened those steely blue eyes on his minister and replied, "Alex, I want us to accelerate the construction on the Coquihalla and have it opened in time for Expo."

Alex knew when to simply nod. His deputy didn't, and replied: "Well, we can make every effort, Premier, but it is not likely, wouldn't bet on it, couldn't take it to the bank."

Bennett replied: "Let's break for lunch. It's a buffet, so help yourselves. Alex, perhaps you and your deputy can join Bud and me."

Bud Smith had just joined Bennett's staff as principal secretary. The night before, during happy hour, he had sauntered around, bow-legged, pigeon-toed in his cowboy boots, being friendly and meeting the deputies he did not know, and scaring the hell out of most of them with his frank manner. One deputy, an old friend from university, asked Bud why he had come down from Kamloops to Victoria to take the job, "and how long are you staying?"

Bud replied: "Till we can get the Coquihalla highway built. So, not long."

After lunch the premier opened the meeting by saying: "Alex, we were talking about some highway expenditures that could possibly be accelerated. Any ideas?"

Alex replied: "Yes, Premier, I believe we can get to work today, my deputy will be leaving right after our presentation, and we will open the Coquihalla prior to Expo by accelerating construction. You agree, deputy?"

"Absolutely! We'll find a way, and it will open before Expo, Premier. I give you my word."

The opening of the Coquihalla was accomplished by accelerating the construction and paying for it through the imposition of temporary tolls. Bud Smith travelled to all the affected municipalities and encouraged them, by explaining the deal, to pass resolutions to impose the tolls—but only to pay for the acceleration of the Merritt connector.

The day it opened, Bennett proudly rode the scenic route in an open convertible, knowing the economic activity generated by this infrastructure expenditure would pay for itself hundreds of times over. Bud Smith explains:

> Premier Bennett held the view very strongly that we had to do something to get away from the notion of having three economies in British Columbia: Greater Vancouver, the Island and the rest. His view was that if you tied together, through the completion of the Coquihalla, the four communities of the Thompson–Okanagan—Penticton, Kelowna, Kamloops and Vernon—there would be, in ten or fifteen years, a population of 500,000 people in that area. And the Coquihalla would be the umbilical cord that would tie them to the southwest corner of British Columbia, the Vancouver corner. And if you have a significant amount of density of economic activity and massive population in one area connected to another area, those two things themselves generate additional economic activity.
>
> So the idea of the Coquihalla highway was to build a road that would tie together those communities and that they, in turn, would be connected to the Lower Mainland. In fact, even without completing the Coquihalla highway system, which hasn't yet been done, there is in excess of half a million people in that area now. And the economy has grown dramatically, particularly the recreation economy, which simply would not have grown without the Coquihalla.

OPENING EXPO WAS A different challenge. It was a marketing opportunity and, if handled correctly, would put Vancouver and Expo 86 on the front pages of the world's papers.

The Queen of Canada, Elizabeth II, had graciously agreed to visit Vancouver in 1984 and officially invite the world to participate in the exhibition. She had told the premier she would gladly come back to open the fair in 1986.

This presented Bennett with a problem. He loved his queen dearly, but he didn't want her to open Expo. He wanted the Prince and Princess of Wales. They were a hot property, especially Diana. But how do you uninvite the queen?

The answer, if there was to be one, lay with Stu Hodgson. Stu was the current chair of transit, put there to ensure that SkyTrain was built and opened on time. But, more importantly, Bennett recalled that Stu had been invited by Prince Charles, personally, to his wedding. The prince called him "Uncle Stu." And Stu was one of the few Canadians to receive a personal invite.

Prince Charles, while growing up, had spent many pleasurable summers in the Northwest Territories, loving the land and the people. And Stu had been commissioner of the Northwest Territories for many years. If anyone could get the queen uninvited without ruffling feathers or causing hurt feelings, and the prince and princess to attend, it was Uncle Stu.

Off to London he went. Pleasant chats and a cup of tea, and the deal was done. The prince politely asked his mother if she would mind, *terribly,* stepping aside and letting him and Diana relieve her of the onerous duty of travel. Not only gracious but smart, the queen, aware that the Prince and Princess of Wales were doing much to restore people's confidence in the future of the monarchy, wisely agreed.

Now it just had to happen.

WHILE ALL THE PLANNING for Expo was going on and the excitement was building, business went on in the capital. The cabinet had now been working together for ten years, and the ministers were a team that knew each other well. Good results sometimes flowed from small beginnings, as cabinet member Stephen Rogers remembers:

> I was the minister of environment and Don Phillips was doing the expansion of the Roberts Bank. At that time it was one pod, and they were going to double it because the coal exports were going to get bigger. And just as a quip, I said, "You know, Don, if you quadruple it you

can probably get the environmental permit. But ten years from now when you want to go and quadruple, you'll never get it," because we knew that sort of anti-growth was going.

Every time I'd fly over that terminal and look down at what now is essentially one of North America's most successful and biggest terminals...

For the first three or four years they put a few containers out in that field to see if the coal dust got in them, and then all of a sudden the growth came and we were ready. You can look down and smile when you're flying over and say, "We got that one right."

EXPO 86 WAS TO open on May 2, 1986, at 2:00 PM, precisely, before more television viewers worldwide than had witnessed the opening of the Los Angeles Olympics in 1984. At that exact moment the Prince and Princess of Wales had to be standing in a pre-chosen spot on Granville Island for the live coverage to begin.

The deputy provincial secretary was put in charge of the royal visit on behalf of the province. Former member of Parliament Bill Clark, who had lost his seat to John Turner, headed the federal team. In practical matters this meant that Clark as the representative of the senior government was responsible for the Prince of Wales. The provincial rep was left to make do with Diana. Sometimes life is fair.

In effect, the province ran the show and determined where the royal couple would visit and who they would see, all subject to the approval of Buckingham Palace. Six months before the visit, the first step was to gain Premier Bennett's general approval of the plan for the visit. Obviously, the prince and princess would start in Victoria with the official welcome at the legislative buildings. The deputy provincial secretary then proposed, on the second page of the briefing note, a stop in Nanaimo. Bennett looked at it, and then up over his half-glasses.

"Nanaimo?"

"Kelowna is on page three."

"Nanaimo is where you ran as a Liberal. Back in '69. You got fewer votes than you have relatives living there, didn't you?"

Half-smiles all around the room.

"Yes, after that I decided to go where the real power lies. The bureaucracy."

Bennett looked up sharply over his glasses.

"Well, Premier, that is, power that of course does not include, or rather comes from, this office and, ummmm...Kelowna is on page three. And Nanaimo gives us an opportunity to sail from Departure Bay to Horseshoe Bay on the *Queen of the North,* and you might invite several hundred guests."

"No. I want it to sail into downtown Vancouver and to dock at the Canada Pavilion."

"Yes, sir."

The plan was approved and included stops in Kamloops, then Kelowna and back to Vancouver. Then up to Prince George. Bennett wanted the people of the province, not just Vancouver, to see Charles and Diana. He had wanted more time upcountry, but from his experience with the queen he knew we would have to work hard to gain approval for these trips.

An immense planning session then began. When significant changes were contemplated, they were discussed with the premier. He respected protocol and knew marketing.

He was, however, not above having some mischief with some of the more arcane issues. The height of the podium for the speakers who would open the exhibition became a behind-the-scenes issue. Prime Minister Brian Mulroney's staff insisted that the speaking surface on the podium be thirty-one inches from the floor to enable him to read the text without glasses. Governor General Jeanne Suavé, a former Liberal cabinet minister, was short, and she demanded that the podium be set at twenty-nine inches. Higher, and she would not be seen. The federal staff haggled over this for days. Bennett, when told about this, laughed and insisted on thirty inches. The province gracefully gave in to the prime minister after the governor general, in a pique, refused to come to the opening.

The plans finally completed, and after a second "recce," as Buckingham Palace called the reconnaissance, and many practice runs, including some that used stand-ins for the Royals, the event was arranged and approved. These plans filled huge three-ring binders in which every movement was timed, scripted, practised and followed.

And off it went, for the next ten days. At the end of each day the Royals would go back to their rooms and stand and chat for ten or fifteen minutes. At first, the staff thought this was a very kind gesture. But soon they realized that while they, the staff, could now retire to the bar for a tall scotch and then go out for dinner, the Royals were trapped. A nice jail. But the lack of freedom to go out and do what a normal person might do is work that some are simply not cut out for.

The trips upcountry went splendidly, as did the events in Vancouver. It had been a stretch to get the premier to agree to the Royals visiting city hall. He reminded the planners that the mayor, Mike Harcourt, had written the International Bureau of Expositions advising it to cancel the event and had not been especially co-operative in other matters.

However, Bennett's good sense prevailed, and once the point was made a stop at city hall was arranged. He was mildly amused when Harcourt, mid-visit, told the media that he had been dropped from several venues. Harcourt used the occasion to take a cheap shot at the premier for dropping him, he claimed, after he had been invited.

Bennett said nothing. He knew Harcourt had not been dropped. He had earned the right never to be asked.

It is unusual for the host-city mayor not to be included in many events, but once the mayor's position had been explained to the senior staff in Buckingham Palace they got it. They just shook their heads and never mentioned it again.

The visit went off without a hitch, at least none that the public noticed. All the planning paid off, and the crowds around the province were gratifying to Charles and Diana as they demonstrated their love and affection for the royal family. They were both magnificent.

The second-to-last day was busy with visits on the Expo site to the pavilions of Saudi Arabia, Britain, the United States and California. The Saudi pavilion was interesting, but the staff there got carried away with the incense being burnt, and the short boat journey over to the British pavilion was welcome for the crisp, salt air that cleared a few heads.

As part of the planning every visited site was re-inspected many times before the royal visit, and always twenty-four hours before, six hours before and thirty minutes before to ensure that everything was following the master plan. The visit to the British pavilion was to follow the winding path through the exhibit. Because of the problems Diana experienced when turning corners in crowds, the numbers in the pavilion were to be limited to about thirty.

As soon as the advance person from the thirty-minute inspection left, the British consul in charge opened the doors and invited about three hundred of his closest friends and associates inside. Then closed the doors. The temperature rose fiercely.

When the Royals arrived, the doors were open and into the throngs they went. When they finished the visit thirty minutes later, the princess was not feeling well and the prince was not amused. The Royals' principal secretary asked the deputy provincial secretary how could this have happened, the two of them dropping back slightly from the Royals to have the unpleasant conversation. But because it was the British pavilion, it was soon passed over.

Next, the USA pavilion. The Americans were justly proud of their pavilion, particularly a theatre that simulated the feeling of weightlessness one felt in space. They wanted to show off this display. It had originally been vetoed by the deputy provincial secretary because it could make people nauseous, and when revisited by the Americans with the principal secretary to the Royals on one of his recces, it was firmly rejected again.

Because the Royals were ahead of the principal secretary and the deputy provincial secretary, when the Royals met the U.S. ambassador to Canada at the pavilion door, they could not intervene when the Americans changed the route. By the time they caught up, the entourage was clearly en route to the space theatre. To backtrack would create an incident, and the Americans knew that would not happen.

As Prince Charles said: "There really is no such thing as protocol, there just are good manners."

Into the theatre and out after experiencing weightlessness, the princess was not in good shape. But with the short, brisk walk to the California pavilion, it was hoped that she would gain her sea legs. So, into the California pavilion, which had followed the agreed plan to the letter, and trouble.

The Princess of Wales fainted. She was caught on the way down, before she fell to the floor, and rushed into a small office. Security, medical staff, ambulances were immediately called. Her husband was worried and anxious.

Given smelling salts, she came around. A quiet moment, then Vic Chapman, the Royals' public-relations person, stepped in.

"Ma'am, I need to know the answer to one question, because the media are already speculating. Are you pregnant?"

"No."

"Ma'am, I really need to know, to defuse this or shift the story."

She looked at him for a moment. "Vic, I can tell you categorically as of this morning I know I am not pregnant."

Chapman went off to deal with the media. Diana recovered, and under her own power she walked out and returned to the hotel. The ride back was not comfortable for her, nor for the deputy provincial secretary, who was riding with the principal secretary.

Once back at their hotel, with the Royals comfortable in their suite, the deputy provincial secretary got on the phone. First the premier's office. He was in a meeting; call back in fifteen minutes. Next, Jimmy Pattison, who took the call immediately.

"Is she all right? Anything wrong?"

"She's fine. Just overtaxed."

The deputy went on to tell Jimmy what had happened on the site and argued that someone's ass needed to be severely kicked around the block. This cavalier treatment of the Royals by two significant participating countries, Britain and the USA, was completely unacceptable.

Jimmy replied: "Look at it this way. No one was hurt. She's okay. And, you know, their presence here is no longer front-page news in North America, Canada or elsewhere. But this will put us back on page one tomorrow morning. It's probably worth ten million dollars in free advertising."

The deputy provincial secretary hung up, shaking his head, and phoned for his appointment with the premier. He repeated his conversation with Jimmy, including Jimmy's response, which annoyed him. The premier responded, "Well, Jimmy's right. No harm done. And the advertising for Expo will really help. Go back and fix it without making a fuss or telling the media about the behaviour of the Brits or the Yanks. They only wanted to meet her and show off."

The deputy did so, recognizing that these two successful men had forgotten more about advertising and marketing than he would ever know, and for sure he should try to keep his day job.

IN THE FALL OF 1985 Bill Bennett began to travel around the province, making speeches in key constituencies. Prince George, Cranbrook, the Fraser Valley, Kamloops and Quesnel. The speeches received little media coverage. They had one theme: renewal.

The Social Credit Party had to renew itself again. Standing pat was not an option that would guarantee long-term political success. New people, new ideas were absolutely necessary. He encouraged Bud Smith, in Kamloops, to run. Also Kim Campbell, who was working in his office as a senior policy adviser and brilliant foil to Norman Spector, in Vancouver.

Bennett asked his cabinet one day early in 1986 to tell him, individually, if they were going to run again. They all knew that if they said they were not going to run he would likely remove them from cabinet before the next election. This would give a new face a cabinet position, and thus give the person an easier run at re-election.

Three honourable men stepped forward: Don Phillips, Harvey Schroeder and Jim Chabot. Others kept quiet. The three were removed from cabinet and kept a stiff upper lip in public. Privately, they were hurt and angry. Phillips puts it this way:

> I was annoyed because I was in charge of the business enterprise program, where we sent individual letters to all the businesses we knew in England, Germany, France and Japan. I forget how many we sent out; the first one was "The world is coming to Canada," the second was "The world is coming to British Columbia," the third was "The world is coming to Vancouver" and the fourth was an invitation to come to Expo and get VIP treatment if you want us to pick you up at the airport. That was to be done just for the business enterprise program part of Expo: "Okay, you're coming here, we want to tell you all about British Columbia,

> 'cause then we don't have to go visit you." I thought it was a great program, and then I don't have anything to do with it. I'm no longer chief. I invited all these guys here, and I'm not going to be here to welcome them. I was pissed off, I was really pissed off. But I knew why.

The ones who kept quiet kept their cabinet posts, and this added some bitterness to the pill the three had swallowed.

THE DAY AFTER EXPO closed, some left-wing academics presented a paper describing the disaster Expo had been and the terrible legacy it would create in the future. The major networks and papers presented the criticism as top of the news. It quickly disappeared as a story, because the people knew. No one needed this crap.

Jimmy Pattison sums up the fair:

> The five and a half months were a blur as we went from success to success. In August, which was almost continuously sunny, we broke our original target of 13.75 million. In September, when people expected the crowds to slacken, they held and built through October. The word of mouth had raced around the world. Some of the very top executives from American and Japanese companies started arriving in the fall. Meanwhile, all the local people who were going to savour the quiet off-months descended en masse. On the second-last day, 341,000 flooded the site. The final attendance was 22,111,578 visits.
>
> And best of all, we came in under the budget that we had committed to Premier Bennett and his cabinet and the people of British Columbia. The total deficit was $279 million—which was $32 million better than we'd promised the government.

Perhaps more important was the sense of pride and "can do" that enveloped the province.

THE BOMBSHELL THAT was his resignation sent Bennett's ministers scrambling. The leadership race was on, and what a race. There was no clear replacement. And the ministers could not agree among themselves who they should support. Familiarity does breed contempt; they knew each other too well, were too aware of their strengths and weaknesses.

This was exacerbated by the perception that in the last few years Bennett had relied too much on senior staff in his office and too little on his ministers. This was certainly true on issues like the Constitution repatriation and the fight with Solidarity over the restraint program. But the premier couldn't be blamed. His ministers respected and loved him.

His staff was blamed, and many of the leadership candidates ran against the premier's office on the platform that the membership was no longer in control of the party—the hired guns at the centre were running things.

Bud Smith bore part of this dislike, because some people thought the premier had laid his hands on him: he was the chosen one. Jim Nielsen saw it this way:

> There was an anger about Bud Smith among many members of cabinet. Some felt that Bud seemed to have an inside track. He had been going around the province having meetings with members of the party.
>
> I got a phone call from someone in Richmond one day, and they said, "Are you going to the wine and cheese party?" I said, "What wine and cheese party?" They said, "The one Bud Smith is having in Richmond."
>
> I inquired about it, and I was told, "Bud's trying to get yuppies to become part of Social Credit, and Mike Bailey and he are going around the province on tour."
>
> Anyway when the premier made his announcement some members of cabinet wondered what the hell was going on. And there was a thought that we sure as hell didn't want Bud Smith.
>
> I said, "I'm going to run." I didn't have a hope in hell, I knew that because I didn't have any organization, didn't have money and I wasn't Mister Friendly."

Bud Smith refutes the charge that he was hand-picked by Bennett: "The proof he didn't favour me rests with one fact. Had he been in my camp, I would have won."

IRRESPECTIVE OF THIS DEBATE, the Bennett years in government had seen dramatic changes in the makeup of the major political parties in B.C. since the days of W.A.C. Bennett. The authors Donald Blake, R.K. Carty and Lynda Erickson, in their book *Grassroots Politicians: Party Activists in British Columbia,* chronicle these events, and their empirical evidence strongly supports the anecdotal evidence.

Bill Bennett rebuilt the party that he inherited from his father to create an 80,000-member-strong centre-right party. His father had lost the support of the federal Liberal and Conservative Party stalwarts that had made up his coalition for his twenty years in power. This translated in the 1972 election to the election of five Liberals and two Conservatives.

Bill Bennett's aggressive marketing strategy, coupled with Grace McCarthy's party organization efforts, soon recruited the political elites in the Liberal and Conservative parties. They recognized the need to unite under one banner or face repeated NDP victories. And they did unite. Only two MLAS from the traditional parties were elected in 1975 and none in 1979.

Bennett consolidated his support of the anti-NDP vote and downplayed the populist past of his father because it did not fit his personal style. True to form, having analyzed the issue, he recognized his failing in 1979—when he had ignored his role as party leader as well as head of government—and had gone on to build a modern political machine.

The professional team he built was recruited from the best people in Canada, namely those in Ontario, where Pat Kinsella and Jerry Lampert joined the team. He switched pollsters to Allan Gregg and Decima, the best person in Canada not just to poll but to explain what the polling meant in political-action terms. Polling was not just carried out around election time; it was a year-round activity that Bennett shared with a tight circle both in government and in the party.

Bennett agreed with the professionals to set up more sophisticated fundraising mechanisms, and people like Mike Burns created "the top twenty club." Not a club that only the top twenty businesspeople could join, but a club named after the twenty swing constituencies where extra funding would tip the balance. For a five-thousand-dollar annual donation, people could join the premier for a private dinner three times a year. These and other efforts resulted in large sums of money being raised every year, up to $4 million in the peak year. Pat Kinsella explains:

> The top twenty was, well, I think a lot of people thought it was twenty people. You know, top twenty supporters of Bill Bennett, who would in fact write a cheque for the party. But the top twenty was a Mike Burns idea. And the twenty represented the ridings. It wasn't people. It was the top twenty ridings. There's a number of ridings that we win no matter what, unless we lose the election.
>
> You take out Bennett's riding in Kelowna, you take out Bob McClelland's in Langley, because they were slam-dunks, and a bunch more, and then there'd be twenty that were swing ridings, or close ridings. We would pay attention to those.
>
> What was lacking in most of those was money. Maybe a hundred guys would put in at least a couple of thousand dollars a year.

To parallel the party-building, Bennett changed the structure in his office in Victoria. He appointed Pat Kinsella as deputy minister. This was changed shortly thereafter into a new position called principal secretary. Several months after the 1983 election, he moved Pat out to head up the party apparatus and imported Bud Smith. Then, by reviewing government communications with expert private-sector individuals and attracting Doug Heal, who had led the overview, and then Dave Laundy, he got government messaging consistent and on target. Never an easy task, as getting government ministers and the caucus on the same page is a lot like herding thirty tomcats to the same feeding dish.

Finally Bennett strengthened the internal discipline in the bureaucracy by situating in his office Norman Spector as his deputy minister, one who brought a high level of intellectual rigour and an outspoken mind to government policy.

However, this centralization and modernization was not without detractors. Memberships in the party fell to about thirty-five thousand. Old-time, fundamentalist grassroots Socreds felt alienated from the slick party machine, yearned for the good old populist days when the party was a movement and blamed a lack of local input for policies like restraint, which, in their view, had disproportionately affected local rural services.

The NDP had also been changing in various ways. Its popular support base had continued to grow as Bennett's resource development policies were more successful, thereby providing more unionized resource workers in rural B.C., and these workers were natural NDP followers. Also, as the public service grew with more teachers, health care workers and social services, these workers, particularly after the restraint program, moved squarely into the NDP camp.

As an example, during the Bennett years the number of NDP candidates who came from blue-collar backgrounds fell from over 15 percent to under 5 percent, while public-sector representation rose from under 20 percent to over 40 percent.

But the NDP trends were of little concern to the Socred leadership candidates. To them this was an internal fight. As Blake, Carty and Erickson comment:

> The battle for succession in the party involved subtle and sometimes not so subtle efforts by many candidates to distance themselves from Bennett and the record of his government. Observers of the contest not only saw the distancing by many candidates from the incumbent leader, they saw a struggle for control of the party between advocates of closer ties to the Progressive Conservative party and those wishing to preserve the tradition of federal neutrality; between the inheritors of the party's populist tradition and modern organization men and women; and between neo-conservatives and centrists.

THE AVERAGE PROVINCIAL leadership race in Canada usually attracts fewer than four candidates. Only once in Canadian history had there been more than six candidates in a provincial leadership race (there were six in the 1973 Socred race). But this was only the second leadership contest for Social Credit; W.A.C. had never faced one. When Bill Bennett entered the first one in 1973, there was really no contest. But there was a contest in 1986, and after all, this was Lotus Land: twelve candidates threw their hats in the ring. When the dust cleared, though, the race came down to four candidates: Bill Vander Zalm, Brian Smith, Grace McCarthy and Bud Smith.

A significant trend in choosing the winner was geographic. The minor candidates' support was almost all constituency and personally based. Of the major candidates, Brian Smith cleaned up on Vancouver Island. Bud Smith relied heavily on the Interior. Grace McCarthy's constituency was in the Lower Mainland. Only Bill Vander Zalm had support in every region. He won support from 64 percent of the ridings, Grace from about half, and the rest much lower.

Grace had encouraged Vander Zalm to enter the race to stop Bud Smith. She was half right. He did stop Bud Smith. But by doing so, he gained province-wide support and was able to defeat her on the third ballot, leaving only Brian Smith to face the broad support of the winner on the fourth go-around.

The die was cast when Bud Smith moved his support to Vander Zalm. This left voters a choice of Grace or Brian. Grace's delegates were passionately committed to her. She had run second on the first two ballots. But her growth was limited, because for everyone who loved her, others, led by her former cabinet colleagues, could not see her as a leader. They led the gradual shift to Brian Smith, so by the third ballot he had passed her. She dropped out. It wasn't that people were wild about Brian; they just could not bring themselves to support Grace.

The race between Brian Smith and Bill Vander Zalm was no contest. Two-thirds of Grace's delegates went with the other candidate who had run against party centralization—a return to the old populist days, which she also symbolized. Her support from the elites of society went to Smith; the rest flooded over to Vander Zalm, and he won easily with nearly double the vote. His appeal to populists and old-time party members carried the day. As Blake *et al.* note, "Bill Vander Zalm's victory ultimately represented the recapturing of Social Credit by party activists who yearned for a return to the original populist party of W.A.C. Bennett."

Bill Bennett had wanted change and renewal. A Vander Zalm victory was not the outcome he had hoped for. He felt the party was in danger.

The best he could do was offer to sit down with premier-elect Vander Zalm and talk with him about the immediate and long-term issues he would face. Bennett offered to meet the next morning.

The meeting never happened. Vander Zalm did not show up. Instead, Peter Toigo came over, apologized for Vander Zalm and asked the outgoing premier if he had any advice he wanted to pass along to the incoming premier.

Bennett looked at Toigo for a minute, was polite and outlined a few generalities. In ten minutes, the coffee meeting was over. Bennett never knew whether Vander Zalm heard from Toigo or not. He did not, however, ever hear from Vander Zalm again.

Minutes later, he discussed his concerns with Audrey. He said, "I guess he knows everything he thinks he needs to know to lead the province."

"Lead it where, is the question," Audrey replied.

"I fear where. But I've done all I can. We should go… home."

A FINAL WORD

"He was in it for principled reasons; he was motivated by principle, not personal gain or partisan advantage."

NORMAN SPECTOR

One problem in judging Bill Bennett's performance as premier is the polarized nature of B.C. politics. The partisan nature of politics west of the Rockies will prejudice any measure of his worth.

It is also still too soon to judge. If you marched with Solidarity, Bennett won't be very high on your list. If you were an old Socred, he probably comes in second, after his father.

Most of the down-home kind of folks I talk to pay little attention to politics. Those who practise it remember Bill Bennett fondly. He does look better and better to them as they look back, but that may have more to do with the premiers who followed him.

But I don't think that is all there's to it. People remember Expo and the hope it gave B.C. for a bright future, and the more thoughtful ones think that perhaps they don't give Bennett enough credit for it. They remember the Coquihalla highway, the SkyTrain, B.C. Place, North East Coal and

BCRIC shares, the ombudsman and the auditor general, the Summer and Winter Games. They also remember Solidarity. Some fondly, some not. As issues arise again today, many ask, why are we going through this again: didn't we go through this before?

There are various ways to measure Bill Bennett's place.

He was the third-longest-serving premier in the province, behind his father, who served for just over twenty years, and Richard McBride, who governed for twelve and a half years. Bennett served for almost eleven years.

Since the beginning of the twentieth century, B.C. has had twenty-eight elections. W.A.C. Bennett won six of them. Richard McBride, a Conservative, won four. Bill Bennett won three times. Four other premiers won twice. The rest, one time each.

Popular vote is also a way to judge. In a democracy, it is the people who are the final arbiters. The data here from our early years is a bit murky, and the rules were different. For example, it was common for people to run in more than one constituency to ensure that senior members, such as premiers, were elected in at least one riding.

In one election, the Conservatives elected seven members by acclamation, and therefore it is difficult to rely on voting data. In another, in 1933, the Conservatives, after winning 53.3 percent of the vote in the previous election in 1928, ran no official candidates. The Great Depression knocked them out, at least for one election.

As well, during and shortly after the Second World War (including the 1945 and 1949 elections) there was a coalition government, an alliance between the Liberals and Conservatives that skews voting percentage outcomes. Some would argue that the war had nothing to do with the formation of the coalition, that it really was about keeping the CCF out of power.

The popular vote since 1950 in the next half-dozen record-holders (out of sixteen electoral contests) looks like this:

W.A.C. Bennett—46.79 percent in 1969.

Bill Bennett—48.23 percent in 1979.

Bill Bennett—49.25 percent in 1975.

Bill Vander Zalm—49.32 percent in 1986.

Bill Bennett—49.76 percent in 1983.

Gordon Campbell—57.62 percent in 2001.

The popular vote judges Bill Bennett's administrations well—three of the top five results. Most people would think that the populist Vander Zalm would have done better than Bennett. Wrong. Many people would have thought that W.A.C. with his unbeatable record of six victories would have done better than the son. Wrong.

To try and get a grip on this enigmatic man, I found it useful to review a sample of folks who worked with him or studied him.

Bennett asked Jimmy Pattison to take on a part-time, half-day-a-week job for two years in 1981, to get Expo off on the right foot. When the two years were up, Jimmy wanted to go back to running his business, and he told Bennett that one night as the two of them were having dinner on his boat. Bennett asked him to stay, and he did. Pattison has a unique view of Bennett:

> I had lots to do with Bill Bennett. And the more I saw him, the more I respected him. He really cared about people's money. He was thrifty to the point that he was very conscious of the taxpayers' dollars. To me he was first-class. If politicians everywhere cared about the people's money like Bill Bennett did, this country would be in a lot better shape financially.
>
> He had his own common-sense way, from working with his dad in a hardware store. They had to take in more than they spent. The hardware business is a penny business. He understood pennies and he understood business. Bill Bennett understood a lot about big-picture stuff as well.
>
> When push came to shove, he was always there. I seldom met anybody that I respected more than Bill Bennett.

David Mitchell has studied the Bennett family intensely. Author, historian, MLA, university administrator and political commentator, he compared the father and son in the *Financial Post* on July 26, 1986:

> *As government leaders.* W.A.C. Bennett directed a highly centralized government during a prosperous period. His balanced budgets were the order of the day. Bill Bennett served as premier during a much more complicated period, socially, economically and politically. The roller-coaster economy of the 1970s dove steeply downward in the 1980s as the province's resource-based economy struggled against a serious world oversupply of its primary commodities.
>
> Governing during this period of collapsing assumptions about life in Lotus Land with strong political opposition, increasing demands for public expenditures, and social turmoil, was by far the toughest job in public administration in Canada. Bill Bennett's accomplishments during those ten years are, therefore, possibly greater than his father's in twenty...
>
> *As politicians.* There is no question that W.A.C. Bennett was the more natural politician. Politics were his life...
>
> For Bill Bennett, politics never came as naturally...He never had the *joie de vivre* of his father...
>
> But his years in public office were, he has declared, only one part of his life. And although those years were extremely tough in political terms, his record makes them look easy. In fact, he never lost a nomination, leadership convention, by-election or general election. His father, while we remember his many victories, lost all of the above at different times in his career. Bill Bennett played to win, and he leaves public life undefeated.

Liberal Gordon Gibson was recruited by Bennett to join the new Social Credit Party he built, but he turned it down. Grit blood runs deep in Gibson's veins. Staying on as a Liberal, he succeeded David Anderson as leader of the B.C. Liberal Party. On Bennett's stepping down, he wrote in the *Financial Post* on June 21, 1986:

> It is timely to consider the leadership of retiring Bill Bennett of British Columbia. Make no mistake—over the past few years his leadership of the province has been as bold as Trudeau's on the Constitution or Lévesque's on separatism...

> Bennett's less important leadership has had to do with megaprojects. Whether in the end North East Coal or the Coquihalla Highway or Expo 86 will be pluses or minuses for the province is a question of importance, but only at the margins…
>
> Bennett's real leadership comes in the manner in which he has fundamentally altered the balance of power in British Columbia society. He has taken on some of the most powerful forces in our province and beaten them. In the process, he has reduced their clout by an order of magnitude…
>
> He leaves a province fundamentally changed, for good or ill. His eventual successor of whatever political stripe will have far more financial room to manoeuvre and the ability to be a conciliator rather than a confrontationist—because Bennett did that job for him or her.

Marjorie Nichols, for years the *Vancouver Sun*'s political columnist in Victoria, Ottawa and Washington, was once offered the press secretary job in Bennett's office. She turned him down, but not from disapproval. In her book *Mark My Words*, she observed:

> Bill was very unsure of himself when he started but not afraid to expose himself in that he was always open to advice. The convictions he had were all economic and financial. In the social fields he was at sea.
>
> But unlike most guys I've met, Bennett walked out of politics poorer than he went in. Bill Bennett did not profit personally one iota from his time in office. He was so frugal it was extraordinary. Right after he became premier, I was talking to one of his press secretaries, and I told her that I noticed he had spots on the knees of his suits. I said surely he could afford a better suit than that. She laughed and said: "Those aren't spots—those are his knees." He was wearing this absolutely threadbare suit. This man was a millionaire, and he still had his shoes resoled.
>
> After he came to power in 1975, he kept Barrett's car, a 1973 gold-coloured Chevrolet, and he kept using it right to the end when he stepped out in 1986…

> Up close, Bennett was difficult to dislike. The great battles that I had with him were over the restraint program in 1983...
>
> It wasn't so much the restraint program that I disagreed with, but the accompanying legislation. It went so far beyond where it had to go that it seemed to me to be deliberately provocative.

In their book *The Reins of Power: Governing British Columbia,* a team of University of Victoria political scientists—Terry Morley, Norman Ruff, Neil Swainson, Jeremy Wilson and Walter Young—judged Bennett this way:

> More than either of his two predecessors, Bill Bennett took the business of the leader's image seriously. He was the least experienced of the three, and when he first assumed office lacked those skills that enabled him to handle audiences easily...The personal image he sought to display was that of a serious, hard-working and knowledgeable provincial leader whose approach was dedicated and businesslike. Initially the objective was to demonstrate a contrast with the previous premier. Ultimately, it became the preferred style.
>
> The contrast that Bill Bennett was determined to demonstrate was simply that his government was capable where the previous government was not...
>
> It was under the aegis of the Bennett government of 1979 that Treasury Board was expanded to become an effective financial management agency; the cabinet was restructured to include an elaborate committee system, and the premier's office was expanded to include both technical and political advisers. After the 1979 election it was evident that the premier was determined to tighten his control over the party as well, and in doing so, direct more attention to the symbolic authority of his office. The appointment of a small team of advisers with television expertise was designed to place more emphasis on the central role of premier. To some extent this was in response to the low point in Bennett's political career marked by the "dirty tricks" affair following the 1979 election...
>
> By contrast W.A.C. Bennett and Dave Barrett were "natural" politicians, though in their different leadership styles. W.A.C. Bennett

emphasized the formality of the office and typified the image of authority that was characteristic of the 1940s and 1950s... He also recognized the importance of overt symbols in establishing a sense of provincial pride and loyalty—a loyalty that would also enhance his authority as head of government and putative father of the province's prosperity... Astride the western empire stood the colossus that was Bennett, respected and feared by his colleagues who never argued with the "old man."

If the Bennett style was paternal, the Barrett style was fraternal. The government was a collegial apparatus, management was casual, Treasury Board kind of a bazaar at which ministers would attempt to out-quip the premier in order to increase a departmental budget...

The contrast between W.A.C. Bennett and the easy casualness of Dave Barrett backfired when it appeared to corroborate the opposition view that government was too serious, too complicated and too costly a matter to leave to a premier who seemed at times to be a genial incompetent. To be premier of a province one must, presumably, be more than "just plain folks"—the wise leader knows when to mingle and when to stand apart. Behind the common touch must lie the uncommon grasp.

Norman Spector was Bennett's closest adviser in the later years of his government. The two worked very closely together; Bennett introduced Spector to Prime Minister Brian Mulroney, who subsequently hired him after Bennett stepped down. Spector comments:

A couple of overall impressions. First of all, the way he ran his cabinet. He was like a teacher, he would never use the gavel and say this is the way it's going to be, he would explain the politics and the policy of an issue to them, and they'd listen, after the usual characters had sounded off. Pat McGeer had done his act and Gardy had been sticking his pen in his ear, and Jack Heinrich with his nervous jumping-around way of talking, they were all personalities and they all had their individual character.

Ultimately they'd be waiting for Bennett, and he would then sum it up. Sometimes he'd take fifteen minutes explaining—it'd be like a class, sitting at the knees of a master—explaining to them the realities of the situation, it was incredible. And so no votes, obviously; there never had to be.

The second overall impression was the way he dealt with his staff. Always respectful. Take Kim Campbell as the example. Here's a guy who hires a woman who turns out to be a federal minister of justice and a future prime minister of Canada as his adviser, and a strong woman. I always saw this as symbolic of the fact that he was not afraid to have smart, aggressive people around him, so in that sense he was a good leader. Ultimately he would make the decisions, but he would get the best advice. He didn't surround himself with yes people. Kim's the best example of that.

The third thing is the way he ran the government. The myth that I think caused part of Vander Zalm's ultimate downfall was that it was a centralized operation, that the premier's office held a whip to the ministers and ruled by fear. The reason for this misconception was that he was the outrider, he was the one minister who actually did have to be supervised, because he was such a cowboy. And so I think that he got the impression of the way the government ran and then sought to do that when he became premier, to an even greater extreme.

Bennett basically allowed ministers to do their own thing. Big issues were brought to cabinet, decisions were taken collectively, and Bennett played on three or four issues. Even on those issues, he brought in a range of advice from the public service.

He'd bring them in because he wanted to hear from his professionals, so in that sense it was not a centralized operation. I always thought that part of my role was to make sure that these people did get to come in and were made to feel comfortable, made to feel that they could be honest with the premier about what they thought. As far as I can remember no one ever suffered, no one ever got sent to Coventry as a result of telling the premier what they thought.

One other thing: he had a tough time with the media. The media then were a lot more aggressive towards the government than they are these days, they were a lot leftier. I think part of his problem with the media was that his skills were not verbal skills. Journalists' skills are verbal skills, and they tend to judge people's intelligence on the basis of the verbal facility.

I've never seen somebody look at a balance sheet like Bennett, and understand it so quickly, and I doubt that there would have been one or two journalists in the press gallery who would have had the analytical skills that Bennett had. But that was not something they judged him on. Similarly, he was on top of the budget, it was instinctive almost.

The last thing: of all the politicians I've known, he is number one in my book for standing on principle. Obviously he's a politician, they're all politicians. But you always felt that he was in it for principled reasons; he was motivated by principle, not personal gain or partisan advantage.

Jack Munro, head of the IWA, the largest union in the province during most of Bennett's days in office, was a staunch New Democrat. No friend of Bennett, he still had grudging respect for the man he cut the Kelowna Accord with, as he noted in his book *Union Jack*:

Even after all the goddamn fights I had with Premier Bill Bennett over the years, I would still get edgy every time I had to deal with him. I would always think to myself, "How am I going to handle this? He's the goddamn premier."

Usually when I'm dealing with people, I kind of win them over. I never really felt that I did that with Bennett. He was really cold. I don't think you could ever really get close to him. He put a shield around himself. So I would try and joke with him, and he would joke with me. But hell, when the premier cracks a joke, you have to laugh, even if it isn't goddamn funny. He always laughed at his own jokes...

It was in January 1978 when MacMillan Bloedel announced out of the clear blue they were going to shut down their Vancouver plywood plant, which would have thrown seven hundred people out of work.

First we tried meeting with Calvin Knudsen, CEO of MacMillan Bloedel...

> When that failed, we got Bill Bennett involved. Bennett was far out in goddamn right field, as far as his politics were concerned. But he was the kind of premier that I could have decent meetings with.
>
> The day before MacBlo was going to publicly announce that they were shutting the plant down, I phoned Bennett and told him that we'd like to have a meeting the next morning. We couldn't tell him what about, because MacBlo had only told us on the understanding that we wouldn't tell anyone else until the next day, when they made their public statement. Even though he didn't know what it was about, Bennett agreed to meet us. He said, "Sure, if you're that serious, I'll fly over to Vancouver tomorrow morning and we'll have breakfast." So we had breakfast. We told Bennett our version, and he said that the situation was unacceptable to his government.
>
> Then he met with MacMillan Bloedel. He laid the heavies on Knudsen. After Bennett did that, Knudsen told us that they wouldn't shut the place down...But their heart wasn't in it...So eventually we lost it, but due to Bennett's intervention we ended up saving Vancouver Plywood for an additional two years.
>
> You don't ask for frivolous meetings with the premier. Whenever we met, I sure as hell didn't always get what I wanted, but I always came away feeling that at least the guy had listened. He had a sense of humour as well. One day he was on his way over here to meet with me, and his aides in the car were kind of concerned about what would happen between us. Bennett apparently said to them: "Don't worry. I know the first thing Munro's going to say is, "Well, what did you fuck up today?"

Every former cabinet minister I spoke to enjoyed working with Bill Bennett. Everyone said similar things. He left you alone to run your department. He was there when you needed him. He had shrewd political judgement. He was funny in private, stiff in public. He learned in office and grew into a great premier. They share a view that Brian Smith puts to words: "There were two great premiers in B.C. in the twentieth century. Both were named Bennett."

Is this to be expected from former colleagues? I don't believe you would get the same feedback on premiers from ministers who served over the rest of the twentieth century.

That leaves the Mandarin who wrote this book to have a view. I come at it slightly differently. Comparing Bennett, Bennett and McBride is impossible. Their times were so different. The three enjoyed the most electoral successes, winning three or more times each. This isn't the only measure that should be used, but it's a useful one, which I will now discard.

Governments are living organisms. They evolve, grow and change. They adapt as society's expectations change and evolve. In British Columbia, the government W.A.C. Bennett ran was completely different from the one his son Bill ran. This is where I draw the distinction.

Bill Bennett is the father of modern government in British Columbia. W.A.C. represented the last, and the greatest, of the builders. Dave Barrett was the transition, partially because his own administrative style would not let him grasp the opportunity a new era presented. Bill Bennett is today's man, the premier who transformed the old-style, one-person government into a modern, complex administration.

He was a builder in his own right. He revitalized Vancouver with B.C. Place Stadium, SkyTrain, SeaBus and a land site around False Creek that helps make the city the most liveable in the world.

The Coquihalla highway opened up and tied together the Interior. North East Coal led to infrastructure development from Tumbler Ridge to Prince Rupert, and the port there still awaits other leaders of vision to complete it.

Whistler will host the 2010 Olympics because of the vision of the Bennett government. The other ski hills around the province that were part of the era reap uncountable millions in tourist and recreation spending.

Bennett's strategic thinking led to the development of the Pacific Rim as a trading destination for B.C., followed by Alberta and then the rest of Canada. For the first time in Canadian history, during Bennett's time in office, people in B.C. as well as in the east began to recognize the untold opportunities in the Pacific Rim.

A provincial premier also must play on the federal stage. Bennett's role in the repatriation of the Constitution and the passage of the Canadian Charter of Rights and Freedoms was central, significant and important for Canada. He protected B.C.'s interests. He turned around Ottawa's perception of B.C. governments. He set the stage for future premiers to reap the benefits or squander the gains.

The impact of Expo on the psyche, imagination and economy of B.C. is a lasting legacy, unsurpassed by anything. The industrial spinoffs, the establishment of one of the first commercial arbitration centres in Vancouver, a sense of "can do." The benefits of putting B.C. on the world map, combined with the sense of pride and accomplishment we all felt, runs down through generations.

Running government itself in these times was difficult. We faced the worst recession Canada has known since the Great Depression. This led to dealing with government spending that produces the Achilles heel that Bennett will be judged on.

During restraint he cut programs. His critics forget the large increases in spending, in the first half of his administration, on education, health and social services, and focus on these few years. But the truth is that community college and university spending rose sharply, as did the amounts spent on health care, doubling in his time in office.

The real problem wasn't restraint, all of us pulling in our belts a couple of notches; it was the onslaught of legislation that went further than most British Columbians were prepared to go. That was eventually corrected, but it was not forgotten.

Also, Bennett had his share of scandals to deal with. He learned how to manage them: timing, judgement, decisive action. But they left scars on his administration.

But the B.C. government has never been the same since Bill Bennett. The Financial Administration Act modernized government. The quality and professionalism of staff improved with high standards set at Treasury Board. The auditor general and the ombudsman were created to protect people's interests over government interests. Cabinet committees forced rigour and discipline on an unwieldy government. Modern administrative practices in British Columbia started with the Bennett administration. These are the systems that make taxpayers' dollars safe and at least attempt to see them spent wisely.

Bennett was a strategic premier. He saw the big picture and acted upon it. The other side of this coin is that he could not always communicate the big picture clearly, especially in the beginning. But this points to another strength. More than any premier I have known, he learnt from his mistakes. He was never afraid to analyze what had gone wrong as well as right, and to accept criticism. Then, in a businesslike way, he would lay out a plan, act on it and see it carried out to completion.

He thought long-term, strategically, and then put in place the plans that members of his cabinet and staff tactically carried forward. He revisited the decisions as they went forward, changed them if necessary but only as required. He had patience, based on experience and principle. Once the cycle was complete he reviewed it, learnt from it and planned the next two, three or five years down the line.

Bennett was fiercely partisan. He learnt that he had to be the head of his party as well as head of the government. Both had to be successful to ensure that his particular philosophy of what was good and right for British Columbia was carried forward.

At the same time, Premier Bennett was respectful of the public service and the role of his professional advisers. However, in matters of salary and benefits, he always wanted government employees to be treated in the same way as private-sector workers. And it bothered him that they were treated better.

You always knew where you stood with him. He had a role, his ministers had roles, and you had a role. It was all directed to the success of the government, not to his success. He was a public servant with a high sense of purpose and a commitment to give back to the wonderful province that he loved and that had been good to him. Here are Bill Bennett's views on his role:

> If you go out and tell everybody what they want to hear, you're going to eventually lose everybody. If you go out with your head stuck up with

> politics and office and you want to be loved, you'll end up being hated, because people will think you let them down.
>
> They understand from the beginning that there are some tough issues, so you tell them, "Here's why we're doing it."
>
> Then I think they will at least give you grudging respect, and that's about all that anyone gets out of politics.

I can't judge further than that, other than what I said at the outset of this book. Of all the premiers I worked with, he was head and shoulders above the rest. Nothing I have seen since changes that view.

ACKNOWLEDGEMENTS

Scott McIntyre felt this was an important book to get written, was surprised when it appeared and supportive throughout. His assignment of John Eerkes-Medrano as editor to work with me was a perfect choice. John's experience and gentle hand were invaluable in helping me trim the text while preserving my peculiar writing style.

Of course, I couldn't have done this without the co-operation of former Premier Bill Bennett. We spent seven half-days talking, and he spun stories, explained the politics and provided direction. He was as open as he is able or wanted to be; lifetime habits do not fall away easily. I believed almost everything he told me—he wouldn't have expected me to accept it all.

My interviews with his former ministers were equally revealing. Everyone has benefited from 20–20 hindsight. I wish I could have included all their stories here.

The staff guys I spoke to remember the Bennett days fondly and enjoy recalling the politics of the day and the man who was their premier. Most still call him Premier Bennett as a mark of respect.

The staff at the B.C. Provincial Archives were incredibly helpful and friendly. Likewise the staff at the Vancouver Public Library, Main Branch.

My virtual office assistant, Cindy Greenaway, never failed to meet impossible deadlines.

This book will be widely distributed to B.C. libraries thanks to the generosity of British Columbians. A $25,000 grant from Weyerhaeuser formed the cornerstone of this initiative, which was completed by donations from many others, unfortunately too numerous to mention specifically.

Meldy Harris provided some wonderful material from the "early days," and she and many others provided many photographs. I enjoyed them all. Again I wish I could have included more photographs and the names of everyone who sent them to me. It was very hard to make a final selection.

Bud Smith was always there to lend a helping ear, and to tell another story.

I turned regularly to my friend Norman Spector for advice, and this book would not have been written without his help.

SOURCES

As I noted in the Introduction to this book, I am neither a political scientist nor a historian, but a storyteller. I am the source for much of the information provided here. I lived it, and my personal observations colour the material. Some readers may wish to pursue my other sources in more detail. I list my principal sources for each chapter below.

I have used some sources that provide excellent renditions of the events as I or others I interviewed recalled them. For example, I supplied one chapter of Robert Sheppard and Michael Valpy's book *The National Deal* to a few of the people who were to be interviewed, to focus their comments. It worked; most said, "You know, they got it pretty much right, but don't present it from a B.C. perspective." I have used their observations as signposts and supplemented them with the B.C. inside view.

I have also received great assistance from two of Stan Persky's books. Obviously Stan speaks with his own ideological voice, but his books are based heavily on newspaper clippings, which are highlighted in his endnotes, and those endnotes were very useful in directing me to the appropriate newspaper stories and gaining the media's view.

Most of my interviews were recorded, and they will find their way into the B.C. Archives and perhaps into a university library. I will wait a few years, but they will be made public because part of what I wanted to do was capture an oral history for scholars to use as a primary source.

One last story. In the spring of 1984 Stu Hodgson, chair of Transit and Ferries, came into my office. He said he had a present for me. On several carts were huge 24″×36″ binders, filled with clippings from Canada's major newspapers, chronicling the summer and fall of discontent that was known as Operation Solidarity, or Restraint.

I lugged those damn things around for years, and when I left government they went home with me. My wife put up with this four-foot pile for a decade, until we moved. She convinced me to give them to the B.C. Archives. I did, and there they sat for five years.

When I came to write this book and wanted to prepare a chapter on that summer and fall of discontent, back to the archives I went. I spent days poring through these clippings to once again get the chronology right. Stu, you must have known something.

NOTE: Full citations of the books, periodicals and journals cited below appear in the Bibliography, beginning on page 290.

CHAPTER 1

B.C. Archives: Interviews by David Mitchell of May Bennett, R.J. Bennett, W.R. Bennett, A. Toser, T. Toser; Barrie Clark interview of W.R. Bennett on his radio program.

Author Interviews: W.R. Bennett, Audrey Bennett, Meldy Harris, Don Phillips.

Books: Keene and Humphreys; Mitchell; Nichols and Krieger; Rayner.

Newspapers and Magazines: Vancouver Province, September 5, 1970; *Vancouver Sun,* June 13, 1973; *Equity,* April 1994, May/June 1984; *Today,* August 1980; *Weekend Magazine,* February 21, 1976.

CHAPTER 2

B.C. Archives: Interview by David Mitchell of Dave Barrett.

Books: Barrett and Miller; Blake; Blake, Carty and Erickson; Carty; Kavic and Nixon; Nichols and O'Hara; Rayner; Webster.

Periodicals and Journals: Cairns; Tennant.

Newspapers and Magazines: Victoria Times, May 31, 1970; *Vancouver Sun,* July 24, 1959; September 8, 1972 (James K. Nesbitt column); *Chinese-Canadian Bulletin,* November–December 1972;

Vancouver Sun, August 30, 1972 (Allan Fotheringham column); April 7, 1973; March 7, 1974 (Marjorie Nichols column).

CHAPTER 3

Author Interviews: W.R. Bennett, Grace McCarthy, Meldy Harris, Don Phillips.

Books: Campbell; Mitchell; Nichols and Krieger; Nichols with O'Hara.

Newspapers and Magazines: Star, Fall 1975; *Vancouver Sun*, May 5, 1975; September 8, 1973 (general and Allan Fotheringham column); *Daily Courier*, September 8, 1973; *Vancouver Sun*, September 26, 1973; October 11, 1973, November 13, 1973; November 22, 1973 (special column on Socred leadership race by Marjorie Nichols); Vancouver *Province*, November 22 (special interview with Peter McNally); *Vancouver Sun*, November 26, 1973.

CHAPTER 4

Author Interviews: W.R. Bennett, Audrey Bennett, Grace McCarthy, Allan Williams.

Books: Barrett and Miller; Blake; Blake, Carty, Erickson; Campbell; Kavic and Nixon; Mitchell.

Periodicals and Journals: Blake; Kristianson.

Newspapers and Magazines: Vancouver Sun and Vancouver *Province*, November 3 to December 12, 1975.

CHAPTER 5

Author Interviews: W.R. Bennett, Grace McCarthy, Bob McClelland, Rafe Mair, Jim Nielsen.

Books: Campbell; Morley, Ruff, Swainson, Wilson and Young; Nichols with O'Hara; Persky; Rayner.

Newspapers and Magazines: Vancouver Sun, December 18, 1975; *Vancouver Sun* and Vancouver *Province*, February 21, 1976; November 1, 1976; *Vancouver Sun*, May 13, 1978.

Government Documents: Clarkson, Gordon Report.

CHAPTER 6

Author Interviews: W.R. Bennett, Hugh Curtis, Bud Smith, David Emerson.

Books: Barrett and Miller; Ohashi, Roth, Spinder, McMillan and Norrie; Persky.

Newspapers and Magazines: Vancouver Sun, January 16, 1976; May 21, 1976; May 25, 1976.

Government Documents: Hansard (debates on Auditor General and Ombudsman); W.R. Bennett, "Towards an Economic Strategy for Canada: The British Columbia Position."

CHAPTER 7

Author Interviews: W.R. Bennett, Hugh Curtis, Bud Smith, Allan Williams, Jim Matkin.

Books: Barrett and Miller; Blake; Blakeney and Borins; Campbell; Carty; Nichols with Krieger; Weiler.

Periodicals and Journals: Axworthy.

Newspapers and Magazines: Vancouver Sun and Vancouver *Province* (*Vancouver Express,* as the *Sun* and *Province* were on strike); January 3–February 3, 1979 and May 7, 1979, and many other articles on B.C. labour relations; *Maclean's,* February 12, 1979 (column by Allan Fotheringham).

CHAPTER 8

Author Interviews: W.R. Bennett, Grace McCarthy, Don Phillips, Brian Smith, Allan Williams, Larry Bell, Paul Manning, Jack McKeown.

Books: Barrett and Miller; Holmes and Northrop; Mulgrew; Persky.

Newspapers and Magazines: Vancouver Sun, February 16, 1978 (Frances Russell column) and September 22, 1979. From September 22, 1979, when the "dirty tricks" scandal broke. news reports seemed to appear at least several times a week until the end of the year, ending with the "Scrooge" story on December 5, 1979. All local newspapers during that period were reviewed. Similarly, when the "Gracie's Finger" story broke on January 10, 1980, it filled many pages until the legislature rose in August. Again, for background purposes, I worked my way through the microfiche coverage of these interesting times.

CHAPTER 9

Author Interviews: W.R. Bennett, Jack Heinrich, Rafe Mair, Jim Nielsen, Brian Smith, Jim Matkin, Norman Spector.

Books: Romanow, Whyte and Leeson; Persky; Sheppard and Valpy.

Periodicals and Journals: Meekison, Romanow and Moull.

Newspapers and Magazines: Again, when the First Ministers Conferences were underway the daily coverage in all major newspapers was extensive. I relied on this source to gain a sense of what the media were thinking.

Government Documents: Canadian Intergovernmental Conference Secretariat, "Federal–Provincial Conferences of First Ministers" (various materials); W.R. Bennett, "Submission on Behalf of B.C. to the Special Joint Committee on the Constitution of Canada" and "B.C.'s Constitutional Proposals"; Ministry of Intergovernmental Relations, Annual Reports; British Columbia *Hansard.*

CHAPTER 10

Author Interviews: W.R. Bennett, Hugh Curtis, Bob McClelland, Jim Nielsen, Don Phillips, Bud Smith, Mike Bailey, Larry Bell, David Emerson, Jim Hume, Pat Kinsella, Dave Laundy, Jim Matkin, Norman Spector.

Books: Barrett and Miller; Blake; Garr.

Periodicals and Journals: Blake.

Newspapers and Magazines: Vancouver, January 1984 (article by Peter Ladner).

CHAPTER 11

Author Interviews: W.R. Bennett, Mike Bailey, Hugh Curtis, Jim Nielsen, Don Phillips, Jim Matkin, Norman Spector.

Books: Garr; MacMinn; Mitchell; Munro and O'Hara, Neufeld and Parnaby; Nichols and Krieger; Nichols and O'Hara; Webster.

Periodicals and Journals: Blake.

Newspapers and Magazines: As mentioned in the introduction to this section, I was lucky to have Stu Hodgson provide the newspaper clippings from all the major newspapers in Canada on this subject. They lie in the B.C. Provincial Archives in half a dozen large binders, and they helped keep my story chronologically on track.

CHAPTER 12

Author Interviews: W.R. Bennett, Hugh Curtis, Grace McCarthy, Bob McClelland, Jim Nielsen, Don Phillips, Stephen Rogers, Senator Jack Austin, Bob Exell, Pat Kinsella, Jimmy Pattison, Bud Smith.

Books: Blake, Carty and Erickson; Mitchell; Pattison with Grescoe.

Periodicals and Journals: Tennant.

Newspapers and Magazines: Vancouver Sun, March 19, 1984; May 2, 1986; *Vancouver Sun* and *Province,* end of April until mid-May 1986, when Expo opened, and again in late September until the first week in October 1986, when it closed.

Government Documents: Officials Report, "General Report on the 1986 World Exposition"; Mayor's correspondence, Vancouver Archives.

A FINAL WORD

Author Interviews: W.R. Bennett, Brian Smith, Jimmy Pattison, Norman Spector.

Books: Nichols with O'Hara; Morley, Ruff, Swainson, Wilson and Young; Munro with O'Hara; Pattison with Grescoe.

Newspapers and Magazines: Financial Post, June 21, 1986; July 26, 1986.

Government Documents: Reports of the Electoral Office of B.C.

BIBLIOGRAPHY

BOOKS

Anderson, R., and E. Wachtel. *The Expo Story.* Madeira Park, B.C.: Harbour, 1986.

Barrett, D., and W. Miller. *Barrett: A Passionate Political Life.* Vancouver: Douglas & McIntyre, 1995.

Blake, D. *Two Political Worlds: Parties and Voting in British Columbia.* Vancouver: UBC Press, 1985.

Blake, D., R.K. Carty, and L. Erickson. *Grassroots Politicians: Party Activists in British Columbia.* Vancouver: UBC Press, 1991.

Blakeney, A., and S. Borins. *Political Management in Canada: Conversations on Statecraft.* 2nd ed. Toronto: University of Toronto Press, 1998.

Campbell, D. "Dedicated to My Friends on the Road." Unpublished manuscript. B.C. Provincial Archives, 1990.

Carty, R.K., ed. *Politics, Policy and Government in British Columbia.* Vancouver: UBC Press, 1996.

Covey, S. R. *Principle-Centered Leadership.* New York: Free Press, 1990.

Garr, A. *Tough Guy: Bill Bennett and the Taking of British Columbia.* Toronto: Key Porter, 1985.

Holmes, W.L., and B.L. Northrop. *Where Shadows Linger: The Untold Story of the RCMP's Olson Murders Investigation.* Surrey, B.C.: Heritage House, 2000.

Kavic, L.J., and G.B. Nixon. *The 1200 Days, A Shattered Dream: Dave Barrett and the NDP in BC 1972–75.* Coquitlam, B.C.: Kaen, 1978.

Keene, R., and D.C. Humphreys. *Conversations with W.A.C. Bennett.* Toronto: Methuen, 1980.

MacMinn, George. *Parliamentary Practice in British Columbia.* Victoria: Queen's Printer, 1981.

Mair, R. *Rafe: A Memoir.* Madeira Park, B.C.: Harbour, 2004.

Mason, G., and K. Baldrey. *Fantasyland: Inside the Reign of Bill Vander Zalm.* Toronto: McGraw-Hill Ryerson, 1989.

Mitchell, D.J. *W.A.C. Bennett and the Rise of British Columbia.* Vancouver: Douglas & McIntyre, 1983.

Mitchell, D.J. *Succession: The Political Reshaping of British Columbia.* Vancouver: Douglas & McIntyre, 1987.

Morley, J.T., N. Ruff, N. Swainson, J. Wilson, and W. Young. *The Reins of Power: Governing British Columbia.* Vancouver: Douglas & McIntyre, Vancouver, 1983.

Mulgrew, I. *Final Payoff: The True Price of Convicting Clifford Robert Olson.* Toronto: Seal Books, 1990.

Munro, J., and J. O'Hara. *Union Jack: Labour Leader Jack Munro.* Vancouver: Douglas & McIntyre, 1988.

Neufeld, A., and A. Parnaby. *The IWA in Canada: The Life and Times of an Industrial Union.* Vancouver: IWA Canada/New Star Books, 2000.

Nichols, M., and B. Krieger. *Bill Bennett: The End.* Vancouver: Douglas & McIntyre, Vancouver, 1986.

Nichols, M., with J. O'Hara. *Mark My Words: The Memoirs of a Very Political Reporter.* Vancouver: Douglas & McIntyre, 1992.

Ohashi, T., T. Roth, A. Spinder, M. McMillan, and K. Norrie. *Distributing Shares in Private and Public Enterprises.* Vancouver: Fraser Institute, 1980.

Pattison, Jimmy, with Paul Grescoe. *Jimmy: An Autobiography.* Toronto: Seal Books, 1987.

Persky, S. *Son of Socred.* Vancouver: New Star Books, 1979.

Persky, S. *Bennett II.* Vancouver: New Star Books, 1983.

Rayner, W. *British Columbia's Premiers in Profile.* Surrey, B.C.: Heritage House, 2000.

Romanow, R., J. Whyte, and H. Leeson. *Canada... Notwithstanding: The Making of the Constitution 1976–1982.* Toronto: Carswell/Methuen, 1984.

Sheppard, R., and M. Valpy. *The National Deal: The Fight for a Canadian Constitution.* Toronto: Fleet Books, 1982.

Tennant, P. *Aboriginal Peoples and Politics.* Vancouver: UBC Press, 1991.

Webster, J. *Webster! An Autobiography by Jack Webster.* Vancouver: Douglas & McIntyre, 1990.

Weiler, P. *Reconcilable Differences.* Toronto: Carswell, 1980.

GOVERNMENT DOCUMENTS

Bennett, W.R. "Submission on Behalf of British Columbia to the Special Joint Committee on the Constitution of Canada." Ottawa, January 9, 1981.

Bennett, W.R. "Towards an Economic Strategy for Canada: The British Columbia Position." 1978.

British Columbia. *Hansard* and *Reports* of the Electoral Office of B.C.

British Columbia. Ministry of Intergovernmental Relations. "First, Second Annual Report." Province of British Columbia, 1981 and 1982.

"British Columbia's Constitutional Proposals," presented to the First Ministers Conference on the Constitution. October 1978.

Canadian Intergovernmental Conference Secretariat. Federal–Provincial Conferences of First Ministers. Selected materials.

Clarkson, Gordon & Co. "Report, Financial Information: for the year ending March 31, 1976." February 18, 1976, Vancouver.

Officials Report. "General Report on the 1986 World Exposition." Official Publication of EXPO Corporation. Vancouver, 1986.

Provincial Archives, Royal British Columbia Museum. Archival materials.

Vancouver Archives, City of Vancouver. Mayor's correspondence.

PERIODICALS AND JOURNALS

Annesley, P. *Equity* (April 1984), (May/June 1984).

"Audrey Bennett." *United News* (May 1975).

Axworthy, T. "Of Secretaries to Princes." *Canadian Public Administration* 31 (Summer 1988).

Blake, D. "Sources of Change in the B.C. Party System." *B.C. Studies* 50 (Summer 1981).

Blake, D. "The Electoral Significance of Public Sector Bashing." *B.C. Studies* 62 (Summer 1984).

Cairns, A.C. "Review of *The 1200 Days: A Shortlived Dream* by L.J. Kavic and G.B. Nixon, and *Son of Socred* by S. Persky." *B.C. Studies* 49 (Spring 1981).

Fotheringham, A. "Bennett the Second: Horatio Alger With a Head Start." *Weekend* (February 21, 1976).

Grescoe, P. *Today* (August 1980).

Kristianson, G.L. "The Non-Partisan Approach to B.C. Politics: The Search for a Unity Party." *B.C. Studies* 33 (Spring 1977).

Meekison, J.P., R.J. Romanow, and W.D. Moull. "Origins and Meaning of Section 92A: The 1982 Constitutional Amendment on Resources." Institute for Research on Public Policy, 1985.

Mitchell, D. "Audrey Bennett: Backing Up the Boss." *Equity* (October 1985).

Tennant, P. "The NDP Government of B.C.: Unaided Politicians in an Unaided Cabinet." *Canadian Public Policy* (Autumn 1977).

Tennant, P., ed. "British Columbia: A Place for Aboriginal Peoples?" Special issue of *B.C. Studies* 57 (Spring 1983).

NEWSPAPERS AND MAGAZINES

Extensive reading of the *Vancouver Sun* and its columnists Allan Fotheringham and Marjorie Nichols.

Secondary support—Newspapers: Vancouver *Province, Victoria Times-Colonist, Central Okanagan Capital News, Daily Courier, Star* and *Financial Times*. Magazines: *Maclean's, Saturday Night, Alberta Report, Weekend Magazine, Equity, Dick MacLean's Guide, Vancouver* and *Today.*

SPEECHES

Kube, A. "Operation Solidarity/Solidarity Coalition—Common Cause." Toronto, 1984.

Mickleburgh, R. "Operation Solidarity: How It Was." Toronto, 1984.

INTERVIEWS (FROM B.C. PROVINCIAL ARCHIVES)

Dave Barrett PABC 1704 (D. Mitchell)

May Bennett PABC 2703 (D. Mitchell)

R.J. Bennett PABC 2703 (D. Mitchell)

W.R. Bennett PABC 1707 (D. Mitchell)

Barrie Clark PABC 3973

A. Toser PABC 2706 (D. Mitchell)

T. Toser PABC 3358 (D. Mitchell)

INTERVIEWS (CARRIED OUT BY AUTHOR)

Jack Austin

Mike Bailey

Larry Bell

Audrey Bennett

W.R. (Bill) Bennett (7 occasions)

Hugh Curtis

Bob Exell

Meldy Harris

Jack Heinrich

Jim Hume

Pat Kinsella

Dave Laundy

Rafe Mair

Paul Manning

Jim Matkin

Grace McCarthy (2 occasions)

Bob McClelland

Jack McKeown

Jim Nielsen

Jimmy Pattison

Don Phillips

Stephen Rogers

Brian Smith

Bud Smith

Norman Spector

Allan Williams

INDEX

Aberhart, William, 15–16
Anderson, David, 28–29, 58, 60, 61, 82–83, 272
Andrews, Ron, 58
Andstein, Cliff, 216–17, 220–21, 223, 225, 227
Austin, Jack, 240–42

Bailey, Mike, 170, 184–85, 196, 209, 263
Barber, Charles, 181–82, 187
Barnes, Emery, 43, 187
Barrett, Dave, 3–4, 23–26, 28, 115–16, 274–75, 279; as MLA and opposition leader, 24, 26–29, 99, 108–9, 111–12, 135, 146–47, 179–80, 185–89, 191–92, 213–14, 234–35; as premier, 29–38, 41–42, 57, 61–70, 76–78, 107–8, 131, 249
Barrett, Shirley, 25, 29, 69, 187
Barton, Vi, 137
Bell, Larry, 127–29, 174–77, 233–34, 238
Bennett, Anita, 11, 12
Bennett, Audrey, 18, 52–53, 69, 80, 104, 124, 190, 192, 196–97, 208–9, 268
Bennett, Brad, 208
Bennett, Elizabeth, 11
Bennett, R.J., 4, 10–11, 13, 15, 21
Bennett, W.A.C.: assessment and legacy, 16–17, 235, 266, 270–72, 274–75, 279; and Bill Bennett's career, 43, 47; character of, 7, 13, 14–15; death, 106; as financial manager, 35, 57, 233; political career, end of, 20, 32, 39–40, 44; political style and influences, 15–16, 26–27, 28, 29, 95, 106, 145; and Social Credit, 15–16, 40–42, 48
Bennett, W.R. (Bill): aboriginal land claims, 249–51; accused of insider deals, 4, 21; assessment and legacy, 3–4, 264–66, 269–82; character, 3, 11–12, 19, 21–22, 104, 106–7, 123–24, 171, 184–85, 232, 277, 278; early years, 10–15, 17–21; family life, 18–19, 51–53, 80, 208–9; image and media

relations, 50–51, 85–86, 186, 216, 276–77; management style, 275–76, 279; political strategist, 20, 40, 59–61, 107, 117, 138, 151, 184, 186, 235–36, 279, 281
Bennett, W.R. (Bill), as MLA and opposition leader, 7–10, 21–22, 43–51, 52–58, 59–61, 63–70, 122–23, 213
Bennett, W.R. (Bill), first term: election (1979), 111–12; financial discipline, 77–80, 91–93; intergovernmental relations, 93–97, 103, 146–47; labour relations, 109–11; MacMillan Bloedel sale, 104–6; management style, 71–77, 80–86, 87–91, 104; privatization program and BCRIC, 97–102; scandals, 123, 124–26
Bennett, W.R. (Bill), second term: election (1983), 179–84, 188–93; financial discipline, 117, 170–77, 181; intergovernmental relations and constitution, 132, 141–44, 149–69, 170–74, 280; international investments program, 131–33; labour relations, 116–17, 144–45; management style, 117, 127–28, 144, 148–49, 177, 182, 184–85; Olson affair, 122; party leader, 112–17; restraint plans, 170–79; scandals, 129–31, 133–38; stadium project, 126–29
Bennett, W.R. (Bill), third term: Coquihalla Highway, 252–54; Expo 86, 237–49, 254–55, 256–62, 280; management style, 195–97, 261–62; party leader, 261–62; restraint and Solidarity, 193–209, 211–21, 223–32, 234–36, 280; retirement and succession, 251–52, 262–63, 267–68; and ski resorts, 232–33; trade talks with China, 133
Berger, Thomas R., 26–28, 249
Bird, Chris, 136
Blakeney, Allan, 158–59, 160–62
Bonner, Robert, 23–24
Bourassa, Robert, 141
Brown, Dave, 50
Bruce, Donald, 136
Bryson, Gerry, 30, 32, 72, 233
Buchanan, John, 159
Burns, Mike, 181, 264, 265

Calder, Frank, 67, 112, 123
Cameron, Art, 125
Campbell, Dan, 40–42, 50–51, 53, 113, 116, 137, 142, 144
Campbell, Gordon, 271
Campbell, Kim, 220, 261, 276
Campbell, Meryl, 31
Chabot, Jim, 31, 47–48, 74, 89, 198–99, 209, 216–18, 261–62
Chapman, Vic, 260
Chapple, Clem, 133–35, 191–92
Charles, Prince of Wales, 255, 256–61
Chrétien, Jean, 96, 154, 158, 166–69
Clark, Bill, 256
Clark, Joe, 127, 239
Cocke, Yvonne, 40, 108
Curtis, Hugh, 60; finance minister, 132, 176, 178, 194, 198, 201–2, 209, 218, 233–34; municipal affairs minister, 73; provincial secretary, 242

Dalglish, Brenda, 129
Davidson, Mike, 199, 219–20
Davidson, Walter, 213–14
Davis, Jack, 126
Davis, William (Bill), 158–59, 160–62, 172–73, 181
DeHart, Frank, 14
Diana, Princess of Wales, 255, 256–61
Diefenbaker, John, 140
Doman, Herb, 4

Douglas, C.H., 15
Douglas, T.C. (Tommy), 26, 112, 140
Dunn, Jack, 213–14

Earle, Winnie, 11, 13
Eckardt, Lawrence, 104, 134, 135, 137
Eliesen, Marc, 38, 62
Elizabeth II, Queen of Canada, 254–55
Emerson, David, 87, 94–95, 171, 175–76
Eriksen, Bruce, 87–89
Esson, William, 136
Exell, Bob, 250, 251

Filmer, Alan, 120–21
Fotheringham, Allan, 44, 52, 64, 105–6, 169
Fraser, Alex, 47, 72, 252–54
Froese, Russ, 133–34

Gaglardi, Phil, 9, 40
Gardom, Garde, 61, 275; attorney general, 72, 84–85, 125, 143; intergovernmental relations minister, 144–46, 149, 199
Garr, Allen, 183, 221
Gautier, Roy, 228, 244–48
Gibson, Gordon, 58, 61, 67, 100, 272–73
Goard, Dean, 81
Good, Bill, Jr., 136
Gorie, Bill, 210–11
Gotlieb, Allan, 151–52
Greene, Justis, 189–90
Greene Raine, Nancy, 233
Gregg, Allan, 179–80, 186, 264
Greig, Ron, 130
Grossman, Larry, 172–73
Guibault, George, 89–90

Hackman, Shirley. *See* Barrett, Shirley
Hall, Ernie, 31, 37–38
Hannah, Daryl, 190
Harcourt, Mike, 235, 242–43, 246, 247–48, 258
Hardwick, Walter, 80–81
Harris, Hugh, 19–20, 43–45, 48, 69–70, 180–81, 185
Harris, Meldy, 19–20, 43
Hatfield, Richard, 160
Heal, Doug, 182, 265
Hean, Arnold, 55
Heinrich, Jack, 144–45, 275
Helliwell, David, 99, 101
Hodgson, Stu, 222, 255
Howard, Frank, 136
Hume, Jim, 122, 184–85, 216
Hyndman, Peter, 58, 60

James, Audrey. *See* Bennett, Audrey
John, Eddie, 250
Jordan, Don, 209, 222, 229–30
Jordan, Pat, 47, 187

Kaiser, Edgar, Jr., 101
Kelleher, Steven, 219–20, 225
Kelly, Jack, 129–30
Kempf, Jack, 129–30
Kiernan, Ken, 48
King, Bill, 23, 32–34, 36, 38, 107, 108, 135
Kinnaird, Jim, 108, 111, 177
Kinsella, Pat, 179–80, 181–82, 186, 191–92, 264–65
Kirby, Michael, 152–53, 155–56, 157, 159
Knudsen, Calvin, 277–78
Kramer, Mike, 214, 225–26, 231
Krasnick, Mark, 145, 146, 159–61
Kube, Art, 203, 206–10, 211–12, 215, 225, 227–28, 232
Kuehn, Larry, 225–26, 228

Lampert, Jerry, 185–86, 251, 264
Laskin, Bora, 154
Lauk, Gary, 131, 137

Laundy, Dave, 182–83, 265
Lea, Graham, 187
Leggatt, Stu, 187
Lenko, George, 130
Lesage, Jean, 140
Lévesque, René, 96, 139, 147, 150–51, 154, 158–59, 163–69, 172, 272
Levi, Norm, 33, 38
Loffmark, Ralph, 39
Lougheed, Peter, 44, 133, 151, 154, 158–59, 164–69
Lyon, Sterling, 150–51

McBain, Sharon, 87–89
McBride, Richard, 270, 279
McCarthy, Grace, 85; advises young Bill Bennett, 19; deputy premier, provincial secretary, 72–73; "Gracie's finger" scandal, 133–38; leadership race (1986), 267–68; Remembrance Day and restraint, 229; and Social Credit, 39–42, 48, 50, 53–54, 56, 60, 63–64, 264; tourism minister, 237
McClelland, Bob, 251, 265; election campaign (1975), 69–70; health minister, 72, 82; labour minister, 193–94, 198, 247; leadership race (1973), 47–48
MacDonald, Alex, 187
McEachern, Allan, 223
McGeer, Pat, 27–28, 61, 72, 80–81, 84, 87, 148, 275
MacKay, Ellen, 130
McKeown, Jack, 131–32
McMurtry, Roy, 166
Madigan, Sean, 120
Maile, Fred, 119–20
Mair, Rafe, 55, 73–75, 84, 143, 147–48, 183–85
Manning, E.C., 16
Manning, Paul, 126–29, 238
Mason, Jim, 47, 48
Matkin, Jim: constitutional negotiations, 151–52, 154–56, 159–62; labour deputy, 110, 145–48; leaves public service, 198–99; restraint program, 174, 176–77, 210, 220, 225–26; union negotiations for Expo, 246
Morin, Claude, 147, 160, 162
Mulroney, Brian, 257, 275
Munro, Jack, 224–32, 246, 277–78

Nichol, John, 83
Nichols, Marjorie: on Barrett administration, 41–42, 63–64; on Bennett administrations, 76, 129, 183, 188, 217, 222, 273–74; on Social Credit, 47
Nicol, Dick, 213–14
Nielsen, Jim, 73, 86, 148–49, 193, 210–11, 234–35, 263

Olson, Clifford, 119–22
Owen, Walter, 62

Palmer, Vaughn, 212, 249
Parks, John, 213–14
Passeral, Al, 112, 189–90
Pattison, Jimmy, 53, 148, 242, 244–49, 260–62, 271
Pearse, Peter, 83–84
Pearson, Lester, 141, 240
Peck, Ed, 178, 220, 221–22, 225–26
Peckford, Brian, 168
Peel, Sandy, 94, 132
Perrault, Ray, 240
Phillips, Don: economic development minister, 72, 74, 75, 124–25, 131–33, 184–85, 218, 233, 255–56; and MLA Bill Bennett, 22, 46, 47, 67; retirement, 261–62

Radford, Jack, 37–38
Ready, Vince, 178, 220, 225–27

Reid, Patrick, 237
Rhodes, Al, 253
Richards, May, 11
Richards, Norm, 31, 216, 220
Richardson, Art, 31
Richmond, Claude, 185, 247
Rigby, Norman, 210–11
Roach, Bill, 213–14
Roberts, Jim, 207, 215
Rogers, Forrest, 53
Rogers, Stephen, 255–56
Romanow, Roy, 157–58, 166–69

Sauvé, Jeanne, 257
Schroeder, Harvey, 47, 48, 89, 213, 261–62
Shearer, Renate, 207, 215
Shelford, Cyril, 28
Sihota, Moe, 212
Sinclair, Ian, 105–6, 238
Smith, Brian, 124, 149–50, 198, 229, 267–68, 278
Smith, Bud, 90, 114, 184, 251; leadership race (1986), 261, 263, 267–68; principal secretary, 247–48, 253–54, 265; "wagonmaster" (1983), 179–80, 188–92
Smith, Ed, 47, 48, 75, 123
Smith, Mel, 145, 147–48, 166, 250
Smith, Walter Kirke, 125
Spector, Norman, 146, 182, 183, 261, 265, 269, 275–77; intergovernmental relations and constitution, 132, 139, 151–56, 159–62, 167–69, 171; restraint program, 174–75, 197–200, 211, 219–21, 225, 227, 229–30; union agreement for Expo, 247–48
Stanfield, Robert, 19
Stephens, Vic, 104, 135
Stevenson, Don, 160–62
Strachan, Bob, 26, 36
Stupich, Dave, 77

Tamoto, Florence, 135–37
Tassé, Roger, 152–53
Taylor, Austin, 60, 98
Thomson, Susan, 137
Timmis, Denis, 69
Toigo, Peter, 268
Trudeau, Pierre Elliott, 97, 272; constitutional negotiations, 139–40, 141–44, 149–50, 153–69; Expo support, 239–42; First Ministers conferences, 94–96, 172–74; wage and price controls, 37

Vander Zalm, Bill, 60, 235–36; confrontational style, 83, 115, 276; minister of social services, 73, 82–83, 87–88, 91; popular vote (1986), 270–71; snubs Bill Bennett, 267–68
Vogel, Richard, 136–37, 152–53
Volrich, Jack, 243

Wallace, Lawrie, 29, 30, 146, 181, 237
Wallace, Scott (Dr.), 58, 67
Warren, Derril, 20, 29, 44–45, 54
Waterland, Tom, 73, 83–84
Webster, Jack, 99
Weeks, Arthur, 124–25
Weiler, Paul, 109–10, 160–62
Wicks, Lyle, 23, 26
Williams, Allan, 61, 72, 81, 84, 109–10, 121–22, 136–37, 144
Williams, Bob, 21, 26, 33, 34, 38, 62, 108, 111, 187
Wolfe, Evan, 72, 84, 92, 106–7, 135–36

Zhao Ziyang, 133